GRAPHIS POSTER 93

. . . .

THE INTERNATIONAL ANNUAL OF POSTER ART

DAS INTERNATIONALE JAHRBUCH DER PLAKATKUNST

LE RÉPERTOIRE INTERNATIONAL DE L'ART DE L'AFFICHE

EDITED BY · HERAUSGEGEBEN VON · REALISÉ PAR:

B. MARTIN PEDERSEN

PUBLISHER AND CREATIVE DIRECTOR: B. MARTIN PEDERSEN

EDITORS: HEINKE JENSSEN, ANNETTE CRANDALL, MICHAEL O'CONNOR

ART DIRECTORS: B. MARTIN PEDERSEN, RANDELL PEARSON

PHOTOGRAPHER: WALTER ZUBER

GRAPHIS PRESS CORP. ZÜRICH (SWITZERLAND)

GRAPHIS PUBLICATIONS

GRAPHIS, THE INTERNATIONAL MAGAZINE OF DESIGN AND COMMUNICATION

GRAPHIS DESIGN, THE INTERNATIONAL ANNUAL OF DESIGN AND ILLUSTRATION

GRAPHIS PHOTO, THE INTERNATIONAL ANNUAL OF PHOTOGRAPHY

GRAPHIS POSTER, THE INTERNATIONAL ANNUAL OF POSTER ART

GRAPHIS NUDES, AN INTERNATIONAL COMPILATION OF THE BEST IN
     CONTEMPORARY NUDE PHOTOGRAPHY

GRAPHIS PACKAGING, AN INTERNATIONAL SURVEY OF PACKACKING DESIGN

GRAPHIS LETTERHEAD, AN INTERNATIONAL SURVEY OF LETTERHEAD DESIGN

GRAPHIS DIAGRAM, THE GRAPHIC VISUALIZATION OF ABSTRACT, TECHNICAL AND
     STATISTICAL FACTS AND FUNCTIONS

GRAPHIS LOGO, AN INTERNATIONAL SURVEY OF LOGOS

GRAPHIS PUBLICATION, AN INTERNATIONAL SURVEY OF THE BEST
     IN MAGAZINE DESIGN

GRAPHIS ANNUAL REPORTS, AN INTERNATIONAL COMPILATION OF THE BEST DESIGNED
     ANNUAL REPORTS

GRAPHIS CORPORATE IDENTITY, AN INTERNATIONAL COMPILATION OF THE BEST IN
     CORPORATE IDENTITY DESIGN

ART FOR SURVIVAL: THE ILLUSTRATOR AND THE ENVIRONMENT, A DOCUMENT OF ART
     IN THE SERVICE OF MAN.

THE GRAPHIC DESIGNER'S GREEN BOOK, ENVIRONMENTAL CONCEPTS FOR THE DESIGN AND PRINT INDUSTRIES

GRAPHIS PUBLIKATIONEN

GRAPHIS, DIE INTERNATIONALE ZEITSCHRIFT FÜR DESIGN UND KOMMUNIKATION

GRAPHIS DESIGN, DAS INTERNATIONALE JAHRBUCH ÜBER DESIGN UND ILLUSTRATION

GRAPHIS PHOTO, DAS INTERNATIONALE JAHRBUCH DER PHOTOGRAPHIE

GRAPHIS POSTER, DAS INTERNATIONALE JAHRBUCH DER PLAKATKUNST

GRAPHIS NUDES, EINE AUSWAHL DER BESTEN ZEITGENÖSSISCHEN AKTPHOTOGRAPHIE

GRAPHIS PACKAGING, EIN INTERNATIONALER ÜBERBLICK ÜBER DIE PACKUNGSGESTALTUNG

GRAPHIS LETTERHEAD, EIN INTERNATIONALER ÜBERBLICK ÜBER BRIEFPAPIERGESTALTUNG

GRAPHIS DIAGRAM, DIE GRAPHISCHE DARSTELLUNG ABSTRAKTER TECHNISCHER UND
     STATISTISCHER DATEN UND FAKTEN

GRAPHIS LOGO, EINE INTERNATIONALE AUSWAHL VON FIRMEN-LOGOS

GRAPHIS MAGAZINDESIGN, EINE INTERNATIONALE ZUSAMMENSTELLUNG DES BESTEN
     ZEITSCHRIFTEN-DESIGNS

GRAPHIS ANNUAL REPORTS, EIN INTERNATIONALER ÜBERBLICK ÜBER DIE GESTALTUNG
     VON JAHRESBERICHTEN

GRAPHIS CORPORATE IDENTITY, EINE INTERNATIONALE AUSWAHL DES BESTEN
     CORPORATE IDENTITY DESIGNS

ART FOR SURVIVAL: THE ILLUSTRATOR AND THE ENVIRONMENT, EIN DOKUMENT
     ÜBER DIE KUNST IM DIENSTE DES MENSCHEN

THE GRAPHIC DESIGNER'S GREEN BOOK, UMWELTKONZEPTE FÜR DIE DESIGN- UND DRUCKINDUSTRIE

PUBLICATIONS GRAPHIS

GRAPHIS, LE MAGAZINE INTERNATIONALE DU DESIGN ET DE LA COMMUNICATION

GRAPHIS DESIGN, LE RÉPERTOIRE INTERNATIONAL DE LA COMMUNICATION VISUELLE

GRAPHIS PHOTO, LE RÉPERTOIRE INTERNATIONAL DE LA PHOTOGRAPHIE

GRAPHIS POSTER, LE RÉPERTOIRE INTERNATIONAL DE L'AFFICHE

GRAPHIS NUDES, LE MEILLEUR DE LA PHOTOGRAPHIE DE NUS CONTEMORAINE INTERNATIONALE

GRAPHIS PACKAGING, LE RÉPERTOIRE INTERNATIONAL DE LA CRÉATION D'EMBALLAGES

GRAPHIS LETTERHEAD, LE RÉPERTOIRE INTERNATIONAL DU DESIGN DE PAPIER À LETTRES

GRAPHIS DIAGRAM, LE RÉPERTOIRE GRAPHIQUE DE FAITS ET DONNÉES ABSTRAITS,
     TECHNIQUES ET STATISTIQUES

GRAPHIS LOGO, LE RÉPERTOIRE INTERNATIONAL DU LOGO

GRAPHIS PUBLICATION, LE RÉPERTOIRE INTERNATIONAL DU DESIGN DE PÉRIODIQUES

GRAPHIS ANNUAL REPORTS, PANORAMA INTERNATIONAL DU MEILLEUR DESIGN DE RAPPORTS
     ANNUELS D'ENTREPRISES

GRAPHIS CORPORATE IDENTITY, PANORAMA INTERNATIONAL DU MEILLEUR DESIGN D'IDENTITÉ CORPORATE

ART FOR SURVIVAL: THE ILLUSTRATOR AND THE ENVIRONMENT, L'ART AU SERVICE DE LA SURVIE

THE GRAPHIC DESIGNER'S GREEN BOOK, L'ÉCOLOGIE APPLIQUÉE AU DESIGN ET À L'INDUSTRIE GRAPHIQUE

PUBLICATION NO. 213 (ISBN 3-85709-393-5)
© COPYRIGHT UNDER UNIVERSAL COPYRIGHT CONVENTION
COPYRIGHT © 1993 BY GRAPHIS PRESS CORP., DUFOURSTRASSE 107, 8008 ZURICH, SWITZERLAND
JACKET AND BOOK DESIGN COPYRIGHT © 1993 BY PEDERSEN DESIGN
141 LEXINGTON AVENUE, NEW YORK, N.Y. 10016 USA
FRENCH CAPTIONS BY NICOLE VIAUD

PRINTED IN JAPAN BY TOPPAN PRINTING CO., LTD.

CONTENTS · INHALT · SOMMAIRE

ARGENTINA	ARG	ARGENTINIEN	ARG	ALLEMAGNE	GER
AUSTRIA	AUT	AUSTRALIEN	AUS	ARGENTINE	ARG
AUSTRALIA	AUS	BAHAMAS	BAH	AUSTRALIE	AUS
BAHAMAS	BAH	BRASILIEN	BRA	AUTRICHE	AUT
BRAZIL	BRA	DÄNEMARK	DEN	BAHAMAS	BAH
CANADA	CAN	DEUTSCHLAND	GER	BIÉLORUSSIE	WRU
CROATIA	CRO	FINNLAND	FIN	BRÉSIL	BRA
CZECHOSLOVAKIA	CFR	FRANKREICH	FRA	CANADA	CAN
DENMARK	DEN	GRIECHENLAND	GRE	CORÉE	KOR
FINLAND	FIN	GROSSBRITANNIEN	GBR	CROATIE	CRO
FRANCE	FRA	HONGKONG	HKG	DANEMARK	DAN
GERMANY	GER	IRAN	IRN	ESPAGNE	SPA
GREAT BRITAIN	GBR	ISRAEL	ISR	ETATS-UNIS	USA
GREECE	GRE	ITALIEN	ITA	FINLANDE	FIN
HONG KONG	HKG	JAPAN	JPN	FRANCE	FRA
IRAN	IRN	JUGOSLAVIEN	YUG	GRANDE-BRETAGNE	GBR
ISRAEL	ISR	KANADA	CAN	GRECE	GRE
ITALY	ITA	KOREA	KOR	HONG KONG	HKG
JAPAN	JPN	KROATIEN	CRO	IRAN	IRN
KOREA	KOR	MEXICO	MEX	ISRAEL	ISR
MEXICO	MEX	NIEDERLANDE	NLD	ITALIE	ITA
NETHERLANDS	NLD	NORWEGEN	NOR	JAPON	JPN
NORWAY	NOR	ÖSTERREICH	AUT	MEXIQUE	MEX
PORTUGAL	POR	PORTUGAL	POR	NORVEGE	NOR
RUSSIA	RUS	RUSSLAND	RUS	PAYS-BAS	NLD
SLOVENIA	SLO	SCHWEDEN	SWE	PORTUGAL	POR
SPAIN	SPA	SCHWEIZ	SWI	RUSSIE	RUS
SWEDEN	SWE	SLOVENIEN	SLO	SLOVENIE	SLO
SWITZERLAND	SWI	SPANIEN	SPA	SUEDE	SWE
TURKEY	TUR	TSCHECHOSLOWAKEI	CFR	SUISSE	SWI
USA	USA	TÜRKEI	TUR	TCHÉCOSLOVAQUIE	CFR
VENEZUELA	VEN	USA	USA	TURQUIE	TUR
WHITERUSSIA	WRU	VENEZUELA	VEN	VENEZUELA	VEN
YUGOSLAVIA	YUG	WEISSRUSSLAND	WRU	YOUGOSLAVIE	YUG

REMARKS

WE EXTEND OUR HEARTFELT THANKS TO CONTRIBUTORS THROUGHOUT THE WORLD WHO HAVE MADE IT POSSIBLE TO PUBLISH A WIDE AND INTERNATIONAL SPECTRUM OF THE BEST WORK IN THIS FIELD.

ENTRY INSTRUCTIONS MAY BE REQUESTED AT:
GRAPHIS PRESS CORP.,
DUFOURSTRASSE 107,
8008 ZÜRICH, SWITZERLAND

ANMERKUNGEN

UNSER DANK GILT DEN EINSENDERN AUS ALLER WELT, DIE ES UNS DURCH IHRE BEI- TRÄGE ERMÖGLICHT HABEN, EIN BREITES, INTERNATIONALES SPEKTRUM DER BESTEN ARBEITEN ZU VERÖFFENTLICHEN.

TEILNAHMEBEDINGUNGEN:
GRAPHIS VERLAG AG,
DUFOURSTRASSE 107,
8008 ZÜRICH, SCHWEIZ

ANNOTATIONS

TOUTE NOTRE RECONNAISSANCE VA AUX DESIGNERS DU MONDE ENTIER DONT LES ENVOIS NOUS ONT PERMIS DE CONSTITUER UN VASTE PANORAMA INTERNATIONAL DES MEILLEURES CRÉATIONS.

MODALITÉS D'ENVOI DE TRAVAUX:
EDITIONS GRAPHIS,
DUFOURSTRASSE 107,
8008 ZÜRICH, SUISSE

MAKOTO SAITO

PORTRAIT OF MAKOTO SAITO
BY KAZUMI KURIGAMI

. . . .

The avant-garde is seldom to be found in Japan's poster art. Most graphic art is valued for such things as overall taste, detail, a tranquil air, ease of comprehension, or texture. In the work of only a few graphic designers can one see a true sense of personal style. When I design something, I want it to be new. I ignore existing designs, and I have no interest in designing in accordance with rules that other people have laid out. I want to create designs and graphic art that have never been seen before. □ I studied philosophy, not design. I didn't want to be influenced by what had been done in the past. As far as I am concerned, the design we have had so far is for the things we have had so far. For me, it is what I am making now that is important. I don't need the support of the crowd, and it doesn't matter what they think of my work. When the average person looks at one of my designs and says, "That's neat!" I feel a little disappointed. I don't think there are all that many people who are actually able to see what they look at, who are able to catch the nuances and details of something truly new. This is not to say that the common run of people are irrelevant. Their opinions are valid at their own level. But when I design something, I do so with those special people— the ones who can see things clearly—in mind. □ Advertisements in Japan are valued for their effectiveness as marketing tools, but in their creative dimen-

sion they leave much to be desired. This is inevitable when decisions are made on the basis of mass appeal. If there are, say, 70 people in a group, probably only 10 will understand what the designer is doing. The people with an esthetic sense will be outvoted 60 to 10 when it comes to making a decision. (Though a group of 70 people who all understood design would be overwhelming, and, I must admit, I often belong to the larger group when it comes to doing business.) □ Design arises from the interaction of a company and the society in which it exists. A company's owner has a great deal to do with the overall impression given by the company, and when the owner has a refined sense of style something very positive can result. But when a person with no sense of style owns the company, the company and its products will also lack style. Of course a company must seek profit, but there are some companies that seek something else, something beyond profit. A company may want to convey a sense of romance, or of polish and sophistication. □ Companies with a distinct sense of their own esthetic are the ones that give shape to a culture. These are the companies I want to work with. I want to separate myself as far as possible from what is called "graphic design," but I don't want to make "pure art." I want to express something between art and design—something that transcends them. ■

. . . .

MAKOTO SAITO, BORN IN 1952 IN FUKUOKA PREFECTURE, JAPAN, IS ONE OF THE WORLD'S LEADING POSTER ARTISTS IN ADDITION TO ENJOYING COMMERCIAL SUCCESS, HE HAS WON NUMEROUS AWARDS, INCLUDING FOUR GOLD AWARDS FROM THE NEW YORK ART DIRECTORS CLUB, A SPECIAL PRIZE AND A GRAND PRIZE AT THE LAHTI POSTER BIENNIAL, HIGHEST AWARD AT THE COLORADO INTERNATIONAL POSTER INVITATIONAL AND A GOLD PRIZE AND PROJECT PRIZE AT THE WARSAW INTERNATIONAL POSTER BIENNIAL. ■

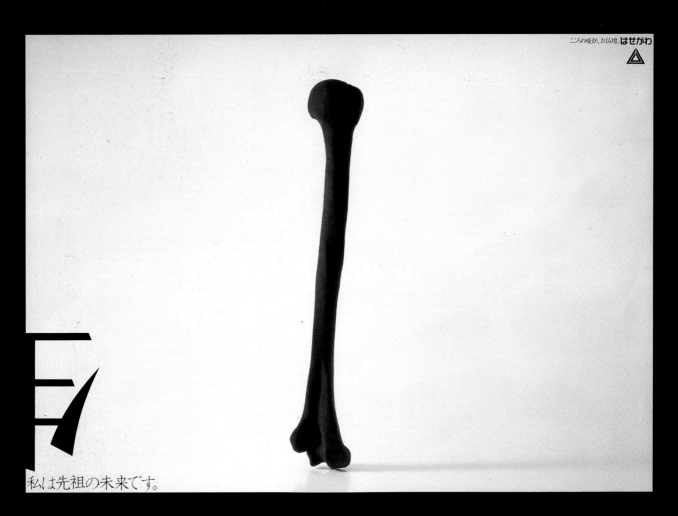

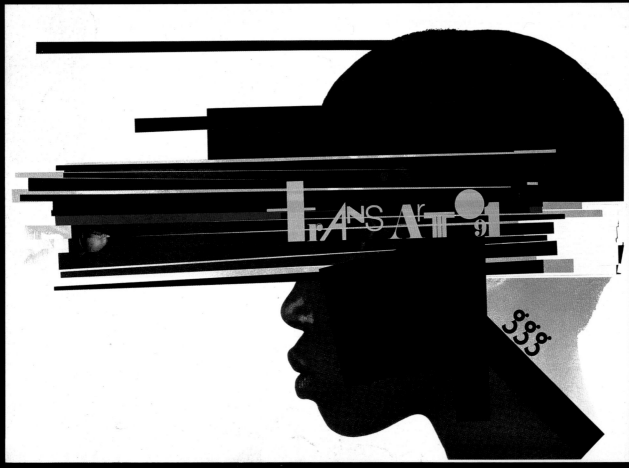

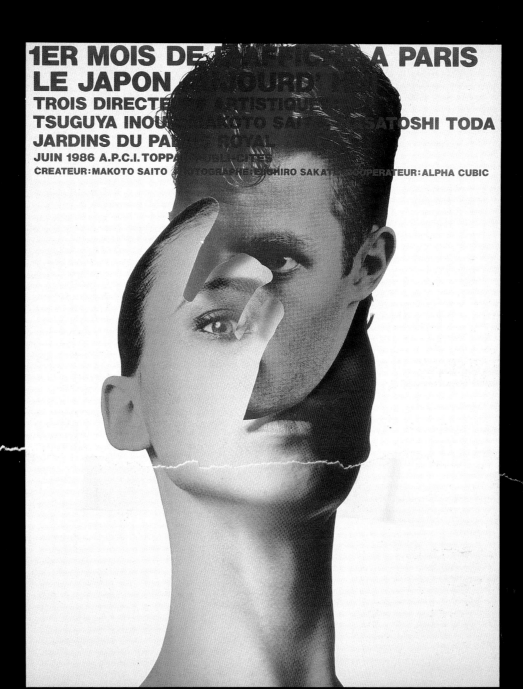

MAKOTO SAITO

PORTRÄT MAKOTO SAITO
VON KAZUMI KURIGAMI

. . . .

Die Plakatkunst in Japan hat wenig mit Avantgarde zu tun. Die Kriterien, nach denen Graphik-Design beurteilt wird, sind vor allem die geschmackvolle Gestaltung, Ausarbeitung von Details, die ruhige Ausstrahlung, Verständlichkeit oder interessante gestalterische Aspekte. Nur sehr wenige Graphik-Designer haben einen wirklich eigenen Stil. Wenn ich etwas entwerfe, will ich etwas Neues machen. Ich kümmere mich nicht um das, was im Bereich des Graphik-Designs geschieht, und es interessiert mich nicht, nach den von anderen aufgestellten Regeln zu arbeiten. Ich will etwas gestalten, das noch nie dagewesen ist. □ Ich habe mich mit Philosophie befasst, nicht mit Design. Ich wollte mich nicht von dem beeinflussen lassen, was man in der Vergangenheit gemacht hat. Für mich ist das Design der Vergangenheit für Dinge der Vergangenheit. Wichtig ist für mich, was ich jetzt mache. Ich brauche die Anerkennung der Masse nicht, und es ist mir gleichgültig, was man von meiner Arbeit hält. Wenn sich jemand meine Arbeiten anschaut und sie als «nett» bezeichnet, bin ich enttäuscht. Es gibt meiner Meinung nach nicht sehr viele Leute, die wirklich sehen, was sie vor sich haben, die auch die Nuancen und Details von etwas erfassen, das wirklich neu ist. Das soll nicht heissen, dass die Meinung des Durchschnittsbürgers irrelevant ist. Auf seiner Ebene hat sie durchaus Gültigkeit. Wenn ich etwas entwerfe, denke ich aber an die wenigen, die sehen, worum es geht. □ Werbung wird in Japan nach ihrer Wirksamkeit als Marketinginstrument beurteilt, in kreativer Hinsicht lässt sie leider viel zu wünschen übrig. Wenn man die Wirkung auf die Masse als Massstab wählt, kann nichts anderes dabei herauskommen. In einer Gruppe von 70 Leuten werden höchstens 10 begreifen, was der Designer tut. Also werden die Leute mit einem Gefühl für Ästhetik im Verhältnis 60:10 überstimmt, wenn es darum geht, eine Entscheidung zu treffen. (Ich muss zugeben, dass es ziemlich überwältigend wäre, wenn alle 70 dieser Gruppe etwas von Design verstünden. Und wenn es ums Geschäft geht, schliesse selbst ich mich dieser grösseren Gruppe an.) □ Design basiert auf der Wechselwirkung zwischen den Unternehmen und der Gesellschaft, in der sie existiert. Der Inhaber einer Firma hat grossen Einfluss auf den Firmenauftritt, und wenn er ein sicheres Gefühl für Stil hat, kann sich sein Einfluss sehr positiv auswirken. Umgekehrt wirkt sich sein Mangel an Stilgefühl negativ auf die Firma und ihre Produkte aus. Natürlich muss ein Unternehmen nach Gewinn streben, aber es gibt einige Firmen, die noch etwas anderes suchen, etwas, das über den Gewinn hinausgeht. Es geht ihnen z.B. darum, ein Gefühl von Romantik zu vermitteln oder etwas Glanz und Raffinesse. □ Dieses Gespür für eine eigene Ästhetik ist es, das die Firmenkultur ausmacht. Mit solchen Firmen möchte ich zusammenarbeiten. Ich möchte mich so weit wie möglich von dem entfernen, was man Graphik-Design nennt. Aber ich will auch nicht «reine Kunst» machen. Was ich erreichen möchte, ist eine Ausdrucksform, die zwischen Kunst und Design liegt, die darüber hinausgeht. ■

. . . .

MAKOTO SAITO, 1952 IN DER PRÄFEKTUR FUKUOKA IN JAPAN GEBOREN, IST EINER DER INTERNATIONAL BEKANNTESTEN PLAKATGESTALTER UNSERER ZEIT. SEINE PLAKATE WURDEN BEI INTERNATIONALEN WETTBEWERBEN MIT ZAHLREICHEN PREISEN AUSGEZEICHNET: U.A. MIT GOLDMEDAILLEN DES NEW YORK ART DIRECTORS CLUBS IN DEN JAHREN 1987, 1988, 1989 UND 1992; EBENFALLS GOLD ERHIELT ER BEI DER INTERNATIONALEN TRIENNALE IN TOYAMA (1985, 1988, 1991) SOWIE 1989 DEN GRAND PRIX UND 1991 DEN SONDERPREIS DER POSTER BIENNALE IN LAHTI. ■

M A K O T O   S A I T O

En ce qui concerne la création d'affiches au Japon, on ne peut pas dire qu'elle soit d'avant-garde. La plupart des créations du design graphique sont jugéés selon des critères de bon goût, suivant l'élaboration des détails, le calme qu'elles émanent, la lisibilité ou d'autres aspects intéressants au niveau de la composition. Or, seuls quelques designers font vraiment preuve d'un style personnel. A chaque fois que j'esquisse quelque chose, je désire faire quelque chose de complètement nouveau. C'est pourquoi je ne me préoccupe pas de ce qui se passe dans le secteur du design graphique. Travailler à partir de principes établis par d'autres ne m'intéresse pas le moins du monde. Je veux concevoir des images qu'on n'a encore jamais vues auparavant. ☐ J'ai fait des études de philosophie, et non pas de design. Je ne voulais pas me laisser influencer par ce qui avait été fait dans le passé. Je dirais que le design du passé appartient au passé. Seul importe pour moi ce que je fais maintenant. Je n'ai pas besoin de la reconnaissance des masses et ce qu'elles pensent de mon travail m'est totalement égal. Si quelqu'un regarde l'une de mes affiches et dit que c'est «bien», je suis plutôt déçu. A mon avis, rares sont les gens qui savent véritablement voir ce qu'ils ont sous les yeux, qui sont capables de saisir toutes les nuances et les détails de quelque chose qui est vraiment nouveau. Cela ne veut pas dire pour autant qu'il faille négliger le jugement de l'homme de la rue. A son niveau, il est aussi valable. Lorsque je crée quelque chose, c'est toutefois à ces quelques rares personnes qui savent vraiment voir que je pense. ☐ Au Japon, la publicité est jugée en fonction de son efficacité en tant qu'instrument de marketing; pour ce qui est des qualités de création, cela laisse malheureusement à désirer. C'est inévitable quand les décisions sont prises sur la base de l'effet qu'elles produisent sur les masses. Dans un groupe de 70 personnes par exemple, dix au maximum vont sans doute comprendre ce que le designer a fait. Les gens qui ont un sens de l'esthétique seront donc mis en minorité à 60 contre10, lorsqu'il sera question de prendre une décision. (Je dois toutefois admettre que ce serait vraiment extraordinaire si les 70 personnes comprenaient quelque chose au design. Mais quand il s'agit de faire des affaires, je me range à l'avis de ce groupe.) ☐ Le design se base sur l'interaction de l'entreprise et de la société dans laquelle elle se trouve. Le propriétaire d'une entreprise joue un rôle considérable sur la façon dont celle-ci est perçue: s'il est raffiné et qu'il a un goût sûr, cela peut avoir des répercussions tout à fait positives. Mais si au contraire, il n'a aucun sens du style, cela aura des conséquences négatives sur la firme et sur ses produits. Naturellement, une entreprise est tenue de réaliser des bénéfices, mais il existe des firmes qui cherchent encore autre chose, quelque chose qui dépasse le simple niveau du profit. Il leur tient à cœur par exemple de transmettre un sentiment de romantisme, ou bien un certain éclat, un certain raffinement. ☐ C'est ce sens prononcé de leur esthétique propre qui détermine la culture des entreprises. J'aimerais pour ma part travailler pour ces firmes. Je souhaiterais me distancer le plus possible du design graphique proprement dit. Mais je ne veux pas non plus faire de «l'art pour l'art». Ce que je désire dans mon travail, c'est découvrir une forme d'expression qui se situe quelque part entre l'art et le design, qui les transcende en quelque sorte. ■

MAKOTO SAITO, NÉ EN 1954 DANS LA PRÉFECTURE DE FUKUOKA AU JAPON, EST L'UN DES CRÉATEURS D'AFFICHES LES PLUS CÉLÈBRES DE NOTRE ÉPOQUE. SES AFFICHES ONT REÇU DE NOMBREUX PRIX DANS LES CONCOURS INTERNATIONAUX, NOTAMMENT LA MÉDAILLE D'OR DU ART DIRECTORS CLUB DE NEW YORK EN 1987, 1988, 1989 ET 1992, LA MÉDAILLE D'OR DE LA TRIENNALE INTERNATIONALE DE TOYAMA EN 1985, 1988 ET 1991, AINSI QUE LE GRAND PRIX (EN 1989) ET LE PRIX SPÉCIAL DU JURY (1991) DE LA BIENNALE DE L'AFFICHE À LAHTI. ■

The room: four walls, a bed, a dresser drawer full of collectibles—a couple of arrowheads, some coins and a few treasured baseball cards. Under the mattress, your favorite baseball glove, ball in the pocket, wrapped in a belt and soaked with Glovoleum. On the nightstand lie the latest issue of *Mad* magazine, a Batman comic book and your Game Boy. □ The room of a 12-year-old kid is where you'll find NIKE posters, not taped inside a shop window announcing a museum opening, or screaming social commentary from a telephone pole. Sports is about youth, the age of innocence, when you take things at face value, when you have heroes, when your thoughts of greatness are not dreams but plans. Think back to your room. It was a sanctuary, a place of independence, the walls covered with images of rock bands, a car calendar, and a sports poster that you would stare at until your gaze drifted to the ceiling, taking you worlds away. This is the field of competition for NIKE posters. □ For some it was Ted Williams, Joe Namath, Bill Russell or Billie Jean King. For others it is Ken Griffey Jr., Michael Jordan or André Agassi. It doesn't matter. Across generations athletes have represented something special to all of us, and it is this intangible sense of connection that is the foundation for our communication with consumers. □ As NIKE celebrates its 20th anniversary, we are still relatively new to the world of sports memorabilia. NIKE posters began in the late '70s with a fresh approach. Unlike other athlete-in-action posters, a NIKE poster played off an athlete's personality. What was it that distinguished this person in the eyes of a child? The other (and often more difficult) part of the question was: How do we communicate this to the consumer? Humor and irreverence have always been exceptionally effective for NIKE, and we made full use of these tools in our early posters. Sets were built to strengthen the concepts— often visual puns setting an athlete's talent, reputation or name against a common phrase or image. During this same period, NIKE developed a series of "inspirational" posters. Unlike our "personality" posters, these generally featured unknown athletes (usually running). The headlines were motivational messages, such as "There Is No Finish Line." □ These early NIKE posters weren't for sale. We designed them for promotional use, printing just enough to give to retailers and to distribute at sporting events. This changed in the early '80s, when we discovered that the posters were being sold on the black market for many times their cost. At the same time, many companies began to market their own sports posters successfully. The time was right for NIKE to step into the business of selling posters. □ The time was also right to try a few new things creatively, to blast out of the comfort zone. Using the foundation formed by the personality poster, we took the athletes out of the studio and placed them on the field. At the same time, technological advances that have since become commonplace, such as the use of high-end computer systems in the separation process, allowed us to expand the possibilities of our posters and to create situations that had previously been impossible to execute. NIKE has also had success with wholly illustrated posters, and with posters combining illustration and photography. □ Whatever the poster ends up looking like, the beginning of the process is always the same. Designers sit down with writers and the name of an athlete. First come the questions: Who is this person? What has he done? What can we say about him? What can't we say? How much can we spend to say it? Sometimes the ideas flow, sometimes they don't. There is as much argument as there is agreement, and everything comes under scrutiny, even the basic definition of a poster. Who said a poster has to be a flat piece of paper 18 by 24 inches? NIKE introduced a three-dimensional poster, die-cut posters, oversize ceiling and door posters, round posters, skewed posters and otherwise unconventional

MOSES

W   I   N   G   S

No bird soars too high,
If he soars with his own wings.
—William Blake

NIKE

Rice Be Nimble, Rice Be Quick,

posters. So far, we haven't been sorry. □ Two things have remained constant in NIKE posters since their beginning: creatively, the use of humor, irreverence and inspiration to create an emotional tie with the consumer; pragmatically, to get as many posters as possible in the public eye (and on kids' walls). This year NIKE has expanded distribution channels to offer more posters to a wide range of consumers. There are 60 new posters, and we're also producing athlete calendars. We plan to expand into other areas, such as trading cards, buttons and possibly T-shirts and other garments. □ Even this brief mention of marketing strategies and consumer potential gets me very excited about the future of NIKE posters. It also makes me a little nervous. Sometimes I worry that the realities of business will permanently fade the dream. Then, while I'm designing a new poster, out of nowhere I get a whiff of Glovoleum. I remember the room, and the heroes. These fleeting connections assure me that I'm still alive, and still dreaming. ■

RON DUMAS IS CREATIVE DIRECTOR OF THE GRAPHIC-DESIGN GROUP AT NIKE, WHERE HE OVERSEES THE EFFORTS OF 17 GRAPHIC DESIGNERS, THREE WRITERS AND FOUR OPERATIONS PEOPLE. HE HAS DESIGNED SOME OF NIKE'S MOST MEMORABLE IMAGES, INCLUDING "WINGS," A POSTER OF THE BASKETBALL STAR MICHAEL JORDAN, WHICH IS NOW ON PERMANENT DISPLAY IN THE LIBRARY OF CONGRESS. AS PART OF HIS CORPORATE-IDENTIFICATION WORK, DUMAS IS RESPONSIBLE FOR NIKE'S LOGO DEVELOPMENT. A NATIVE OF THE PACIFIC NORTHWEST, HE JOINED NIKE IN 1984. ■

Das Zimmer: vier Wände, ein Bett, eine Schublade mit allen möglichen Schätzen – ein paar Pfeilspitzen, einige Münzen und ein paar für den Besitzer kostbare Baseball-Karten. Unter der Matratze der Lieblings-Baseball-Handschuh, ein Ball, der Geruch von Glovoleum-Öl. Auf dem Nachttisch die neuste Ausgabe von *Mad*, ein Batman-Comics-Heft und ein Computerspiel. □ Der Bewohner dieses Zimmers ist ein 12jähriges amerikanisches Kind. Genau hier findet man NIKE-Plakate. Sie haben weder mit Museumseröffnungen zu tun noch mit aufrüttelnden Appellen oder Kommentaren, es geht um Sport und damit um die Jugend. Wenn man jung ist, hat man Idole, man träumt nicht davon, Grossartiges zu erreichen, man ist fest davon überzeugt, dass man es schaffen wird. Erinnern Sie sich an Ihr Zimmer. Es war Ihr Reich, ein Ort der Unabhängigkeit, die Wände vollgepflastert mit Bildern von Rock Bands, einem Autokalender, einem Sportplakat, auf dem die Augen vor dem Einschlafen ruhen, bevor sie zur Decke wandern und man schliesslich in andere Welten versinkt. In diesem Umfeld findet der Konkurrenzkampf der NIKE-Plakate statt. □ Für einige war es Ted Williams, Joe Namath, Bill Russell oder Billie Jean King. Für andere ist es Michael Jordan oder André Agassi. Es kommt nicht darauf an, wer das Idol ist. Für alle Generationen waren Athleten etwas Besonders, hier gibt es eine Gemeinsamkeit, auf der unsere Kommunikation mit den Konsumenten aufbaut. □ NIKE feiert gerade sein 20jähriges Bestehen und ist damit relativ neu in der Welt der Sport-Souvenirs. Die NIKE-Plakate erschienen in den späten siebziger Jahren. Sie waren ganz anders als die üblichen Plakate mit Athleten in Aktion. Bei Nike ging es um die Persönlichkeit eines Athleten. Was macht diese Person in den Augen eines Kindes zu etwas Besonderem? Der andere, oft schwierigere Teil der Frage war: Wie vermitteln wir dies dem Konsumenten? Schon immer hatte NIKE aussergewöhnlich erfolgreich mit Humor und Unbekümmertheit operiert, und bei unseren ersten Plakaten bedienten wir uns ausgiebig dieser Mittel. Oft wurde das Konzept durch visuelle Wortspiele, die sich auf das Können, den Ruf oder den Namen eines Athleten bezogen, unterstützt. In dieser Zeit entwikkelte NIKE auch eine Reihe von «Inspirations»-Plakaten. Im Gegensatz zu den «Persönlichkeits»-Plakaten zeigten diese unbekannte Athleten (gewöhnlich Läufer). Die Headlines waren motivierende Botschaften. □ Diese frühen NIKE-Plakate waren nicht käuflich. Wir entwarfen sie für Promotionszwecke, und die Auflage war gerade gross genug, um Läden und Sportveranstaltungen zu versorgen. Das änderte sich in den frühen achtziger Jahren, als wir entdeckten, dass die Plakate auf dem Schwarzmarkt gehandelt wurden, und zwar zu überhöhten Preisen. Gleichzeitig begannen viele Firmen damit, ihre Plakate zu verkaufen, und sie hatten Erfolg damit. □ Das war der richtige Zeitpunkt für NIKE, sich in das Geschäft des Plakatverkaufs einzulassen. Es war auch der richtige

Zeitpunkt, um etwas in kreativer Hinsicht zu wagen. Als Grundlage dienten die Persönlichkeits-Plakate. Wir brachten die Athleten aus dem Studio hinaus an den Ort des Geschehens. Technische Fortschritte durch neue Computersysteme für die Lithoherstellung erschlossen uns bei den Plakaten neue Möglichkeiten. Wir konnten Dinge machen, die vorher unmöglich gewesen waren. NIKE hatte auch mit zeichnerisch illustrierten Plakaten Erfolg sowie mit Kombinationen von Zeichnung und Photographie. □ Wie immer das Plakat herauskommt, der Anfang des Arbeitsprozesses ist immer der gleiche. Designer setzen sich mit Textern zusammen. Vorgegeben ist der Name des Athleten und die ersten Fragen, die man sich zu stellen hat, lauten: Wer ist diese Person? Was hat sie geleistet? Was können wir über sie sagen? Wieviel können wir dafür ausgeben? Manchmal fliessen die Ideen, manchmal nicht. Es gibt Zustimmung und Ablehnung, und alles wird sorgfältig geprüft, sogar die grundsätzliche Definition eines Plakates. Wer sagt, dass ein Plakat ein flaches Stück Papier in einem bestimmten Format sein muss? NIKE brachte dreidimensionale Plakate heraus, ausgestanzte Plakate, übergrosse Decken- und Türplakate, runde Plakate, schräge und andere ausgefallene

Plakate. Bis jetzt haben wir nichts bereut. □ Zwei Dinge sind seit der Einführung der NIKE-Plakate konstant geblieben: In kreativer Hinsicht der Einsatz von Humor, Respektlosigkeit und das Gespür dafür, wie wir den Konsumenten auf emotionaler Ebene erreichen; in pragmatischer Hinsicht ist es der Wunsch, mit möglichst vielen Plakaten an das Publikum (und die vier Wände der Kinderzimmer) zu gelangen. □ Dieses Jahr hat NIKE die Vertriebskanäle erweitert, um einem breitem Publikum noch mehr Plakate anbieten zu können. Es gibt 60 neue Plakate, und wir stellen auch Athleten-Kalender her. Wir haben vor, auch in andere Bereiche zu expandieren: Wir denken dabei an Sportbilder, Buttons und möglicherweise T-Shirts und andere Bekleidungsstücke. □ Natürlich bin ich von den Marketingstrategien und dem Konsumentenpotential begeistert, aber ich werde auch ein bisschen nervös dabei. Manchmal fürchte ich, dass die Realitäten des Geschäftslebens den Traum für immer auslöschen werden. Doch dann steigt mir beim Entwerfen eines neuen Plakates der Geruch des Glovoleum-Öls in die Nase, und ich sehe plötzlich das Zimmer, die Idole vor mir. Dieses flüchtige Aufsteigen der Kindheit sagt mir, dass ich noch lebe und noch immer träume. ■

RON DUMAS STAMMT VON DER PAZIFIKKÜSTE IM NORDWESTEN DER USA. 1984 KAM ER ALS SENIOR DESIGNER ZU NIKE. HEUTE IST ER CREATIVE DIRECTOR DER GRAPHIK-DESIGN-GRUPPE. ER ARBEITET MIT 17 GRAPHIK-DESIGNERN, DREI TEXTERN UND VIER PROJEKTPLANERN. ALS DESIGNER HAT ER EINIGE DER BESTEN BILDER FÜR NIKE GESCHAFFEN, WIE Z.B. DAS «WINGS»-PLAKAT DES BASKETBALL-STARS MICHAEL JORDAN, DAS JETZT IN DER LIBRARY OF CONGRESS HÄNGT. IM CORPORATE-IDENTITY-BEREICH WAR ER FÜR DIE LOGO-ENTWICKLUNG ZUSTÄNDIG. ■

La pièce: quatre murs, un lit, une étagère sur laquelle s'entassent les objets les plus hétéroclites – deux pointes de flèches, quelques pièces de monnaie et des cartes de base-ball, conservées amoureusement par leur propriétaire. Sous le lit, son gant de base-ball favori, une balle, l'odeur de l'huile Glovoleum. Sur la table de nuit, le dernier numéro de *Mad*, un livre de bandes dessinées de Batman et un jeu électronique. □ Ce lieu n'est autre que la chambre d'un adolescent américain. C'est là que vous trouverez des affiches NIKE. Elles n'ont rien à voir avec ces affiches qu'on voit dans les vitrines et qui annoncent l'ouverture d'un musée, ou bien celles dont le message social déchirant vous interpelle. Elles parlent de sport, et donc de la jeunesse. Quand on est jeune, on

a des idoles; on ne rêve pas de devenir célèbre, on est absolument convaincu qu'on y réussira. Vous vous souvenez de votre chambre d'adolescent? C'était votre royaume, le lieu même de votre indépendance: des murs couverts d'images de groupes rock, un calendrier de voitures et une affiche sportive, sur laquelle les yeux se reposaient avant de s'endormir, avant de s'évader vers d'autres mondes. C'est là le vrai terrain de prédilection des affiches NIKE. □ Les idoles des uns s'appelaient Ted Williams, Joe Namath, Bill Russell ou Billie Jean King, celles des autres Michael Jordan ou André Agassi. Peu importe. Pour toutes les générations, les athlètes ont représenté quelque chose de particulier. Il y a là quelques traits communs avec ce qui est à la base de notre communication avec le consommateur. □ NIKE fête son 20e anniversaire et c'est une marque encore relativement jeune dans la branche. Les premières affiches NIKE furent publiées à la fin des années 70. Elles étaient différentes de toutes les autres affiches, sur lesquelles on voyait des athlètes en pleine action. Ce qui intéresse NIKE, c'est la personnalité de ces athlètes. Qu'est-ce qui fait qu'il est si extraordinaire aux yeux d'un enfant? L'autre aspect, le plus difficile, de la question était: comment allons-nous communiquer cela au consommateur? NIKE avait toujours su procéder avec humour et de manière irrévérencieuse, et dans nos premières affiches, nous avons appliqué ce principe. Souvent, le concept était renforcé par des jeux de mots visuels qui se rapportaient aux performances, à la renommée ou au nom d'un athlète. NIKE produisit à cette époque une série d'affiches «d'inspiration». Au contraire des affiches de personnalités, ces dernières représentaient généralement des athlètes inconnus (des coureurs notamment). Les accroches étaient des messages de motivation. □ Ces premières affiches de NIKE n'étaient pas faites pour la vente. Nous les avions créées pour un usage promotionnel, et les tirages suffisaient à peine pour tous les magasins et les manifestations sportives. Tout a changé au début des années 80, lorsque nous avons découvert que les affiches étaient revendues au marché noir, et qui plus est, à des prix exorbitants. Au même moment, de nombreuses firmes commencèrent, avec succès, à vendre leurs affiches. □ Le moment était venu pour NIKE de se lancer à son tour dans ce commerce. C'était aussi l'occasion ou jamais de montrer plus d'audace dans la création, de sortir des sentiers battus. Les affiches de personnalités fournirent le point de départ: nous avons sorti les athlètes des studios pour les photographier sur le lieu de l'action. En même temps, les derniers progrès technologiques, par exemple l'emploi de systèmes d'ordinateur perfectionnés dans la résolution de l'image, nous ont permis d'étendre le champ de nos possibilités et d'imaginer des situations qu'il aurait été auparavant impossible de concevoir. NIKE a eu également beaucoup de succès avec des affiches complètement illustrées et des affiches combinant l'illustration et la photographie. □ Quelle que soit l'affiche, le processus est toujours le même. Les designers se réunissent avec les rédacteurs. Quelqu'un suggère le nom d'un athlète. Puis les questions fusent: qui est-ce? qu'est-ce qu'il a fait? qu'est-ce qu'on pourrait bien dire de lui? de quel budget dispose-t-on? Parfois les idées coulent de source, parfois c'est le néant. On discute le pour et le contre, tout est soigneusement étudié, y compris la conception fondamentale de l'affiche. Qui a dit qu'une affiche devait être un morceau de papier plat de 18 x 24 inches? NIKE a produit des affiches tridimensionnelles, des affiches découpées, des affiches géantes pour coller aux portes ou aux plafonds, des affiches rondes, taillées en biais et d'autres variations absolument inédites. Nous ne l'avons pas regretté. □ Deux choses sont restées constantes depuis le début: au niveau créatif, l'humour, l'attitude irrévérencieuse et le sens de ce qui saura émouvoir le spectateur; dans un esprit plus pragmatique, le désir de toucher le plus de monde possible (et d'orner les murs des chambres des adolescents). □ Cette année, NIKE a étendu ses réseaux de distribution, afin de pouvoir proposer ses affiches à un plus vaste public. Nous avons créé 60 nouvelles affiches et nous produisons aussi des calendriers d'athlètes. Nous avons l'intention de nous lancer dans d'autres secteurs: nous pensons à des cartes, des badges, peut-être même des T-shirts ou autres vêtements. □ Je suis bien sûr optimiste à l'idée des stratégies de marketing et du potentiel de consommateurs, mais parfois, je suis un peu inquiet. Je redoute que les réalités du business ne finissent par tuer le rêve. Pourtant, quand je suis en train de concevoir une nouvelle affiche, l'odeur de l'huile Glovoleum me remplit les narines et soudain, je revois ma chambre, les idoles sur les murs. Cette bouffée de souvenirs me rassure: je vis encore et je suis encore capable de rêver. ■

RON DUMAS EST DIRECTEUR DE LA CRÉATION CHEZ NIKE; IL A SOUS SA DIRECTION 17 DESIGNERS GRAPHIQUES, TROIS RÉDACTEURS ET QUATRE DIRECTEURS DE PROJET. DESIGNER, IL EST RESPONSABLE DE QUELQUES-UNES DES IMAGES LES PLUS FAMEUSES DE NIKE, NOTAMMENT «WINGS», UNE AFFICHE DE MICHAEL JORDAN, LA STAR DU BASKET-BALL AMÉRICAIN, EXPOSÉE EN PERMANENCE DANS LA LIBRARY OF CONGRESS; IL A ÉGALEMENT CONÇU LE LOGO, PARTIE INTÉGRANTE DE L'IDENTITÉ VISUELLE DE NIKE. NÉ SUR LA CÔTE PACIFIQUE NORD-OUEST, IL A ÉTÉ ENGAGÉ CHEZ NIKE COMME SENIOR DESIGNER EN 1984. ■

CATHERINE BÜRER

PORTRAIT OF CATHERINE BÜRER
BY JAN ZWART

. . . .

A torn poster, behind which parts of the previous poster are visible: This everyday image is a surrealist spectacle, simultaneously poetic, funny and relevant. The image bears witness to the relevance of this medium, as a new message takes the place of the previous one, and the passerby is faced with a new attempt at seduction or provocation. Some may walk past without looking, without being touched, but more often the passerby's attention is caught, and in an instant the poster may have changed his mood or his viewpoint. ☐ The remarkable thing is the dialogue between poster asnd passerby, one provoking, the other reacting. The span of reactions is wide: smiles, laughter, disdain, disgust, interest, admiration. The dialogue determines, for each viewer, the value of the poster, its success in evoking the intended effect. ☐ Why choose the poster to carry a message? To use Marshall McLuhan's famous phrase, "The medium is the message." In other words, to guarantee the effect of the message, one must choose the appropriate channel. Everyone working in advertising knows that a poster has a certain effect on the public, a different effect from any other medium. It is a nonconformist. Today, the audio-visual dominates the world of imagery. Images move, are torn apart, jump, tremble. We go from one picture to the next without taking the time to look at any of them. The clarity of the fixed image is superseded by a blurred succession of images. The concepts of progress and progression condition us, the focus is on ever increasing productivity, and "efficiency" is the key word for everything that happens in politics, business, the intellectual world, the world of advertising and even the world of art. Creative work that does not follow these rules fascinates me now more than ever. ☐ The way we use and understand a medium is defined by different characteristics in different cultures. In Japan, for example, the job of the poster is not to carry information to a potential customer but to carry an esthetic or entertaining message. In the Japanese culture, which is defined by efficiency and earnings, the poster's role is to open the door to imagination, to allow distraction and relaxation. The craziest ideas may be realized. Finesse, sensuality, playful forms, violent colors—everything contributes to astonishing and charming the viewer rather than convincing him. ☐ In our Western culture, it seems that information takes priority over the image. The word dominates. The message comes clothed in different written forms, which change according to the current fashion or business priorities: Dynamism succeeds style, humor or intellectualism follows realism. The function of "buying" the viewer's complicity takes precedence over the pure, free-of-cost spectacle. I remain convinced, however, that the poster can combine advertising messages and esthetic or stimulating qualities, and that the result can etch itself into one's memory and be valued as a work of art. □ How can one not be drawn to A.M. Cassandre's 1925 poster for the French newspaper *L'Intransigeant*? It transmits a message through its simplicity of design, harmony of colors and balanced composition. Words are not the core of the work; they are merely explanation. Similarly in Werner Jeker's 1984 poster for Banzaï. Here also, the spatial element is given priority. The strangeness of this poster provokes strong reactions: curiosity, dread, perplexity, sensuality. Or look at Herbert Matter's photomontages: They evoke a certain atmosphere, the images alone bringing the effect.

CASSANDRE'S L'INTRANSIGEANT

The image carries the message at first sight. These are very different types of posters, but in all of them, the emotion that the poster evokes in the viewer is what counts. □ A poster, Cassandre said, "must carry in itself the solution to three problems: optical, graphic and poetic." It must be seen; its language is "image, the carrier of thought itself." The poster "has only one way to make itself heard: poetic language." Poetry, whether shocking or tender, is always emotion. □ The power of imagination resides within the image. Proof is provided by advertising campaigns, such as the Benetton campaign, which provoked passionate reactions. Without encumbering itself with questions of esthetics or ethics, placing all its force on effect, the poster transmits emotion, whether pleasure, disgust, scandal or amusement. When this occurs, the poster has performed its most important function: to be seen and commented upon. ∎

CATHERINE BÜRER WAS BORN IN GENEVA IN 1957, AND STUDIED ART HISTORY AT THE UNIVERSITY OF GENEVA. SINCE 1990 SHE HAS BEEN DIRECTOR OF THE POSTER COLLECTION AT THE MUSEUM FÜR GESTALTUNG IN ZÜRICH. SHE IS THE EDITOR OF POSTERS FROM JAPAN 1978-1993, TO BE PUBLISHED IN AN ENGLISH/JAPANESE AND A GERMAN/JAPANESE VERSION BY EDITION STEMMLE IN JUNE 1993, TO ACCOMPANY AN EXHIBITION AT THE MUSEUM.∎

Ein zerfetztes Plakat, dahinter ein anderes, älteres Plakat: dieses alltägliche Bild ist ein surrealistisches Spektakel, voller Poesie, amüsant und zugleich bezeichnend. Es zeugt vom Leben und der Aktualität dieses Mediums: unausweichlich löst eine neue Botschaft die vorhergehende ab, konfrontiert den Passanten mit einem neuen Versuch der Verführung oder Herausforderung. Einige mögen achtlos an einem Plakat vorbeigehen, unberührt, doch die meisten sehen hin, und seine blosse Existenz genügt, um für einen Moment ihre Sehweise zu verändern, vielleicht ihre Laune zu beeinflussen. □ Das Erstaunliche an diesem Phänomen ist die Wechselbeziehung zwischen zwei gegebenen Grössen: auf der einen Seite das Plakat, das herausfordert, auf der andern der Passant, der darauf reagiert. Es sind zwei Partner, zwischen denen sich ein Dialog aufbaut. Dabei ist die Palette der Reaktionen sehr unterschiedlich: vom Lächeln zum Lachen, von Geringschätzung bis Abscheu, von Interesse bis Bewunderung. Von dieser

Dialektik hängt, subjektiv gesehen, der Wert ab, der dem Plakat zugesprochen wird, die Wirkung des Plakats im Verhältnis zum angestrebten Ziel. □ Ich persönlich bin für das Emotionale sehr empfänglich. Wir leben in einer Zeit, in der das Audiovisuelle die Bilderwelt dominiert: die Klarheit des fixen Bildes weicht der Verschwommenheit der rasch aufeinanderfolgenden Bilder. Fortschritt und Fortschreiten, das sind die Konzepte, die uns konditionieren. Effizienz ist das Schlüsselwort für alles, was in der Politik, in der Wirtschaft, im intellektuellen Bereich, in der Werbung, und selbst in der Kunst geleistet wird. Ein Werk, das sich nicht diesen Zwängen unterwirft, fasziniert mich daher heute mehr denn je. □ Warum sollte man Bilder einsetzen, um Gefühle hervorzurufen? Und warum sollte man ein Plakat als Träger einer Botschaft wählen? 1964 erklärte Marshall McLuhan: «Das Medium ist die Botschaft.» Im Klartext heisst das: um die Wirksamkeit der zu vermittelnden Botschaft sicherzustellen, muss man das entsprechende

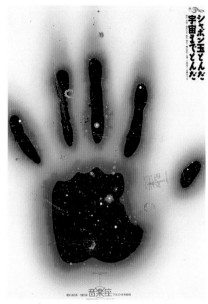  

LEFT TO RIGHT: "BUBBLE" BY KOICHI SATO, 1989; WERNER JEKER'S "BANZAÏ," 1984; A 1934 POSTER BY HERBERT MATTER.

Medium wählen. Insofern ist ein Plakat bereits Träger einer Botschaft. Jeder Werbeschaffende weiss, dass das Plakat eine bestimmte Wirkung auf das Publikum hat, eine Wirkung, die sich von der eines anderen Mediums unterscheidet. Dieses Medienverständnis definiert sich durch verschiedene, kulturabhängige Merkmale. □ Schockwirkung des Bildes oder Schockwirkung der Information, welches ist das dominierende Element? In Japan zum Beispiel werden Plakate nicht in erster Linie als Informationsträger für den potentiellen Konsumenten verstanden, sondern als Träger ästhetischer oder unterhaltender Botschaften. Paradoxerweise ist dieser Aspekt der freien Kreation gerade in einer Kultur, die wie keine andere durch Effizienz und Gewinn bestimmt wird, am stärksten vertreten. Ziel des Plakats ist es, Ausweichmöglichkeiten anzubieten, der Phantasie Tür und Tor zu öffnen, Ablenkung und Entspannung zu ermöglichen. In unserer westlichen Zivilisation hingegen wird die Information offenbar auf Kosten des Bildes bevorzugt. Tatsächlich dominiert das Wort – sei es durch seine alles andere ausschliessende Präsenz, sei es durch seine Bedeutung gegenüber dem Bild. □ Trotzdem bin ich überzeugt, dass Werbebotschaften und ästhetische oder stimulierende Eigenschaften miteinander verbunden werden können und dass so erstaunliche Kreationen entstehen, die sich dem Gedächtnis einprägen und als Kunstwerk geschätzt werden. □ Wie könnte man nicht von Cassandres Plakat für Intransigeant überwältigt sein. Hier wird eine Botschaft durch die schlichte Graphik, die Harmonie der Farben und die ausgewogene Komposition klar vermittelt. Das Wort dient dabei allein als erklärender Zusatz und ist nicht der Kern des Werkes. Denn allein die Gefühle, die beim Zuschauer wachgerufen werden, zählen: Das Bild vibriert und verankert sich im Gedächtnis. Cassandre selbst hat erklärt, dass ein Plakat «die Lösung für drei Problembereiche in sich tragen muss: für den optischen, den graphischen und den poetischen Bereich». Das Plakat muss gesehen werden, seine Sprache ist «das Bild als eigentlicher Vermittler der Idee», seine Rolle ist, mit jedem Individuum zu kommunizieren, «das Plakat hat nur eine Chance, sich Gehör zu verschaffen: durch die Sprache der Poesie». Die Poesie, ob sie als Schock oder als Zärtlichkeit auftritt, ist vor allem Gefühl. □ In der Geschichte des Plakats stossen wir auf viele andere Beispiele, die dieses Gefühl entstehen lassen,

P REAUPAGAND A

"PREAUPAGANDA," A 1991 POSTER BY MARSDEN LACHER STUDER, PLAYS ON THE WORD "EAU," FRENCH FOR "WATER."

zum Beispiel das Plakat für Banzaï von Werner Jeker, dessen Fremdheit schockiert, und das sich im Gedächtnis festsetzt durch die zahlreichen Empfindungen, die es hervorruft: Neugier, Erschauern, Verwirrung, Sinnlichkeit. Wie beim Plakat von Cassandre ist das räumliche Element das Wesentliche, das Wort bleibt Zusatz. □ Auch andere Plakate haben diese Kraft der emotionalen Botschaft. Die Photomontagen eines Herbert Matter drücken eine Stimmung aus, das Bild allein bestimmt die Wirkung. Auf den ersten Blick ist das Bild die Botschaft; Gustav Kluzis, John Heartfield, FHK Henrion, Emil Schulthess oder Klaus Staeck, um nur einige Namen zu nennen, setzten diese Technik mit Erfolg ein. □ Unumstritten ist, dass das Bild eine enorme Macht hat. Beweis dafür liefern Plakatkampagnen wie die für Perrier oder die für Benetton, wobei letztere leidenschaftliche Reaktionen verursachten. Der Sinn des Plakates, die Kommunikation herzustellen, ist damit erfüllt. Ohne sich mit Fragen des Ästhetizismus oder der Ethik herumzuschlagen, sondern alles auf die Wirkung setzend, vermittelt das Plakat ein Gefühl – sei es Freude oder Abscheu; es mag als skandalös oder unterhaltend empfunden werden. Wenn dieses Phänomen eintritt, hat das Plakat seinen wahren Sinn wiedergefunden: gesehen, betrachtet und kommentiert zu werden. ■

CATHERINE BÜRER, 1957 IN GENF GEBOREN, HAT IN GENF KUNSTGESCHICHTE STUDIERT. (THEMA IHRER LIZENZIATSARBEIT: «ZITAT DER KUNST IM WERBEPLAKAT».) SEIT 1990 IST SIE DIREKTORIN DER PLAKATSAMMLUNG DES MUSEUMS FÜR GESTALTUNG ZÜRICH. BEGLEITEND ZU EINER AUSSTELLUNG IN DIESEM MUSEUM WIRD IM JUNI 1993 BEI DER EDITION STEMMLE EIN BUCH VON IHR ÜBER «PLAKATE AUS JAPAN 1978-1993» ERSCHEINEN, UND ZWAR IN EINER DEUTSCH/JAPANISCHEN UND EINER ENGLISCH/JAPANISCHEN VERSION. ■

Une affiche déchirée, à travers laquelle perce une autre plus ancienne, c'est un spectacle surréaliste, poétique, cocasse ou pertinent tout à la fois. Cet état témoigne de la vie et de l'actualité de ce médium: inexorablement, un nouveau message prend la relève du précédent, une nouvelle tentative du séduction ou de provocation «agresse» le passant. Celui-ci peut passer, blasé, sans regarder. Pourtant, dans la majeure partie des cas, il l'aura perçue, et sa présence aura modifié son champ visuel, peut-être influencé son humeur, le temps d'un instant. □ Ce qui est remarquable dans ce phénomène est l'interdépendance entre deux entités: d'une part l'affiche, qui provoque, de l'autre le passant, qui réagit. Ce sont deux partenaires entre lesquels s'instaure un dialogue. La palette des réactions peut être très variable: du sourire au rire, du dédain au dégoût, de l'intérêt à l'admiration. De cette dialectique dépendra, subjectivement, la valeur donnée à l'affiche, son efficacité par rapport au but visé. □ Pour ma part, je suis très sensible à l'émotion. Nous vivons une ère où l'audio-visuel domine le monde de l'image; la netteté de l'image fixe laisse place à la vibration d'images successives. Les concepts de progrès, de progressions nous conditionnent, et «efficacité» est le mot-clé de toute réalisation politique, économique, intellectuelle, publicitaire et même artistique. Une création qui ne s'inscrit pas dans ces registres me fascine donc plus que jamais. □ En fait, pourqoi poser l'image comme révélateur d'émotion? Et pourqoi choisir l'affiche pour véhiculer un message? En 1964, Marshall McLuhan déclarait: «le message c'est le médium». En clair, en fonction du message à faire passer, on choisira le canal approprié. En tant que telle, l'affiche porte déjà un message. Chaque publicitaire sait que celle-ci a un effet déterminé sur le public, differérent de celui d'un autre médium. Cette compréhension du médium se matérialise par des caractéristiques différentes suivant les cultures. □ Choc de l'image ou choc de l'information, quel est l'élément prédominant? Au Japon par exemple, l'affiche n'est pas primairement considérée comme le porteur d'une information au consommateur potentiel, mais plutôt comme d'un message esthétique ou distrayant. C'est paradoxalement dans une culture conditionnée par l'efficacité et le rendement que cet aspect de la création libre est le plus présent. Le but de l'affiche est celui de permettre l'évasion, d'ouvrir la voie aux phantasmes, de distraire et de détendre. Raffinement, sensualité, jeu de formes, violence des couleurs, tout contribue à frapper et à charmer plus qu'à convaincre absolument. Dans notre société occidentale par contre, il semblerait que l'information soit privilégiée au détriment de l'image. Le verbe, en effet, domine soit par sa présence exclusive, soit par son importance face à l'image. □ Il n'en reste pas moins que je suis persuadée que message publicitaire et qualités esthétiques ou stimulantes peuvent être associés et donner lieu à des créations étonnantes qui s'imprègnent dans les mémoires et prennent valeur d'œuvre d'art.

□ Comment en effet ne pas être subjugué par l'affiche de Cassandre pour l'Intransigeant dans laquelle nous voyons un messsage transmis clairement par la simplicité du graphisme, l'harmonie des couleurs et l'équilibre de la composition. Le verbe sert ici uniquement de complément explicatif et ne forme pas le noyau de l'œuvre. C'est l'émotion qu'elle fait naître chez le spectateur qui compte: l'image vibre et s'ancre dans la mémoire. Cassandre lui-même déclarait qu'une affiche «doit porter en elle la solution de trois problèmes: optique, graphique, poétique». Elle doit être vue, son langage est «l'image, véhicule même de la pensée». Son rôle étant de communiquer avec chaque individu, «(elle) n'a qu'une chance de se faire entendre: le langage poétique». La poésie, qu'elle soit choc ou carress, est avant tout émotion. □ Nous trouvons, dans l'histoire de l'affiche, beaucoup d'autres exemples qui suscitent cette émotion, par exemple l'affiche pour Banzaï, de Werner Jeker, qui provoque un choc par son étrangeté et s'inscrit dans la mémoire par les sensations amoncelées: curiosité, frisson, perplexité, sensualité. Comme dans l'affiche de Cassandre, l'élément spatial est primordial, le verbe étant le complément. □ D'autres exemples prouvent cette force du message-émotion. Les photomontages d'un Herbert Matter expriment une ambiance, l'image à elle seule détermine l'effet. Vue au premier degré, elle est le message; Gustav Kluzis, John Heartfield, FKH Henrion, Emil Schulthess ou Klaus Staeck, pour ne nommer que ceux-là, utilisent cette technique avec succès. □ Il est incontestable que dans l'image réside un pouvoir fantastique. Preuve en sont les campagnes de publicité comme celle pour Perrier qui s'affiche sur nos murs ou celle pour Benetton qui suscitent les réactions les plus passionnées. Le but de l'affiche, établir la communication, est atteint. Sans s'encombrer de questions concernant l'esthétisme ou l'éthique, mais en misant tout sur l'effet, elle transmet une émotion, que ce soit plaisir, dégoût, scandale ou amusement. Lorsque ce phénomène se produit, l'affiche retrouve sa valeur première: être vue, regardée et commentée. ■

. . . .
CATHERINE BÜRER, NÉE EN 1957 À GENÈVE, OU ELLE A SUIVI DES ÉTUDES D'HISTOIRE DE L'ART (SUJET DU MÉMOIRE DE LICENCE: «CITATION DE L'ART DANS L'AFFICHE PUBLICITAIRE»), EST DIRECTRICE DE LA COLLECTION D'AFFICHES DU MUSEUM FÜR GESTALTUNG DE ZURICH DEPUIS 1990. ELLE EST L'AUTEUR DU LIVRE «PLAKATE AUS JAPAN 1978-1990», QUI PARAITRA EN JUIN 1993 AUX EDITIONS STEMMLE EN VERSION ALLEMAND/JAPONAIS ET ANGLAIS/JAPONAIS, PARALLELEMENT À L'EXPOSITION ORGANISÉE DANS CE MUSÉE. ■

ADVERTISING

WERBUNG

PUBLICITÉ

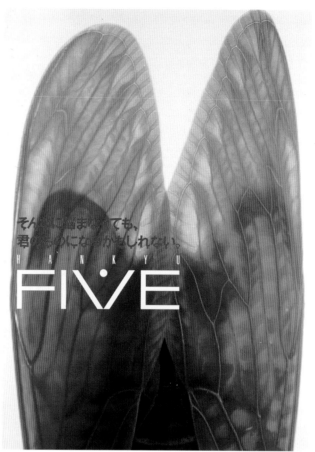

1

2

■ 1, 2 CREATIVE DIRECTOR: TOSHIHIRO KIUCHI ART DIRECTOR: KAZUHIRO SEKI DESIGNERS: KAZUHIRO SEKI, MITSUE MURAKAMI PHO-
TOGRAPHER: SAKAE TAKAHASHI COPYWRITER: TOSHIHIRO KIUCHI AGENCY: OSAKA YOMIURI ADVERTISING INC. CLIENT: HANKYU FIVE
■ 1, 2 FROM A SERIES OF POSTERS FOR THE JAPANESE DEPARTMENT STORE HANKYU FIVE. THE BRIDGE, THE OLDEST ONE IN
OSAKA, SERVES AS A SYMBOL FOR BRINGING PEOPLE TOGETHER. ● 1, 2 AUS EINER SERIE VON PLAKATEN FÜR DAS JAPANISCHE
KAUFHAUS HANKYU FIVE. DIE GEZEIGTE BRÜCKE IST DIE ÄLTESTE VON OSAKA UND DIENT ALS SYMBOL FÜR DAS ZUSAMMEN-
FÜHREN VON MENSCHEN. ▲ 1, 2 D'UNE SÉRIE D'AFFICHES CRÉÉES POUR LE GRAND MAGASIN JAPONAIS HANKYU FIVE. (JPN)

■ 3 CREATIVE DIRECTOR: JOHN C. JAY EXECUTIVE ART DIRECTOR: JIM CHRISTIE ART DIRECTORS: PAUL NISKI, JIM CHRISTIE DESIGNER:
JOHN DUFFY PHOTOGRAPHER: JIM COOPER COPYWRITER: SUSAN COOPER AGENCY: BLOOMINGDALE'S CLIENT: BLOOMINGDALE'S ■ 3
THE SUBJECT OF THIS POSTER FOR BLOOMINGDALE'S DEPARTMENT STORES IS HOME FURNISHINGS IN DIFFERENT REGIONS OF
THE UNITED STATES, OFFERING A FRESH PERSPECTIVE ON AMERICAN DESIGN. ● 3 DAS AMERIKANISCHE KAUFHAUS
BLOOMINGDALE'S BIETET MIT DIESEM PLAKAT EINE ANDERE PERSPEKTIVE AMERIKANISCHEN DESIGNS: HEIMTEXTILIEN AUS
VERSCHIEDENEN REGIONEN DER USA. ▲ 3 CETTE AFFICHE DES GRANDS MAGASINS BLOOMINGSDALE'S PRÉSENTE UN ASPECT
INÉDIT DU DESIGN AMÉRICAIN: DES TISSUS D'AMEUBLEMENT PROVENANT DE DIFFÉRENTES RÉGIONS DES ETATS-UNIS. (USA)

■ 4 ART DIRECTOR: IWAO MATSUURA DESIGNER: HIROSHI TSURUMAKI PHOTOGRAPHER: UMIHIKO KONISHI AGENCY: DAI-ICHI KIKAKU
CO. CLIENT: GINZA CORE CO. ■ 4 SPECIAL SALES ANNOUNCEMENT FOR A JAPANESE DEPARTMENT STORE. ● 4 ANKÜNDIGUNG
DES AUSVERKAUFS IN EINEM KAUFHAUS. ▲ 4 AFFICHE D'UN GRAND MAGASIN JAPONAIS ANNONÇANT LES SOLDES. (JPN)

■ (FOLLOWING SPREAD) **5** ART DIRECTOR/DESIGNER: BILL THORBURN PHOTOGRAPHER: SARAH MOON COPYWRITER: NICKI ROSSI AGENCY: DAYTON'S HUDSON'S MARSHALL FIELD'S DESIGN CLIENT: DAYTON'S HUDSON'S MARSHALL FIELD'S ■ **5** ANNOUNCEMENT OF A FASHION SHOW AT DAYTON'S DEPARTMENT STORE, FOCUSING ON THE SEASON'S TRENDS. ● **5** (FOLGENDE DOPPELSEITE) FÜR EINE MODENSCHAU IM KAUFHAUS DAYTON'S MIT DEN TRENDS FÜR HERBST/WINTER. ▲ **5** (DOUBLE PAGE SUIVANTE) ANNONCE D'UN DÉFILÉ DE MODE OU SONT PRÉSENTÉES LES NOUVEAUTÉS DE LA SAISON DANS LE GRAND MAGASIN DAYTON'S. (USA)

■ (FOLLOWING SPREAD) **6** ART DIRECTOR: MASAHIKO YAMADA DESIGNER: MASAHIKO YAMADA PHOTOGRAPHER: KUNIHIRO TOGAWA STYLIST: MANAMI ISHIKAWA COPYWRITER: SHO SHINKAI AGENCY: WORKSHOP YUI, INC. CLIENT: OPS BODY FACTORY ■ **6** POSTER FOR OPS BODY FACTORY, A FITNESS STUDIO. ● **6** (FOLGENDE DOPPELSEITE) PLAKAT FÜR DIE OPS BODY FACTORY, EIN FITNESS-STUDIO. ▲ **6** (DOUBLE PAGE SUIVANTE) AFFICHE POUR OPS BODY FACTORY, UN STUDIO DE FITNESS JAPONAIS. (JPN)

3

4

We are a people of great diversity. It is what we call upon to define the very nature of being American, yet from every region, there is a unique interpretation. Bloomingdale's celebrates the Spirit of America with a gathering of furnishings for the home that shows us the best.

spiritofamerica

W SALE
JULY/11(thu)–21(sun)

GINZA CORE

Fall Fashion Show

A benefit for The Minneapolis Institute of Arts, featuring a personal appearance by Mary McFadden

Thursday and Friday, September 19 and 20
Eighth Floor Auditorium, Dayton's Minneapolis

Dayton's Oval Room

5

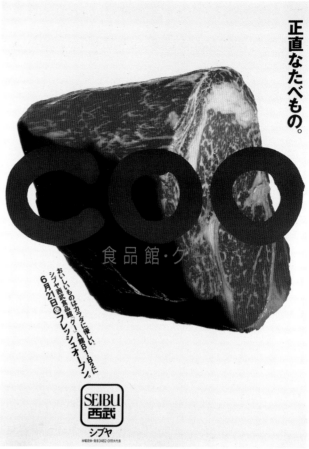

7

8

■ 7, 8 ART DIRECTOR: MASAAKI HIROMURA DESIGNERS: MASAAKI HIROMURA, TOSHIYUKI KOJIMA PHOTOGRAPHER: RYUICHI OKANO COPYWRITER: MASAYUKI MINODA AGENCY: HIROMURA DESIGN OFFICE INC. CLIENT: THE SEIBU DEPARTMENT STORES LTD. ■ 7, 8 POSTERS FOR THE FOOD DEPARTMENT OF SEIBU, A JAPANESE DEPARTMENT STORE. ● 7, 8 PLAKATE FÜR DIE LEBENSMITTEL-ABTEILUNG DES JAPANISCHEN KAUFHAUSES SEIBU. ▲ 7, 8 AFFICHES POUR LES GRANDS MAGASINS JAPONAIS SEIBU. (JPN)

■ 9-12 ART DIRECTOR: MASAAKI HIROMURA DESIGNERS: MASAAKI HIROMURA, TOSHIYUKI KOJIMA, T. KUSAGAYA 9, 10 PHOTOG-RAPHERS: MASAYUKI HAYASHI 9, 10, TOSHIAKI TAKEUCHI 11, 12 STYLIST: JUN YOSHIDA 11, 12 COPYWRITERS: KAZUKO KOIKE, AYAKO KISHI AGENCY: HIROMURA DESIGN OFFICE CLIENT: THE RYOHINKEIKAKU ■ 9-12 TOWELS AND COTTON FABRICS FROM INDIA ARE SHOWN IN THIS POSTER SERIES FOR THE BEST PRODUCTS COMPANY. ● 9-12 HANDTÜCHER UND INDISCHE BAUM-WOLLSTOFFE SIND GEGENSTAND DIESER PLAKATE FÜR DIE BEST PRODUCTS COMPANY. ▲ 9-12 DES SERVIETTES DE TOILETTE ET DES ÉTOFFES DE COTON INDIEN SONT PRÉSENTÉS DANS CETTE SÉRIE D'AFFICHES POUR LA BEST PRODUCTS COMPANY. (JPN)

眠りに
近くなる。
綿百。

ふんわりいろんな綿の特長を
生かしたタオル。しなやかな繊
維、まような打ち込み、やさしい
風合い。眠りにつくときのよう
なやわらかな肌ざわりで、快
適とくつろぎをつれてきます。

無印良品

9

目覚めに
近くなる。
麻混。

シャッキリ、麻と綿を半分
ずつで織り上げたタオル
汗と熱をすばやく逃がす
麻。吸水性が良くやわらか
な綿。熟睡後の目覚めのよ
うな爽快な肌ざわりが、夏
の涼しさをつれてきます。

無印良品

10

目、ニホン。
手、インド。

手織りの綿の良い歴史と、技術をインド
から。日本の空間に合うデザインと、縫
製を日本で。ふたつの国で作った布
と生かし合って。くつろぎ、眠り、いろんな
時間をつくる、無印のファブリックです。

無印良品

11

目、ニホン。
手、インド。

手織りの綿の良い歴史と、技術をインド
から。日本の空間に合うデザインと、縫
製を日本で。ふたつの国で作った布
と生かし合って。くつろぎ、眠り、いろんな
時間をつくる、無印のファブリックです。

無印良品

12

The Westward docks for time between two exciting itineraries.

THE WESTWARD

BERMUDA: ST. GEORGE'S AND HAMILTON   MEXICAN RIVIERA: ACAPULCO   ✕ NORWEGIAN CRUISE LINE.   MAZATLAN   PUERTO VALLARTA   CABO SAN LUCAS   ZIHUATANEJO   IXTAPA
THE BEST THINGS IN LIFE. AT SEA.

THE STARWARD

BARBADOS   ANTIGUA   MARTINIQUE   ST. MAARTEN   SAN JUAN   ✕ NORWEGIAN CRUISE LINE.   TORTOLA   CURAÇAO   VIRGIN GORDA   ST. THOMAS   ARUBA
THE BEST THINGS IN LIFE. AT SEA.

The World's Largest Cruise Ship

T H E   N O R W A Y

ST. MAARTEN   ST. THOMAS   SAN JUAN   ≥ NORWEGIAN CRUISE LINE.   ST. JOHN   PLEASURE ISLAND, BAHAMAS
THE BEST THINGS IN LIFE AT SEA.

15

T H E   S E A W A R D

PLAYA DEL CARMEN   GRAND CAYMAN   COZUMEL   ≥ NORWEGIAN CRUISE LINE.   OCHO RIOS   NCL'S PLEASURE ISLAND, BAHAMAS
THE BEST THINGS IN LIFE AT SEA.

16

■ **13-16** ART DIRECTOR: ANNETTE SIMON PHOTOGRAPHER: JIM ERICKSON AGENCY: MCKINNEY & SILVER CLIENT: NORWEGIAN CRUISE LINE ■ **13-16** SHIPS OF THE NORWEGIAN CRUISE LINE IN DIFFERENT SETTINGS. THE IDEA WAS TO SHOW BOTH THE SHIPS AND THE PORTS: THE LUXURIOUS WESTWARD IS SHOWN IN BERMUDA, THE STARWARD IN CURAÇAO, THE NORWAY IN SAN JUAN AND THE SEAWARD IN COZUMEL. ● **13-16** DIVERSE KREUZFAHRTSCHIFFE DER REEDEREI NORWEGIAN CRUISE LINE SO PRÄSENTIERT, DASS DIE VERSCHIEDENEN SCHIFFE UND DIE ANGELAUFENEN HÄFEN ZUR GELTUNG KOMMEN: DIE WESTWARD LIEGT VOR DER INSEL BERMUDA, DIE STARWARD IN CURAÇAO, DIE NORWAY IN SAN JUAN UND DIE SEAWARD IN COZUMEL. ▲ **13-16** LES DIVERS BATEAUX DE CROISIERE DE LA COMPAGNIE NORWEGIAN CRUISE LINE ONT ÉTÉ PHOTOGRAPHIÉS DEVANT LES PORTS DE DESTINATION: LA WESTWARD AUX BERMUDES, LA STARWARD À CURAÇAO, LA NORWAY À SAN JUAN ET LA SEAWARD À COZUMEL. (USA)

What Better Place To Unwind Than In The Country That Invented The Hammock.

It's Better In The Bahamas.

17

Vacation In A Country Where The Streets Are Lined With Gold.

It's Better In The Bahamas.

18

Uhuhuhu!

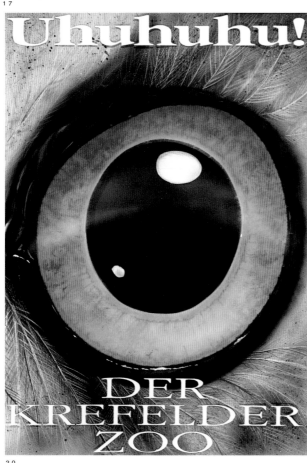

DER KREFELDER ZOO

20

Rrrooaaaaarr...

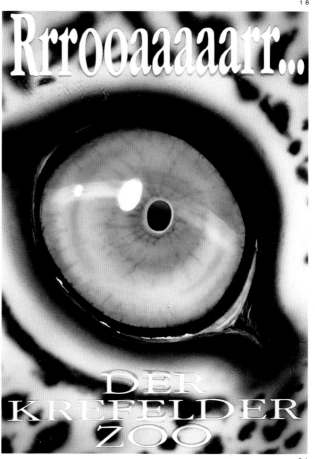

DER KREFELDER ZOO

21

Even In The Bahamas,
The Children Are Spoiled
By Fast Food.

It's Better In The Bahamas.

19

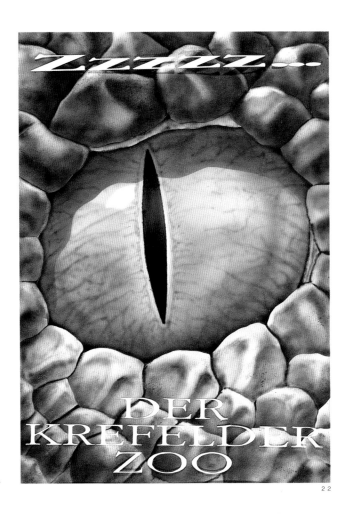

22

■ 17-19 ART DIRECTORS: LARRY BENNETT, BRAD MAGNER PHOTOGRAPHER: JIM ERICKSON COPYWRITER: JOHN RUSSO AGENCY: MCKINNEY & SILVER CLIENT: THE BAHAMAS MINISTRY OF TOURISM ■ 17-19 POSTERS DESIGNED TO DRAMATIZE THE THINGS FOR WHICH THE BAHAMAS ARE BEST KNOWN AND BRING LESSER-KNOWN FEATURES TO THE FOREGROUND. ● 17-19 PLAKATE, DIE SO-WOHL DIE BEKANNTEN ATTRAKTIONEN DER BAHAMAS ALS AUCH WENIGER BEKANNTE DARSTELLEN. ▲ 17-19 CES AFFICHES MON-TRENT LES CHARMES CONNUS QU'OFFRENT LES BAHAMAS ET LES ASPECTS PITTORESQUES QUE L'ON PEUT Y DÉCOUVRIR. (BAH)

■ 20-22 DESIGNER/PHOTOGRAPHER: STEFFI PROBOSZCZ CLIENT: KREFELDER ZOO ■ 20-22 POSTERS FOR THE ZOO OF KREFELD, DESIGNED BY A STUDENT FOR A COMPETITION OF THE FACHHOCHSCHULE DÜSSELDORF. ● 20-22 IM RAHMEN EINES WETTBE-WERBS DER FACHHOCHSCHULE DÜSSELDORF ENTSTANDENE PLAKATSERIE EINER STUDENTIN. ▲ 20-22 AFFICHES POUR LE ZOO DE KREFELD, CRÉÉES PAR UNE ÉTUDIANTE DANS LE CADRE D'UN CONCOURS DE LA FACHHOCHSCHULE DE DUSSELDORF. (GER)

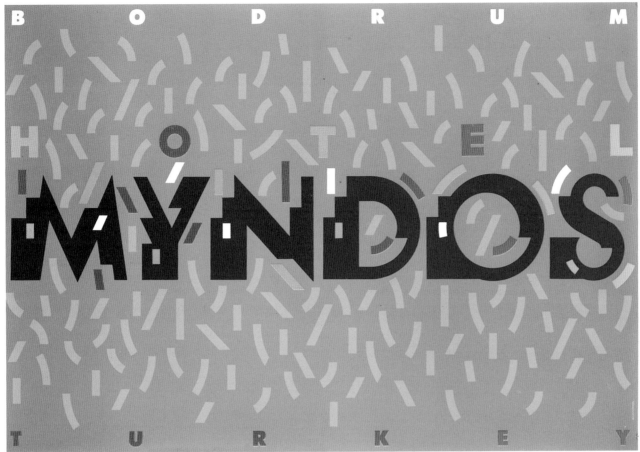

24

■ (THIS SPREAD) **23** Designer: CARLA RUMLER Photographer: HANS GROSCH Agency/Client: TIROL WERBUNG ■ **23** FROM A SERIES OF POSTERS BY ARTISTS FROM THE TIROL REGION OF AUSTRIA, PROMOTING THIS RESORT AREA. ● (DIESE DOPPEL-SEITE) **23** AUS EINER PLAKATREIHE MIT MOTIVEN VON TIROLER KÜNSTLERN. ▲ (CETTE DOUBLE PAGE) **23** D'UNE SÉRIE D'AF-FICHES ORNÉES D'IMAGES CONÇUES PAR DES ARTISTES TYROLIENS, AFIN DE FAIRE LA PROMOTION DE CETTE RÉGION. (AUT)

■ (THIS SPREAD) **24** Art Director/Designer/Illustrator: BÜLENT ERKMEN Agency: REKLAMEVI/YOUNG & RUBICAM Client: HOTEL MYNDOS ■ **24** POSTER PROMOTING THE HOTEL MYNDOS, IN A TURKISH SUMMER RESORT. ● (DIESE DOPPELSEITE) **24** WERBUNG FÜR DAS HOTEL MYNDOS IN EINEM TÜRKISCHEN FERIENORT. ▲ (CETTE DOUBLE PAGE) **24** PUBLICITÉ DE L'HOTEL MYNDOS. (TUR)

■ (FOLLOWING SPREAD) **25** Art Director/Designer: ELIZABETH BRANDT Photographer: CRAIG VANDERLENDE Copywriter: POLLY HEWITT Agency: BURGLER & ASSOCIATES Client: WOLVERINE WORLDWIDE ■ **25** THIS STORE DISPLAY POSTER PROMOTES A NEW LINE OF SHOES TO BE SOLD IN UPSCALE DEPARTMENT STORES. ● (FOLGENDE DOPPELSEITE) **25** LADENPLAKAT FÜR EINE NEUE SCHUHLINIE, DIE FÜR ANSPRUCHSVOLLE KAUFHÄUSER GEDACHT IST. ▲ (DOUBLE PAGE SUIVANTE) **25** AFFICHE POUR LA PUBLICITÉ D'UNE NOUVELLE LIGNE DE CHAUSSURES QUI A ÉTÉ CONÇUE POUR DES MAGASINS HAUT DE GAMME. (USA)

■ (FOLLOWING SPREAD) **26** Art Director/Designer/Agency: TYLER SMITH Photographer: GEORGE PETRAKES Stylist: STEPHANIE KARANDANIS Client: SERGIO BUSTAMANTE ■ **26** THIS POSTER, PROMOTING A NEW LINE OF JEWELRY BY SERGIO BUSTAMANTE, IS BASED ON THE ARTIST'S WORK AS A SCULPTOR. ● (FOLGENDE DOPPELSEITE) **26** DIESES PLAKAT FÜR EINE SCHMUCKLINIE VON SERGIO BUSTAMANTE BASIERT AUF DESSEN ARBEIT ALS BILDHAUER. ▲ (DOUBLE PAGE SUIVANTE) **26** LE CONCEPT DE CETTE AFFICHE POUR UNE COLLECTION DE BIJOUX DE SERGIO BUSTAMANTE EST BASÉ SUR SON ACTIVITÉ DE SCULPTEUR. (MEX)

TOWN & COUNTRY®

25

SERGIO BUSTAMANTE · JEWELRY

26

27

■ **27** ART DIRECTOR/DESIGNER: KENICHI SAMURA PHOTOGRAPHER: YURIKO TAKAGI AGENCY: NUMBER ONE DESIGN OFFICE CLIENT: RENOMA ■ **27** THIS POSTER INTRODUCES THE FALL/WINTER FASHION COLLECTION OF RENOMA, PARIS, TO THE JAPANESE PUBLIC. ● **27** DIE HERBST/WINTER-HERRENKOLLEKTION VON RENOMA PARIS WIRD DEM JAPANISCHEN PUBLIKUM VORGESTELLT. ▲ **27** CETTE AFFICHE QUI S'ADRESSE À UN PUBLIC JAPONAIS ANNONCE LA COLLECTION AUTOMNE/HIVER DE RENOMA, PARIS. (JPN)

■ **28** ART DIRECTOR/DESIGNER/ARTIST: MAKOTO SAITO CLIENT: ALPHACUBIC CO., LTD. ■ **28** A CORPORATE-IMAGE POSTER FOR AN APPAREL MAKER. ● **28** PLAKAT FÜR EINEN KLEIDERHERSTELLER. ▲ **28** AFFICHE POUR UN FABRICANT DE VETEMENTS. (JPN)

ALPHA CUBIC 1991

28

FASHION DESIGN

SPALENBERG 63

Y.F.

29

DESIGN MATSUTANI
TULIPAN TEXTILVERLAG KÖLN

30

Quilts: Handmade Color

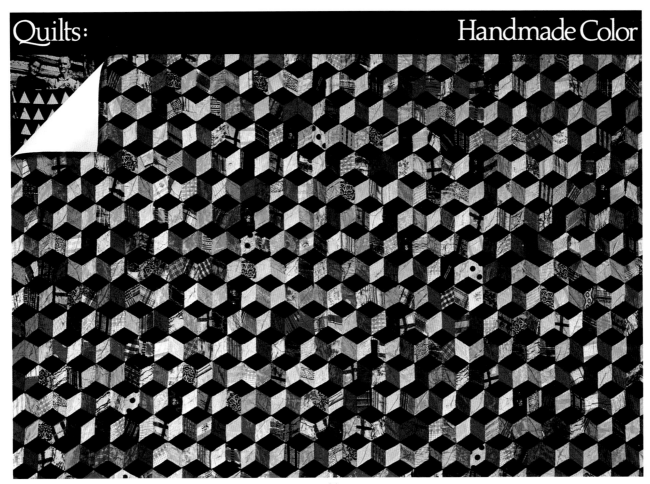

31

■ 29 ART DIRECTOR: CHRISTIAN VOGT DESIGNER: STEFANO DETJEN PHOTOGRAPHER: CHRISTIAN VOGT COPYWRITER: STEFANO DETJEN
AGENCY: STEFANO DETJEN CLIENT: YVONNE FIECHTER ■ 29 POSTER FOR Y.F. FASHION DESIGN, A BOUTIQUE. ● 29 PLAKAT FÜR
Y.F. FASHION DESIGN, EINE MODE-BOUTIQUE. ▲ 29 AFFICHE POUR Y.F. FASHION DESIGN, UNE BOUTIQUE DE MODE. (SWI)

■ 30 ART DIRECTOR: KARL-MARIA HOFER DESIGNER OF FABRICS: MATSUTANI PHOTOGRAPHER: KARL-MARIA HOFER STYLIST:
HEIDEMARIE SCHIFFER CLIENT: TULLIPAN TEXTILVERLAG GMBH ■ 30 POSTER PRESENTING FABRIC DESIGNS BY MATSUTANI. ●
30 WERBUNG FÜR STOFFENTWÜRFE VON MATSUTANI. ▲ 30 PUBLICITÉ POUR DES ÉTOFFES CRÉÉES PAR MATSUTANI. (GER)

■ 31 ART DIRECTOR: JULIUS FRIEDMAN DESIGNERS: JULIUS FRIEDMAN, WALTER MCCORD PHOTOGRAPHER: CRAIG GUYON STUDIO/
PUBLISHER: IMAGES ■ 31 A POSTER DEDICATED THE ART OF MAKING QUILTS. ● 31 DER TRADITIONELLEN AMERIKANISCHEN
QUILT-KUNST GEWIDMETES PLAKAT. ▲ 31 UNE AFFICHE CONSACRÉE AU QUILT, CET ART TRADITIONNEL AMÉRICAIN. (USA)

33

34

35

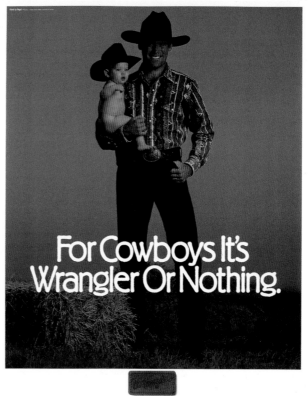

36

32

■ 32 CREATIVE DIRECTOR: KENICHI AKI ART DIRECTOR: MAKOTO SAITO DESIGNER: MAKOTO SAITO PHOTOGRAPHER: HERB RITTS AGENCY: YOMIKO ADVERTISING INC. CLIENT: JAPAN EDWIN, INC. ■ 32 CORPORATE-IMAGE POSTER FOR A JAPANESE APPAREL MAKER. ● 32 IMAGE-PLAKAT FÜR EINEN JAPANISCHEN KLEIDERHERSTELLER. ▲ 32 AFFICHE POUR UN FABRICANT DE VETEMENTS. (JPN)

■ 33, 34 PROGRAM MANAGER: JAIMIE ALEXANDER DESIGNER: PAUL WESTRICK PHOTOGRAPHER: PHILIP PORCELLA TYPOGRAPHER: JOHN KIRK COPYWRITER: WENDIE WULFF PRODUCTION: CAROL KINCAID, SANDY MCKISSICK AGENCY: FITCH RICHARDSON SMITH CLIENT: BASSETT-WALKER, INC. ■ 33, 34 POINT-OF-SALE POSTERS USING PERSONAL IMAGES AND MESSAGES TO EXPRESS THE NATURE OF LEE CLOTHING AND EMPHASIZE THE "SOFTWEAR" CLAIM. ● 33, 34 PLAKATE AUS EINER SERIE MIT AUFNAHMEN VON LEUTEN, DIE SICH ÜBER LEE-KLEIDUNG ÄUSSERN. ▲ 33, 34 EXEMPLES D'UNE SÉRIE D'AFFICHETTES DESTINÉES AUX MAGASINS DE DÉTAIL. DIVERSES PERSONNES DONNENT LEUR AVIS SUR LES VETEMENTS LEE, APPRÉCIÉS À CAUSE DE LEUR CONFORT. (USA)

■ 35, 36 ART DIRECTOR: JERRY TORCHIA PHOTOGRAPHERS: JIM ARNDT 35, DENNIS MURPHY 36 COPYWRITER: STEVE BASSETT AGENCY: THE MARTIN AGENCY CLIENT: WRANGLER JEANS ■ 35, 36 FROM A SERIES OF POSTERS FOR WRANGLER JEANS, STRESSING THE STURDINESS OF THE PRODUCT. ● 35, 36 «WAS GEORGE STRAIT TRÄGT, WENN ER MIT FREUNDEN AUSGEHT»; «FÜR COWBOYS IST ES WRANGLER ODER NICHTS.» WERBUNG FÜR JEANS. ▲ 35, 36 «CE QUE GEORGE STRAIT PORTE QUAND IL SORT AVEC DES COPAINS»; «POUR LES COW-BOYS, C'EST WRANGLER OU RIEN.» PUBLICITÉ POUR LES JEANS WRANGLER. (USA)

37

38

■ **37-39** Art Directors: JAIMIE ALEXANDER, PAUL WESTRICK 38 Designers: PAUL WESTRICK, BETH NOTIVSKY 37, 39, KIAN KUAN 38 Photographers: RON BERG, PHILIP PORCELLA, MARK STEELE Illustrator: JOANIE HUPP Copywriters: JAIMIE ALEXANDER, PAUL WESTRICK Agency: FITCH RICHARDSON SMITH Clients: BASSETT-WALKER, INC. 37, 39 THE LEE COMPANY 37-39 ■ **37-39** POSTERS FROM A SERIES FOR THE LEE BRAND. ● 37-39 PLAKATE AUS EINER SERIE, IN DER LEE ALS «DIE MARKE, DIE ZU DEINEM LEBENSSTIL PASST» POSITIONIERT WIRD. NATÜRLICH WIRKENDE AUFNAHMEN UND PERSÖNLICHE AUSSAGEN UNTERSTÜTZEN DIESEN ANSPRUCH. ▲ **37-39** AFFICHES D'UNE SÉRIE DANS LAQUELLE LEE EST POSITIONNÉE COMME «LA MARQUE QUI VA AVEC VOTRE MODE DE VIE.» CECI EST RENFORCÉ PAR LE STYLE NATUREL ET PERSONNEL DES IMAGES. (USA)

THE BRAND
THAT FITS THE
WAY YOU LIVE.

SINCE **Lee**® 1889

39

40

41

■ **40-42** ART DIRECTORS: JOHN NORMAN 40, JEFF WEITHMAN 41, RON DUMAS 42 DESIGNERS: JOHN NORMAN 40, JEFF WEITHMAN 41, RON DUMAS 42 PHOTOGRAPHERS: ANDREW MACPHERSON 40, 41, PETE STONE 42, STOCK 42 DIGITAL TRANSPARENCY: RAPHAELE INC. COPYWRITER: GUIDO BROUWERS 42 AGENCY: NIKE DESIGN CLIENT: NIKE, INC. ■ **40-42** PROMOTIONAL POSTERS FOR NIKE FEATURING POPULAR ATHLETES: THE GERMAN SPRINTER KATRIN KRABBE; SERGEY BUBKA, THE POLE-VAULTER; AND MICHAEL JORDAN, THE AMERICAN BASKETBALL STAR. ● **40-42** PLAKATWERBUNG FÜR NIKE-SPORTSCHUHE MIT POPULÄREN SPORTLERN: DIE DEUTSCHE SPRINTERIN KATRIN KRABBE, STABHOCHSPRINGER SERGEY BUBKA UND DER AMERIKANISCHE BASKETBALLSPIE-LER MICHAEL JORDAN. ▲ **40-42** PUBLICITÉ POUR NIKE PRÉSENTANT DES SPORTIFS POPULAIRES: LA SPRINTEUSE ALLEMANDE KATRIN KRABBE, LE SAUTEUR À LA PERCHE SERGEY BUBKA ET LA STAR DU BASKET-BALL AMÉRICAIN, MICHAEL JORDAN. (USA)

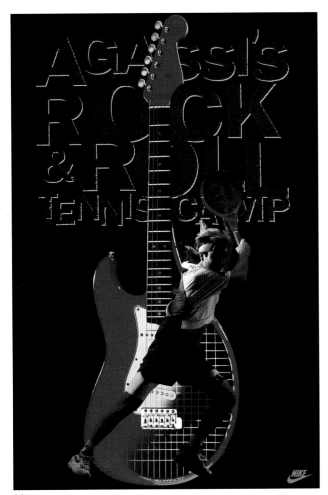

44

45

■ 43 Art Director: JEFF WEITHMAN Designer: JEFF WEITHMAN Photographer: RICHARD CORMAN Agency: NIKE DESIGN Clients: BORUSSIA DORTMUND, NIKE, INC. ■ 43 THE GERMAN SOCCER TEAM BORUSSIA DORTMUND, IN A PROMOTION FOR NIKE. ● 43 DIE DEUTSCHE FUSSBALLMANNSCHAFT BORUSSIA DORTMUND EINMAL ANDERS ALS GEWOHNT, AUF EINEM WERBEPLAKAT FÜR NIKE. ▲ 43 UNE IMAGE INATTENDUE DE L'ÉQUIPE DE FOOTBALL BORUSSIA DORTMUND SUR UNE AFFICHE DE NIKE. (USA)

■ 44 Designer: GUIDO BROUWERS Photographers: JOHN EMMERLING, PETE STONE Agency: NIKE DESIGN Client: NIKE, INC. ■ 44 ANDRÉ AGASSI, THE AMERICAN TENNIS PLAYER, ON A NIKE POSTER. ● 44 DER AMERIKANISCHE TENNISSPIELER ANDRÉ AGASSI AUF EINEM PLAKAT FÜR NIKE. ▲ 44 ANDRÉ AGASSI, LA STAR DU TENNIS AMÉRICAIN, SUR UNE AFFICHE DE NIKE. (USA)

■ 45 Art Director: MICHAEL TIEDY Designer: MICHAEL TIEDY Photographer: STEVE DUNN/ALL-SPORT Illustrator: JOSE ORTEGA Agency: NIKE DESIGN Client: NIKE, INC. ■ 45 PROMOTIONAL POSTER FOR NIKE, FEATURING RAMON MARTINEZ, A PITCHER FOR THE LOS ANGELES DODGERS. ● 45 PLAKATWERBUNG FÜR NIKE MIT DEM BASEBALLSTAR RAMON MARTINEZ. ▲ 45 AFFICHE DE PUBLICITÉ POUR NIKE REPRÉSENTANT LE GRAND JOUEUR DE BASE-BALL AMÉRICAIN, RAMON MARTINEZ. (USA)

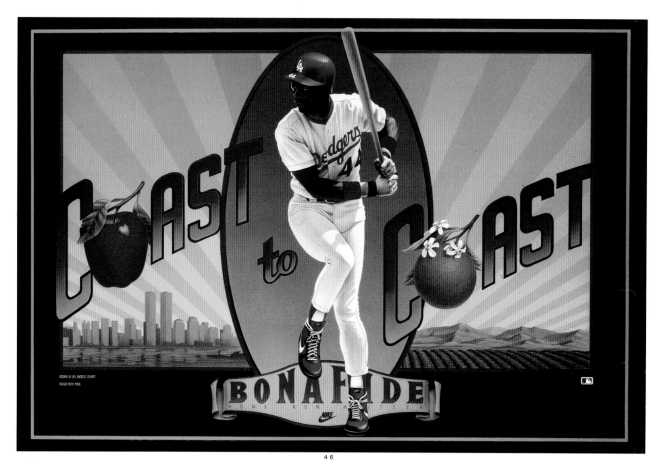

46

■ 46 ART DIRECTORS/DESIGNERS: JIM NUDO, RON DUMAS ILLUSTRATOR: RICK LOVELL, INC. COPYWRITERS: BOB LAMBIE, RON DUMAS
AGENCY: NIKE DESIGN CLIENT: NIKE, INC. ■ 46 THIS POSTER SHOWS THE BASEBALL STAR DARRYL STRAWBERRY, WHO RECENT-
LY MOVED FROM THE NEW YORK METS TO THE LOS ANGELES DODGERS. IT WAS INSPIRED BY THE ART STYLE OF THE 1920S
AND '30S. ● 46 AUS EINER SERIE FÜR NIKE MIT PROMINENTEN SPORTLERN. HIER DER BASEBALLSTAR DARRYL STRAWBERRY IM
STIL DER PLAKATE DER 20ER/30ER JAHRE. ▲ 46 D'UNE SÉRIE D'AFFICHES POUR NIKE MONTRANT LES SPORTIFS LES PLUS
CÉLEBRES. ICI, DARRYL STRAWBERRY, UN JOUEUR DE BASE-BALL, DANS LE STYLE DES AFFICHES DES ANNÉES 20 ET 30. (USA)

■ 47 ART DIRECTORS: CHARLES ANDERSON, DANIEL OLSON DESIGNERS: CHARLES ANDERSON, DANIEL OLSON, HALEY JOHNSON
ILLUSTRATORS: TAKENOBU IGARASHI, ALFONS HOLTGREVE, RALPH STEADMAN, ANDRÉ FRANÇOIS, FELIPE TABORDA AGENCY: C.S.
ANDERSON DESIGN CO. CLIENT: WIEDEN & KENNEDY ■ 47 ANNOUNCEMENT OF THE LATEST AIR-TECHNOLOGY SHOE FROM NIKE.
THE POSTER TIES IN WITH AN EIGHT-PAGE AD INSERT. ● 47 PLAKAT FÜR DIE EINFÜHRUNG DES «180 AIR»-SCHUHS VON NIKE,
DIE NEUSTE ENTWICKLUNG IN DER LUFTPOLSTERTECHNIK. ES KANN MIT EINEM ACHTSEITIGEN INSERAT ALS BEIHEFTER VER-
WENDET WERDEN. ▲ 47 AFFICHE POUR LE LANCEMENT DE «180 AIR» DE NIKE, LA TOUTE DERNIERE NOUVEAUTÉ EN MATIERE
DE CHAUSSURES SUR COUSSIN D'AIR. ELLE PEUT ETRE UTILISÉE COMME ENCART AVEC UNE ANNONCE DE HUIT PAGES. (USA)

ONE EIGHTY
INTERNATIONAL
Air by Nike

ONE
8
ZERO

DESIGN
SPECS

The baskets were for peaches and the ball for bouncing. Dr. Naismith combined the two and created the game. Everyday, from the chain link nets of the school yard to the break away rims of Madison Square Garden, somebody somewhere is shooting hoops. A century has passed, the ball keeps bouncing, and the game is still a peach.

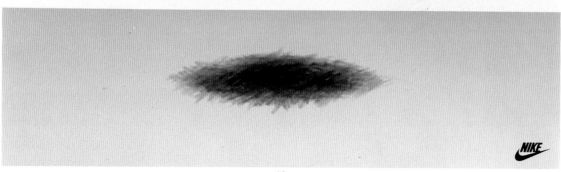

NIKE

48

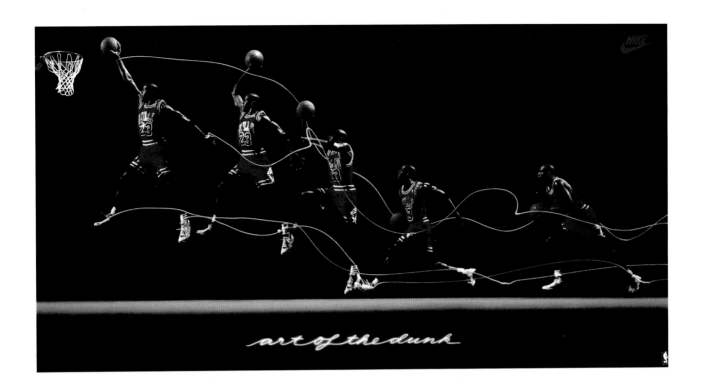

49

50

■ **48-50** Aʀᴛ Dɪʀᴇᴄᴛᴏʀs: JOHN NORMAN 48, 50, RON DUMAS 49, MICHAEL TIEDY 49 Dᴇsɪɢɴᴇʀs: JOHN NORMAN 48, 50, RON DUMAS 49 Pʜᴏᴛᴏɢʀᴀᴘʜᴇʀ: PETE STONE 49 Iʟʟᴜsᴛʀᴀᴛᴏʀs: JOHN NORMAN 48, 50, ANTON KIMBALL 50 Cᴏᴘʏᴡʀɪᴛᴇʀs: BOB LAMBIE 48, RON DUMAS 49, BECKY KATSON 50 Aɢᴇɴᴄʏ: NIKE DESIGN Cʟɪᴇɴᴛ: NIKE, INC. ■ **48-50** PROMOTIONAL POSTERS FOR NIKE, FOCUSING ON BASKETBALL. NUMBER 48 REFERS TO THE GAME'S INVENTION AND ITS INVENTOR, JAMES NAISMITH. NUMBER 49 SHOWS THE LEAPING ABILITY OF MICHAEL JORDAN. NUMBER 50 COMMEMORATES THE GAME'S CENTENNIAL. ● **48-50** DAS THEMA DIESER PLAKATE IST BASKETBALL. BEI ABB. 48 GEHT ES UM DIE ERFINDUNG DES SPIELS, WOBEI DER NAME DES ERFINDERS UND SEIN BILD IN DAS PLAKAT EINBEZOGEN SIND; BEI ABB. 49 UM DAS SPRUNGVERMÖGEN DES SPIELERS MICHAEL JORDAN UND BEI 50 UM DIE 100JÄHRIGE TRADITION DES SPIELS. ▲ **48-50** LE BASKET-BALL EST LE SUJET DE CES AFFICHES POUR NIKE. DANS LA FIG. 48, IL EST QUESTION DE L'INVENTION DE CE JEU ET ELLE COMPORTE LE NOM DE L'INVENTEUR ET SON IMAGE; DANS LA FIG. 50, DES QUALITÉS DU GRAND JOUEUR MICHAEL JORDAN ET DANS LA FIG. 50, DU CENTENAIRE DE CE JEU. (USA)

51

■ (THIS SPREAD) **51** ART DIRECTOR: JEFF WEITHMAN DESIGNER: JEFF WEITHMAN PHOTOGRAPHER: RICHARD CORMAN AGENCY: NIKE DESIGN CLIENTS: OLYMPIQUE LYONNAIS, NIKE, INC. ■ **51** THE OLYMPIQUE LYONNAIS SOCCER TEAM ON A PROMOTIONAL POSTER FOR NIKE. ● (DIESE DOPPELSEITE) **51** DIE FUSSBALLMANNSCHAFT DER STADT LYON AUF EINEM PROMOTIONSPLAKAT FÜR NIKE. ▲ (CETTE DOUBLE PAGE) **51** L'ÉQUIPE DE L'OLYMPIQUE LYONNAIS SUR UNE AFFICHE PROMOTIONNELLE DE NIKE. (USA)

■ (THIS SPREAD) **52** ART DIRECTOR: ERICH JOINER PHOTOGRAPHER: NADAV KANDER COPYWRITER: CLAY WILLIAMS AGENCY: GOODBY, BERLIN & SILVERSTEIN CLIENT: LIBREX COMPUTER SYSTEMS, INC. ■ **52** THIS POSTER TOUTS THE ADVANTAGES OF LIBREX COMPUTER SYSTEMS. THE VIEW IS OF SAN FRANCISCO. ● (DIESE DOPPELSEITE) **52** «KÖNNTE ES SEIN, DASS MAN AM SCHNELL-STEN ZU EINEM BÜRO KOMMT, WENN MAN ÜBERHAUPT KEIN BÜRO HAT.» WERBUNG FOR LIBREX-NOTEBOOK-COMPUTER. DIE AUF-NAHME ENTSTAND VOR SAN FRANCISCO. ▲ (CETTE DOUBLE PAGE) **52** «SE POURRAIT-IL QUE LE MOYEN LE PLUS RAPIDE D'ARRI-VER À SON BUREAU SOIT DE NE PAS AVOIR DE BUREAU DU TOUT?» PUBLICITÉ POUR L'ORDINATEUR LIBREX-NOTEBOOK. (USA)

■ (THIS SPREAD) **53** ART DIRECTOR: RICHARD C. WEISS DESIGNER: CHRISTOPHER LIECHTY PHOTOGRAPHER: CURTIS PEARSON COPYWRITER: CHRISTOPHER LIECHTY AGENCY: WORDPERFECT CORPORATION CLIENT: M-DATA ■ **53** A POINT-OF-PURCHASE

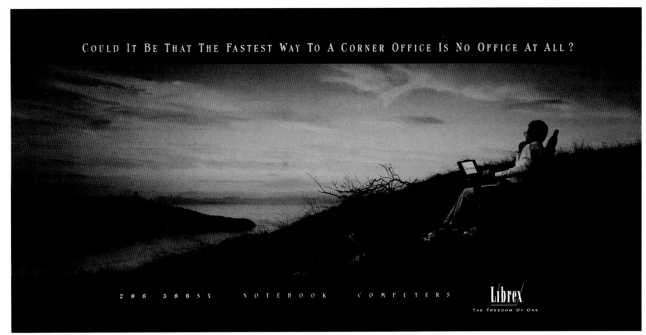

COULD IT BE THAT THE FASTEST WAY TO A CORNER OFFICE IS NO OFFICE AT ALL?

286 386SX NOTEBOOK COMPUTERS Librex
THE FREEDOM OF ONE.

52

CLASSICAL
PERFECTION

WordPerfect
ΕΛΛΗΝΙΚΟ

53

POSTER ANNOUNCING THE SOFTWARE PROGRAM WORDPERFECT IN GREEK. ● (DIESE DOPPELSEITE) 53 «KLASSISCHE PER-
FEKTION.» ANKÜNDIGUNG DES COMPUTER-PROGRAMMS WORDPERFECT AUF GRIECHISCH. ▲ (CETTE DOUBLE PAGE) 53 «LA
PERFECTION CLASSIQUE.» CETTE AFFICHETTE DE MAGASIN ANNONCE LA SORTIE DU LOGICIEL WORDPERFECT EN GREC. (GRE)

■ (FOLLOWING SPREAD) 54 ART DIRECTORS: AKIO OKUMURA, SHUICHI NOGAMI DESIGNER: SHUICHI NOGAMI CLIENT: MORISAWA &
COMPANY LTD. ■ 54 "THE IMAGE IS BORN FIRST"—A PROMOTIONAL POSTER FOR DTP WITH MACINTOSH COMPUTERS. ●
(FOLGENDE DOPPELSEITE) 54 «ZUERST WIRD DAS BILD GEBOREN»—WERBUNG FÜR DESKTOP PUBLISHING MIT MACINTOSH-
COMPUTERN. ▲ (DOUBLE PAGE SUIVANTE) 54 «L'IMAGE EST NÉE D'ABORD»—PUBLICITÉ POUR P.A.O. SUR MACINTOSH. (JPN)

■ (FOLLOWING SPREAD) 55 ART DIRECTOR: CHUL MOON DESIGNER: CHUL MOON ILLUSTRATOR: CHUL MOON CLIENT: DOO SUNG CO. ■
55 THIS POSTER, GENERATED ON A MACINTOSH COMPUTER, ANNOUNCES A KOREAN/JAPANESE PAPER EXHIBITION. ● (FOLGEN-
DE DOPPELSEITE) 55 MIT EINEM MACINTOSH II FX GENERIERTES PLAKAT FÜR EINE KOREANISCH/JAPANISCHE PAPIERAUS-
STELLUNG. ▲ (DOUBLE PAGE SUIVANTE) 55 AFFICHE CONÇUE SUR UN MACINTOSH POUR UNE EXPOSITION DE PAPIER. (KOR)

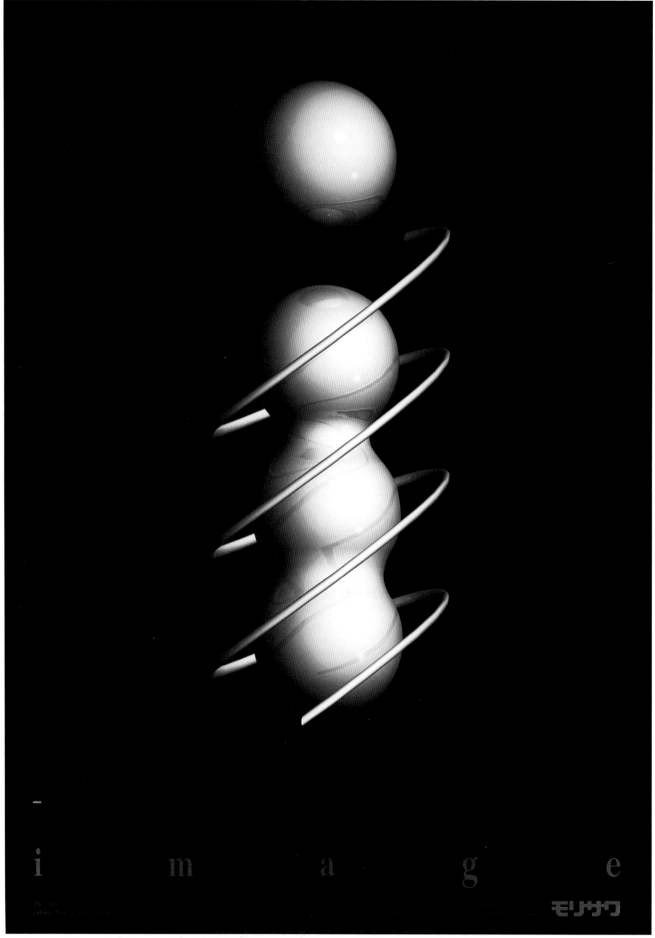

image

モリサワ

Design + Computergraphics Moon Chul Printing Hangun Process

"Design······
the animating
Principle
of all Creative
Processes."
Vasari 1511-1574

55

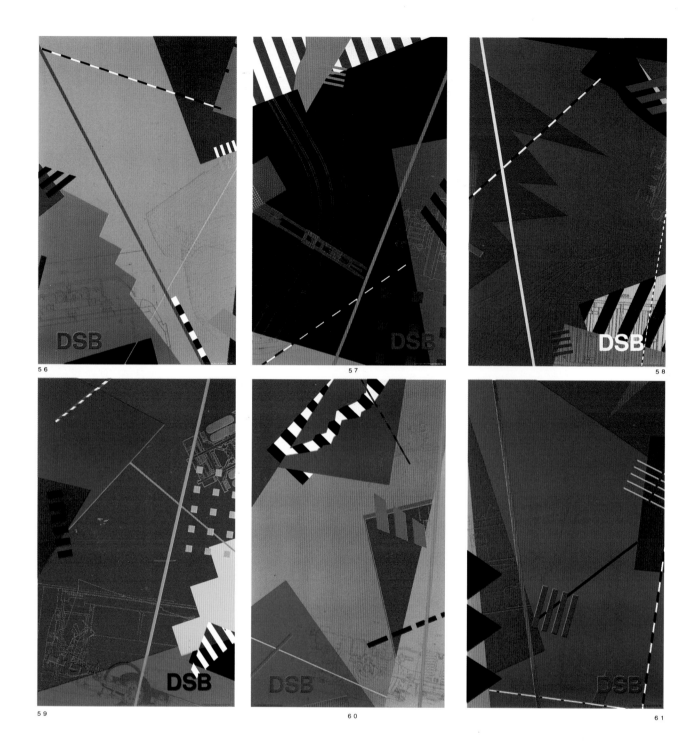

■ **56-61** ART DIRECTOR/DESIGNER/ILLUSTRATOR: ERNST LOHSE CLIENT: DSB ■ **56-61** POSTERS SHOWING THE SERVICES OFFERED BY DANISH RAILWAYS: EXPRESS TRAIN, UNDERGROUND TRAFFIC, CONTAINER TRAFFIC, BUS TRAFFIC, REGIONAL TRAINS AND FERRY TRAFFIC. ● **56-61** PLAKATE FÜR DIE DIENSTLEISTUNGEN DER DÄNISCHEN EISENBAHN: EXPRESSZÜGE, UNTERGRUND-BAHNEN, CONTAINER-VERKEHR, BUSSE, REGIONALZÜGE UND FÄHRVERKEHR. ▲ **56-61** SÉRIE D'AFFICHES VISUALISANT LES SERVICES QU'OFFRENT LES CHEMINS DE FER DANOIS: TRAINS EXPRESS, MÉTRO, BUS, TRAINS RÉGIONAUX ET FERRY-BOATS. (DEN)

62

63

■ 62, 63 ART DIRECTOR: JOHN MULLER DESIGNER: JOHN MULLER PHOTOGRAPHER: MICHAEL REGNIER COPYWRITER: DAVID MARK
AGENCY: MULLER + CO. CLIENT: SPRINT ■ 62, 63 THIS POSTER ANNOUNCES THAT THREE-WAY CONFERENCE CALLS AND GLOBAL
CALLING ARE EASY WITH THE SPRINT FONCARD. ● 62, 63 KONFERENZGESPRÄCHE UND INTERNATIONALE GESPRÄCHE WERDEN
DANK DER SPRINT FONCARD ERLEICHTERT. PLAKATWERBUNG FÜR TELEPHONKARTEN. ▲ 62, 63 LES COLLOQUES ET TOUS LES
ÉCHANGES INTERNATIONAUX SONT FACILITÉS GRACE À SPRINT FONCARD. PUBLICITÉ POUR DES CARTES DE TÉLÉPHONE. (USA)

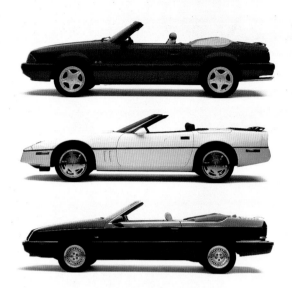

Does your bathroom have to go?
Ask about our home improvement loans.

BANK ONE
Whatever it takes.

Need a new hair dryer?
Ask about our new car loans.

BANK ONE
Whatever it takes.

64

65

■ **64, 65** ART DIRECTOR: BOB MEAGHER PHOTOGRAPHER: JIM ERICKSON COPYWRITER: TRIPP WESTBROOK AGENCY: THE MARTIN AGENCY CLIENT: BANK ONE ■ **64, 65** EXAMPLES FROM A POSTER CAMPAIGN OFFERING SPECIAL LOANS FROM BANK ONE. ● **64, 65** BEISPIELE AUS EINER PLAKATKAMPAGNE EINER BANK, DIE SPEZIELLE KREDITE ANBIETET, WIE ZUM BEISPIEL FÜR WOH-NUNGSRENOVATIONEN ODER AUTOS. ▲ **64, 65** EXEMPLES DE LA CAMPAGNE D'AFFICHES D'UNE BANQUE AMÉRICAINE QUI PRO-POSE DES CRÉDITS SPÉCIAUX, PAR EXEMPLE POUR LA RÉNOVATION D'UN APPARTEMENT OU POUR L'ACHAT D'UNE VOITURE. (USA)

■ **66** ART DIRECTOR/DESIGNER: KAZUMASA NAGAI AGENCY: NIPPON DESIGN CENTER CLIENT: YOKOGAWA ELECTRIC CO., LTD. ■ **66** THE PHILOSOPHY OF THE YOKOGAWA ELECTRIC CO. IS COMMUNICATED IN A SILK-SCREEN POSTER. ● **66** IMAGE-PLAKAT DER YOKOGAWA ELECTRIC CO., DIE HIER VON IHRER TÄTIGKEIT IM BEREICH VON MESSUNGEN, KONTROLLE, INFORMATION ZUM NUTZEN DER ALLGEMEINHEIT UND VON IHRER HALTUNG ALS GUTE BÜRGER MIT DEM MUT ZU INNOVATIONEN SPRICHT. ▲ **66** AFFICHE PROMOTIONNELLE DE LA YOKOGAWA ELECTRIC CO.; L'IMAGE FAIT ALLUSION À L'ACTIVITÉ DE CETTE SOCIÉTÉ DANS LE SECTEUR DES MESURES, DES CONTROLES. INFORME DE SON UTILITÉ PUBLIQUE ET DE SON ESPRIT INNOVATEUR. (JPN)

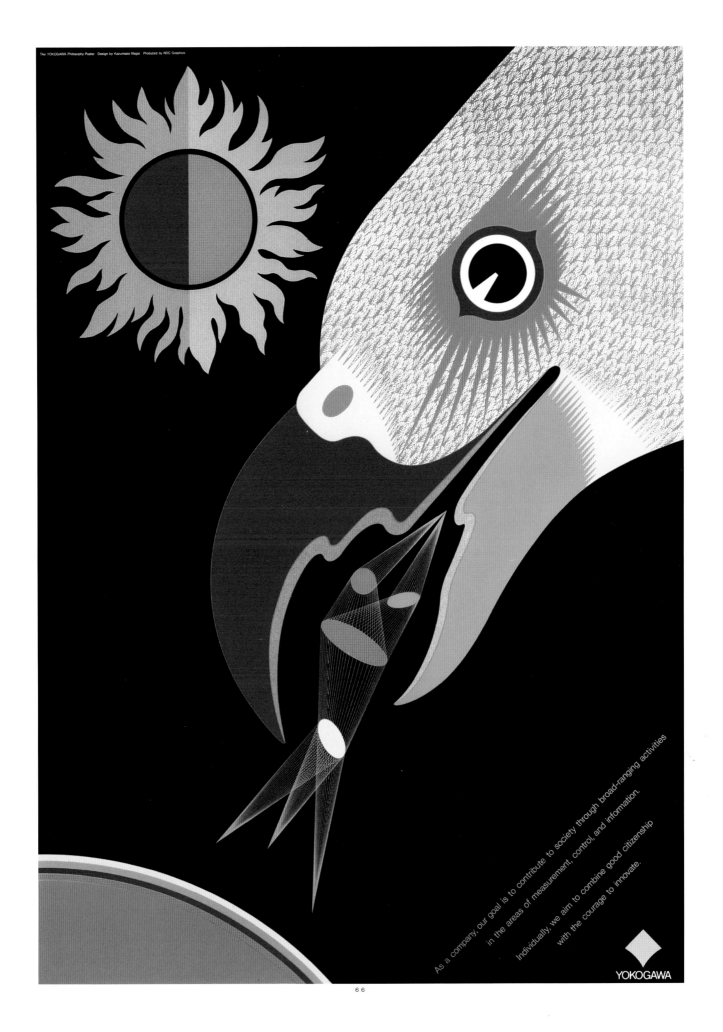

As a company, our goal is to contribute to society through broad-ranging activities in the areas of measurement, control, and information. Individually, we aim to combine good citizenship with the courage to innovate.

YOKOGAWA

RESOURCE 2000. AN ALLIANCE FOR PROGRESS AND PROFIT.

67

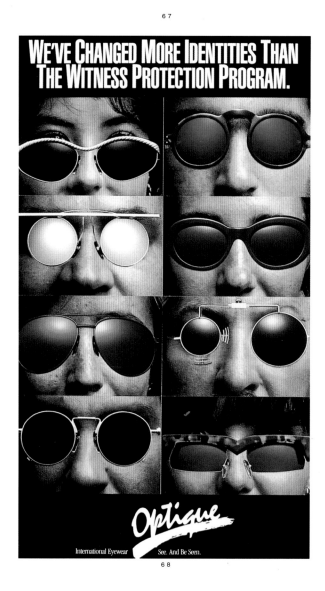

68

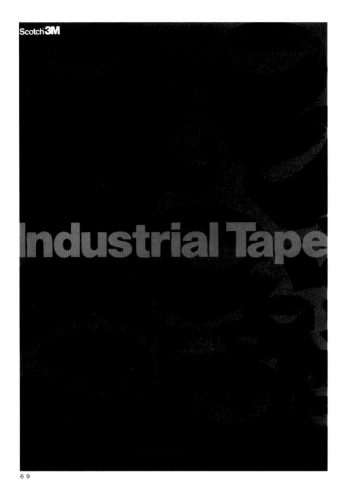

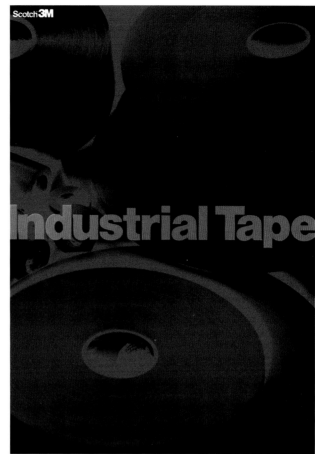

69

70

■ **67** ART DIRECTOR: JANET FRIED DESIGNER: JANET FRIED ILLUSTRATOR: GARY OVERACRE COPYWRITER: DAN MULCAHY AGENCY: ICE COMMUNICATIONS INC. CLIENT: BAUSCH & LOMB ■ **67** BAUSCH & LOMB, PRODUCER OF EYE-CARE PRODUCTS, INTRODUCES AN INITIATIVE TO HELP ITS RETAIL CUSTOMERS REALIZE GREATER PROFITS. THE ILLUSTRATION RECALLS THE STYLE OF THE 1930S, WHEN COOPERATIVE EFFORT HELPED AMERICA THROUGH TOUGH ECONOMIC TIMES. ● **67** BAUSCH & LOMB, HERSTELLER OPTISCHER PRODUKTE, STELLT EIN PROGRAMM VOR, DAS DEN EINZELHÄNDLERN MEHR PROFIT ERMÖGLICHEN SOLL. DIE ILLU-STRATION ERINNERT AN DEN STIL DER DREISSIGER JAHRE, ALS GEMEINSAME ANSTRENGUNGEN IN DEN VEREINIGTEN STAATEN HALFEN, DIE WIRTSCHAFTSKRISE ZU ÜBERWINDEN. ▲ **67** BAUSCH & LOMB, FABRICANT DE PRODUITS OPTIQUES, PROPOSE UN PROGRAMME QUI DOIT PERMETTRE AUX DÉTAILLANTS D'ACCROITRE LEURS PROFITS. L'ILLUSTRATION ÉVOQUE LE STYLE DES ANNÉES 30, L'ÉPOQUE OU DES EFFORTS COMMUNS AIDERENT À SURMONTER LA CRISE ÉCONOMIQUE AUX ETATS-UNIS. (USA)

■ **68** ART DIRECTOR: TED DUQUETTE PHOTOGRAPHER: GEOFFREY STEIN COPYWRITER: GEORGE GOETZ AGENCY: INGALLS, QUINN & JOHNSON CLIENT: OPTIQUE ■ **68** POSTER SHOWING THE WIDE RANGE OF GLASSES OFFERED BY OPTIQUE. ● **68** »WIR HABEN MEHR IDENTITÄTEN VERÄNDERT ALS DAS ZEUGENSCHUTZPROGRAMM.« BEI DIESEM PLAKAT GEHT ES UM DAS GROSSE ANGEBOT MODISCHER BRILLEN VON OPTIQUE. ▲ **68** «NOUS AVONS CHANGÉ PLUS D'IDENTITÉS QUE LE SERVICE OFFICIEL CHARGÉ DE LA PROTECTION DES TÉMOINS DE PROCES.» IL S'AGISSAIT ICI DE PRÉSENTER UN GRAND CHOIX DE LUNETTES DE SOLEIL. (USA)

■ **69, 70** ART DIRECTOR/DESIGNER: ICHIRO MITANI PHOTOGRAPHER: GAKUJI TANAKA AGENCY: MITANI ICHIRO DESIGN CLIENT: SUMI-TOMO 3M ■ **69, 70** POSTERS PROMOTING A BRAND OF INDUSTRIAL TAPE. ● **69, 70** WERBUNG FÜR KLEBBAND, DAS FÜR DEN IN-DUSTRIELLEN GEBRAUCH BESTIMMT IST. ▲ **69, 70** AFFICHES POUR UN RUBAN ADHÉSIF DESTINÉ À L'USAGE INDUSTRIEL. (JPN)

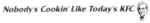

Nobody's Cookin' Like Today's KFC.

71

■ (THIS SPREAD) **71** Art Director: DAVID WOELFEL Photographer: DICK BAKER Copywriter: TOM JORDAN Agency: HOFFMAN YORK & COMPTON Client: KENTUCKY FRIED CHICKEN ■ **71** A POINT-OF-PURCHASE POSTER FOR KENTUCKY FRIED CHICKEN. ● (DIESE DOPPELSEITE) **71** FÜR DEN INNENAUSHANG BESTIMMTES PLAKAT FÜR HÄHNCHEN VON KENTUCKY FRIED CHICKEN. ▲ (CETTE DOUBLE PAGE) **71** AFFICHETTE DESTINÉE AUX POINTS DE VENTE DES POULETS DE KENTUCKY FRIED CHICKEN. (USA)

■ (THIS SPREAD) **72** Art Directors: WARREN EAKINS, STEVE SANDSTROM Designer: STEVE SANDSTROM Photographer: STUDIO 3 Copywriter: STEVE SANDOZ Agency: SANDSTROM DESIGN Client: BURGERVILLE USA ■ **72** PROMOTIONAL POSTER FOR BURGERVILLE, CELEBRATING 30 YEARS OF MAKING HAMBURGERS. THE 1961 CADILLAC CONVERTIBLE IS A CONTEST PRIZE. ● (DIESE DOPPELSEITE) **72** DIESEN CADILLAC VON 1961 GAB ES BEI EINEM WETTBEWERB ANLÄSSLICH DES 30JÄHRIGEN BE-STEHENS DER HAMBURGERKETTE-BURGERVILLE (1961-1991) ZU GEWINNEN. ▲ (CETTE DOUBLE PAGE) **72** A L'OCCASION DES 30 ANS DE LA CITÉ DE BURGERVILLE (1961-1991), ON POUVAIT GAGNER CETTE CADILLAC DÉCAPOTABLE DATANT DE 1961. (USA)

72

■ (FOLLOWING SPREAD) 73 ART DIRECTOR/DESIGNER/ILLUSTRATOR: LANA RIGSBY AGENCY: RIGSBY DESIGN CLIENT: ZOOT RESTAURANT ■ 73 LIMITED-EDITION SILK-SCREEN POSTER, CREATED AS A GIFT FOR PATRONS DURING THE ZOOT RESTAURANT'S FIRST WEEKS. ● (FOLGENDE DOPPELSEITE) 73 SIEBDRUCKPLAKAT IN LIMITIERTER AUFLAGE, DAS NACH DER ERÖFFNUNG EINES RESTAURANTS AN DIE BESUCHER ABGEGEBEN WURDE. ▲ (DOUBLE PAGE SUIVANTE) 73 AFFICHE SÉRIGRAPHIQUE EN ÉDITION LIMITÉE OFFERTE AUX CLIENTS D'UN RESTAURANT TOUT AU LONG DE LA PREMIÈRE SEMAINE SUIVANT SON OUVERTURE. (USA)

■ (FOLLOWING SPREAD) 74 ART DIRECTOR/DESIGNER: JULIUS FRIEDMAN PHOTOGRAPHER: GEOFFREY CARR AGENCY: IMAGES CLIENT: PORCINI RESTAURANT ■ 74 COMMEMORATIVE POSTER FOR THE PORCINI RESTAURANT IN LOUISVILLE, KENTUCKY. ● (FOLGENDE DOPPELSEITE) 74 PLAKAT FÜR EIN RESTAURANT. ▲ (DOUBLE PAGE SUIVANTE) 74 AFFICHE POUR UN RESTAURANT. (USA)

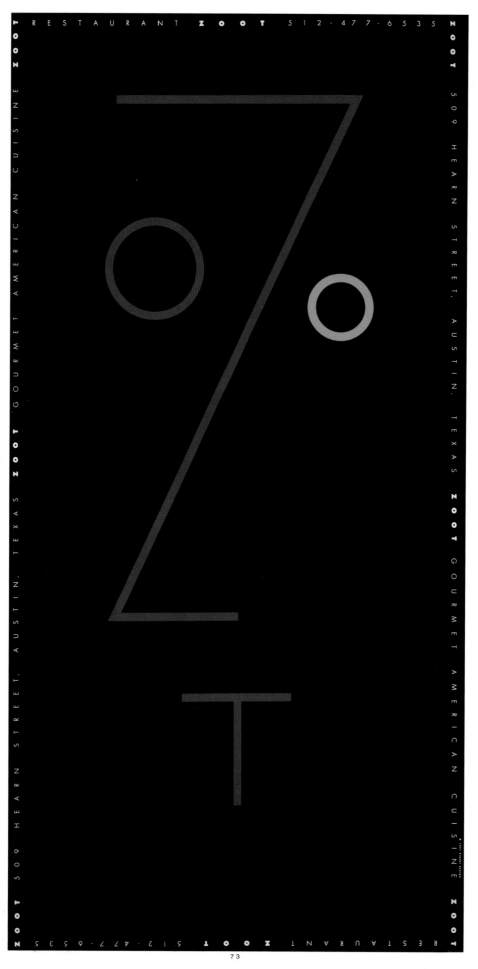

PORCINI

WUNDER BEI McDONALD'S: MILLIONEN-UMSÄTZE OHNE GÄSTE.

Die 365 McDonald's-Restaurants in Deutschland (davon 129 McDrive) sind nach wie vor ein Phänomen. Obwohl sie täglich über 800.000 Gäste bewirten, geht angeblich keiner hin. Besser gesagt, niemand will es gewesen sein. Kein Wunder. Wer gibt schon gern zu, daß er für 10 Mark bestens gegessen hat, wenn sein Gegenüber von 120 Mark teuren Menü im Feinschmeckerlokal erzählt? Wenn überhaupt, dann geht man der Kinder wegen zu McDonald's. Oder aus Zeitgründen, oder weil man zufällig gerade in der Nähe war. Manchmal auch aus Bequemlichkeit, oder weil plötzlich Onkel Norbert in der Tür steht. Das alles sind natürlich Sonderfälle. Insofern ist das Wunder tatsächlich ein Wunder: Wo gibt es schon täglich über 800.000 Sonderfälle?

WIEDER KEIN GOURMET-STERN FÜR McDONALD'S: SERVICE ZU SCHNELL.

Die durchschnittliche Wartezeit bei McDonald's beträgt drei Minuten – vom Moment des Bestellens bis zum Entgegennehmen der Speisen. Das ist zwar für die Gäste angenehm, bringt aber McDonald's regelmäßig um begehrte kulinarische Auszeichnungen (Sterne, Mützen, Löffel usw.). Ein Menü, auf das man nicht 40 Minuten warten muß, kann schließlich nichts Besonderes sein, so frisch es auch sein mag. Erschwerend kommt hinzu, daß man bei 130 McDonald's Restaurants sogar vom Auto aus bestellen und mitnehmen kann. Dies alles ist für den Gourmet absolut unannehmbar. Es sei denn, er kann sich sicher sein, bei McDonald's von keinem anderen Gourmet erkannt zu werden.

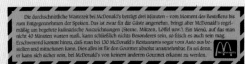

STEUERZAHLER FORDERN: McDONALD'S FÜR ALLE STAATS- EMPFÄNGE.

Wenn Bonn offiziell zu Tisch bittet, kostet das den Steuerzahler zwischen 80 und 150 Mark pro Person. (Der Wiedervereinigungs-Riesling geht extra.) Dagegen würde ein dreigängiges Menü von McDonald's bei etwa 15 Mark liegen. Selbst der teuerste Gang kostet unter 5 Mark. Unser Vorschlag: Chef-Salat als Vorspeise, Hamburger Royal, Pommes Frites und ein erfrischendes Getränk als Hauptgericht. Warme Apfeltasche und einen Kaffee als Dessert. Auf diese Weise wären die werten Damen und Herren nicht nur auf's angenehmste gesättigt. Sie hätten auch reichlich Vitamine, Calcium, Magnesium und Eisen zu sich genommen. Lediglich die Kalorienzufuhr ist ein wenig geringer als bei einem normalen Festmenü. Doch das wäre für die meisten Staatsgäste kaum von Nachteil.

77

PSYCHOLOGE BEHAUPTET: McDONALD'S DISKRIMINIERT ERWACHSENE.

Die einzigen Gäste, die bei McDonald's eine besondere Stellung einnehmen, sind Kinder. In jedem der 365 deutschen McDonald's Restaurants gibt es besondere Stühle für Kinder, auf denen sie ihr besonderes Kinder-Menü essen können und zu dem es immer eine besondere Überraschung gibt: in vielen Restaurants sind besondere Wickelräume eingerichtet und die meisten McDonald's Restaurants haben besondere Spielplätze. Für Kindergeburtstage werden besondere Tische reserviert (nur dafür). Und natürlich dürfen die Kinder besonders laut sein und mit den Fingern essen. Verständlich, daß sich die großen Gäste besonders benachteiligt fühlen und sich fragen, warum sie überhaupt erwachsen geworden sind.

78

■ 75-78 ART DIRECTOR: ALEXANDER BARTEL COPYWRITER: REINHARD SIEMES AGENCY: HEYE + PARTNER GMBH CLIENT: MCDONALD'S GERMANY INC. ■ 75-78 IMAGE CAMPAIGN FOR MCDONALD'S IN GERMANY: "A MIRACLE AT MCDONALD'S: A TURNOVER OF SEVERAL MILLION WITHOUT CUSTOMERS"; "AGAIN NO GOURMET STAR FOR MCDONALD'S: THE SERVICE IS TOO QUICK"; "TAXPAYERS' REQUEST: MCDONALD'S FOR ALL GOVERNMENT RECEPTIONS"; "PSYCHOLOGIST CLAIMS: MCDONALD'S DISCRIMINATES AGAINST GROWN-UPS." ● 75-78 IMAGE-KAMPAGNE FÜR MCDONALD'S. ▲ 75-78 CAMPAGNE D'IDENTITÉ VISUELLE DES RESTAURANTS MCDONALD'S: «MIRACLE CHEZ MCDONALD'S: DES MILLIONS DE CHIFFRE D'AFFAIRES SANS CLIENTS»; «PAS D'ÉTOILE ENCORE POUR MCDONALD'S: SERVICE TROP RAPIDE»; «LES CONTRIBUABLES RÉCLAMENT: MCDONALD'S POUR TOUTES LES RÉCEPTIONS OFFICIELLES»; «UN PSYCHOLOGUE LE PRÉTEND: MCDONALD'S DISCRIMINE LES ADULTES.» (GER)

waiting for a kiss

first kiss

Ahh·····

82

83

84

死ぬまで忘れないと信じて食べた。

Yes, 100%
(Häagen-Dazs)

Shall we Häagen-Dazs?

85

■ **79-81, 85** Art Director/Designer: HISA MATSUNAGA Photographers: ISSAQUE FOUJITA 85, MEGUMU WADA/IMA CORPORATION 79-81 Copywriter: EISAKU SEKIHASHI Agency: J. WALTER THOMPSON JAPAN LTD. Client: HÄAGEN-DAZS JAPAN INC. ■ **79-81, 85** FROM POSTER CAMPAIGNS FOR HÄAGEN-DAZS BARS, CENTERING ON THE KISS. NUMBERS 79 TO 81 GIVE THE PRODUCT'S POINT OF VIEW AS IT IS BEING EATEN: "WAITING FOR A KISS"; "FIRST KISS"; "AHH…"; FIGURE 85 COMMUNICATES THAT THE BARS ARE AS DELICIOUS AS A KISS. ● **79-81, 85** AUS PLAKATKAMPAGNEN FÜR HÄAGEN-DAZS-RIEGEL, DIE DEN KUSS ALS THEMA HABEN. IN ABB. 79-81 SPRICHT DAS PRODUKT, WÄHREND ES GEGESSEN WIRD: «ICH WARTE AUF EINEN KUSS»; «DER ERSTE KUSS»; «AAH…»; IN ABB. 85 WIRD BEHAUPTET, DIE RIEGEL SEIEN SO KÖSTLICH WIE EIN KUSS. ▲ **79-81, 85** AFFICHES POUR LES BARRES HÄAGEN-DAZS SUR LE THEME DU BAISER. DANS LES FIG. 79-81, L'IMAGE EST EXPLICITE: «EN ATTENDANT UN BAISER»; «PREMIER BAISER»; «AAH…»; LA FIG. 85 SUGGERE QUE LE PRODUIT EST AUSSI DÉLICIEUX QU'UN BAISER. (JPN)

■ **82-84** Art Director: JEAN-LOUIS TOURNADRE Account Supervisors: MARC DRILLECH, VÉRONIQUE LOOTEN, VÉRONIQUE LANGLOIS Illustrators: SERGE CLÉMENT 82, 84, JEAN-LUC FALQUE 83 Copywriter: JEAN-FRANÇOIS CRANCE Agency: PUBLICIS CONSEIL Client: FRANCAISE DE BRASSERIE/"33" EXPORT ■ **82-84** POSTER SERIES FOR A FRENCH BEER. ● **82-84** PLAKATREIHE FÜR EIN FRANZÖSISCHES BIER, DAS FÜR DEN EXPORT BESTIMMT IST. ▲ **82-84** D'UNE SÉRIE D'AFFICHES POUR UNE BIERE. (FRA)

■ **86-91** ART DIRECTOR/DESIGNER/PHOTOGRAPHER: ANDRÉAS NETTHOEVEL AGENCY: 2. STOCK SÜD CLIENT: RAUM-DESIGN ■ **86-91** SIMPLE, CLEAR DESIGNS BY CHARLES POLLOCK, PRESENTED IN A CAMPAIGN FOR A FURNITURE HOUSE. THE ILLUSTRATIONS WERE DONE USING THE RAYOGRAPHIC PROCESS, WHICH DOES NOT REQUIRE A CAMERA. ● **86-91** SCHNÖRKELLOSE DESIGNS, VORGESTELLT IN PLAKATEN FÜR EIN MÖBELHAUS. ES WURDE MIT RAYOGRAPHIE (KAMERALOSE PHOTOGRAPHIE) GEARBEITET. ▲ **86-91** LE DESIGN SIMPLE DE CHARLES POLLOCK PRÉSENTÉ DANS UNE CAMPAGNE POUR UN MAGASIN DE MEUBLES; LES IMAGES ONT ÉTÉ RÉALISÉES SELON LA TECHNIQUE DE LA RAYOGRAPHIE, UN PROCÉDÉ PHOTOGRAPHIQUE SANS APPAREIL. (SWI)

■ **92-95** ART DIRECTOR: BRUNO OLDANI DESIGNER: BRUNO OLDANI PHOTOGRAPHERS: BERNARD BLATCH, ROGER FREDERICKS COPYWRITER: ROLF KARLSTRÖM CLIENT: HAG AS ■ **92-95** A SERIES OF SHOWROOM POSTERS FOR A FURNITURE MAKER. THE IMAGES IN THE CENTER ARE HUMOROUS ALLUSIONS TO THE WORKS OF FAMOUS PAINTERS. ● **92-95** EINE REIHE VON SHOWROOM-PLAKATEN FÜR EINEN MÖBELHERSTELLER. DIE BILDER IN DER MITTE SIND HUMORVOLLE ANSPIELUNGEN AUF DIE WERKE BEKANNTER MEISTER. ▲ **92-95** UNE SÉRIE D'AFFICHES DESTINÉES AUX POINTS DE VENTE D'UN FABRICANT DE MEUBLES. LES IMAGES AU CENTRE SONT DES ALLUSIONS PLEINES D'HUMOUR À DES ŒUVRES D'ARTISTES CONNUS. (DEN)

CAPISCO COLLECTION HAG

SIGNÉT COLLECTION HAG

9 2

9 3

AIR COLLECTION HAG

CREDO COLLECTION HAG

9 4

9 5

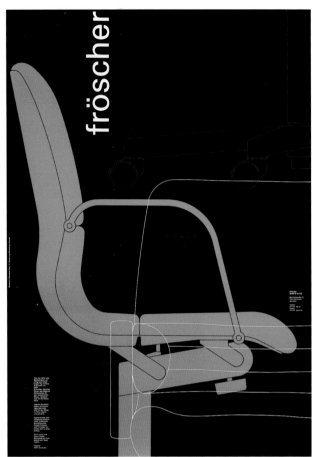

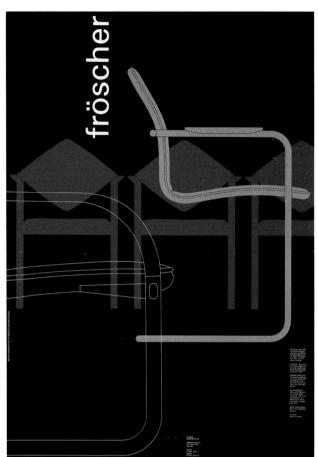

96

97

■ **96, 97** ART DIRECTOR: BAUMANN & BAUMANN DESIGNERS: BARBARA BAUMANN, GERD BAUMANN COPYWRITER: BARBARA BAUMANN AGENCY: BAUMANN & BAUMANN CLIENT: FRÖSCHER GMBH & CO KG ■ **96, 97** POSTERS FOR FRÖSCHER OFFICE FURNITURE. ● **96, 97** PLAKATWERBUNG FÜR BÜROMÖBEL VON FRÖSCHER. ▲ **96, 97** PUBLICITÉ POUR LES MEUBLES DE BUREAUX FRÖSCHER. (GER)

■ **98** ART DIRECTOR: DIRK LONGJALOUX DESIGNER: LUTZ MENZE PHOTOGRAPHER: UDO KOWALSKI AGENCY: HANS GÜNTER SCHMITZ CLIENT: GIRA, GIERSIEPEN GMBH & CO KG ■ **98** POSTER MAILED TO ARCHITECTS, INTERIOR DESIGNERS AND ELECTRIC PLANNERS. ● **98** AN ARCHITEKTEN, INNENARCHITEKTEN UND ELEKTROPLANER GERICHTETES PLAKAT. ▲ **98** CETTE AFFICHE S'ADRESSANT AUX ARCHITECTES, DÉCORATEURS ET ÉLECTRICIENS MONTRE UNE GAMME COMPLETE D'INTERRUPTEURS. (GER)

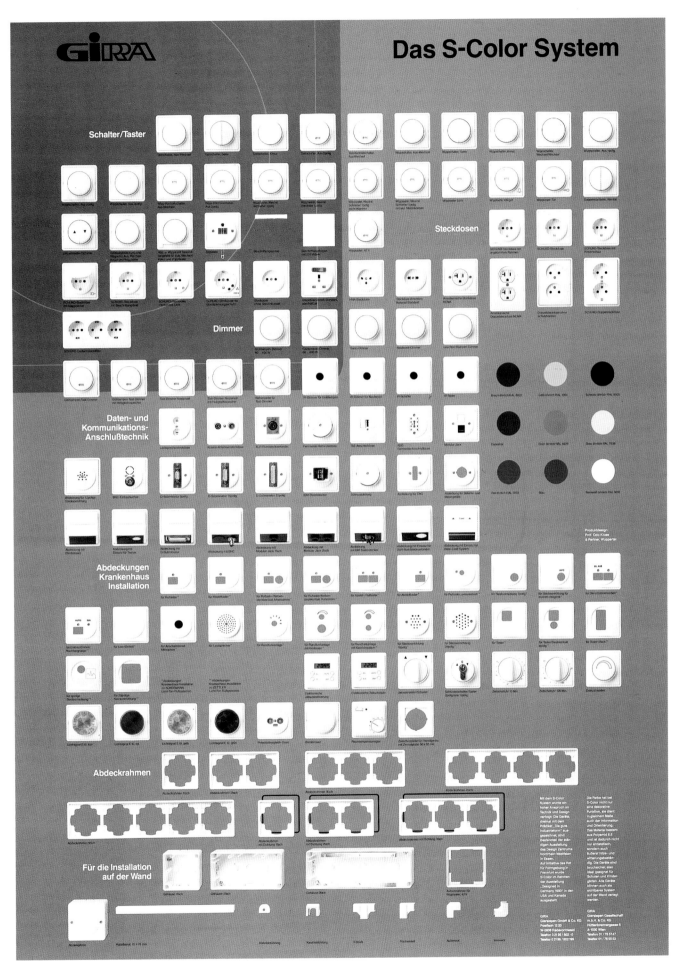

THERE'S MORE TO SEE IN A WEATHER SHIELD WINDOW.

WEATHER SHIELD
WINDOWS & DOORS

THERE'S MORE TO SEE IN A WEATHER SHIELD WINDOW.

WEATHER SHIELD
WINDOWS & DOORS

THERE'S MORE TO SEE IN A WEATHER SHIELD WINDOW.

WEATHER SHIELD
WINDOWS & DOORS

102

103

■ **99-101** ART DIRECTOR/DESIGNER: MIKE WHEATON PHOTOGRAPHER: DENNIS MANARCHY COPYWRITER: REED ALLEN AGENCY: HOFFMAN YORK & COMPTON CLIENT: WEATHER SHIELD WINDOWS & DOORS ■ **99-101** FROM A CAMPAIGN INTRODUCING WEATHER SHIELD WINDOWS TO CONSUMERS. THE WINDOWS, WHICH OFFER ALL-WEATHER PROTECTION, COME IN STANDARD SIZES, OR THEY CAN BE CUSTOM-MADE. ● **99-101** AUS EINER KAMPAGNE, IN DER DEN KONSUMENTEN EINE BISHER RELATIV UNBEKANNTE SPEZIELLE FENSTERART VORGESTELLT WIRD. SIE BIETET SCHUTZ UND KLARE SICHT UNTER ALLEN WETTERBEDINGUNGEN UND IST IN STANDARD- SOWIE SONDERMASSEN LIEFERBAR. ▲ **99-101** D'UNE CAMPAGNE DANS LAQUELLE ON PRÉSENTE AUX CON-SOMMATEURS UN TYPE PARTICULIER DE FENETRE, ENCORE PEU CONNU DU PUBLIC, QUI OFFRE UNE BONNE PROTECTION PAR TOUS LES TEMPS ET UN VERRE BIEN TRANSPARENT. ELLE EST LIVRÉE DANS DES FORMATS STANDARD OU SPÉCIAUX. (USA)

■ **102** ART DIRECTOR: JULIUS FRIEDMAN DESIGNER: JULIUS FRIEDMAN PHOTOGRAPHER: GEOFFREY CARR AGENCY: IMAGES CLIENT: TELL CITY CHAIR COMPANY ■ **102** PROMOTIONAL POSTER FOR AN INDIANA CHAIR MANUFACTURER. ● **102** PROMOTIONSPLAKAT FÜR EINEN AMERIKANISCHEN HERSTELLER VON STÜHLEN. ▲ **102** AFFICHE PUBLICITAIRE POUR UN FABRICANT DE CHAISES. (USA)

■ **103** ART DIRECTOR: WILLIAM REUTER DESIGNERS: WILLIAM REUTER, JOSÉ BILA ILLUSTRATOR: JOSÉ BILA AGENCY: REUTER DESIGN CLIENT: DESIGN 31 CUSTOM FRAMING ■ **103** BILLBOARD FOR A CUSTOM FRAMING SHOP. THE HAND-PAINTED SIGN IS ABOUT 20 FEET SQUARE. ● **103** EIN DIREKT AUF DIE HAUSWAND GEMALTES BILLBOARD FÜR EINEN BILDERRAHMENHERSTELLER. ▲ **103** PANONCEAU PUBLICITAIRE DIRECTEMENT PEINT SUR LE MUR D'UN IMMEUBLE ABRITANT UN FABRICANT DE CADRES. (USA)

TAKEO PAPER WORLD '92

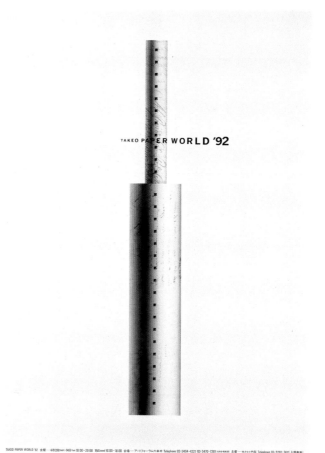

TAKEO PAPER WORLD '92

104

105

■ 104, 105 Art Director/Designer: KENYA HARA Agency: NIPPON DESIGN CENTER Client: TAKEO CORP. ■ 104, 105 ANNOUNCE-
MENTS OF A CORPORATE PROMOTIONAL EXHIBITION OF THE TAKEO PAPER COMPANY. ● 104, 105 ANKÜNDIGUNGEN EINER AUS-
STELLUNG DES PAPIERHERSTELLERS TAKEO. ▲ 104, 105 ANNONCES D'UNE EXPOSITION DU FABRICANT DE PAPIER TAKEO. (JPN)

■ 106 Art Director: AKIO OKUMURA Designer: MAKOTO ITO Client: INOUE PAPER CO., LTD. ■ 106 PROMOTIONAL POSTER FOR
THE INOUE PAPER COMPANY—AN INTERPRETATION OF THE WORD "FLOAT." ● 106 «FLOAT» (SCHWEBEN)—MIT EINER SPE-
ZIELLEN VISUALISIERUNG DIESES WORTES WIRBT DER PAPIERHERSTELLER INOUE PAPER CO. ▲ 106 LE MOT «FLOAT» (FLOT-
TER) EST VISUALISÉ DE MANIÈRE ORIGINALE SUR CETTE AFFICHE POUR LE FABRICANT DE PAPIER INOUE PAPER CO. (JPN)

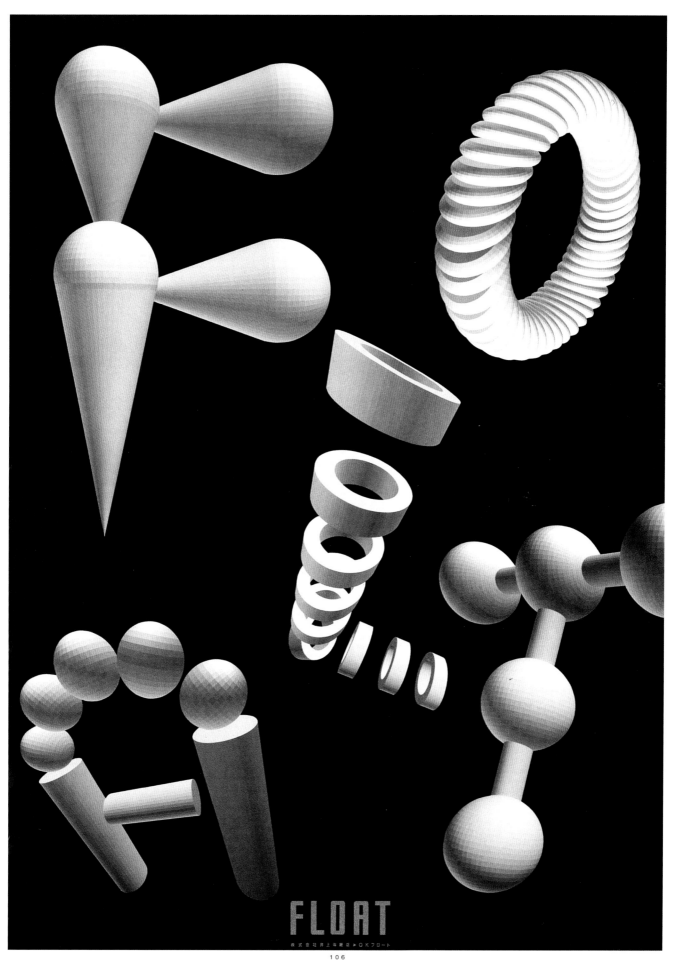

FLOAT

株式会社井上洋紙店 ▶ OKフロート

106

CHAMPION
KROMEKOTE

107

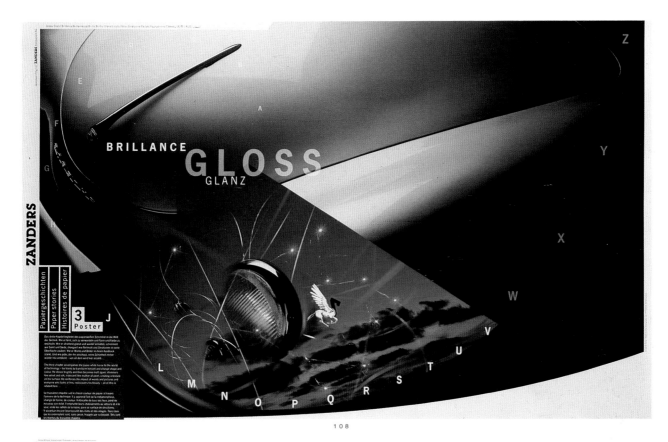

108

109

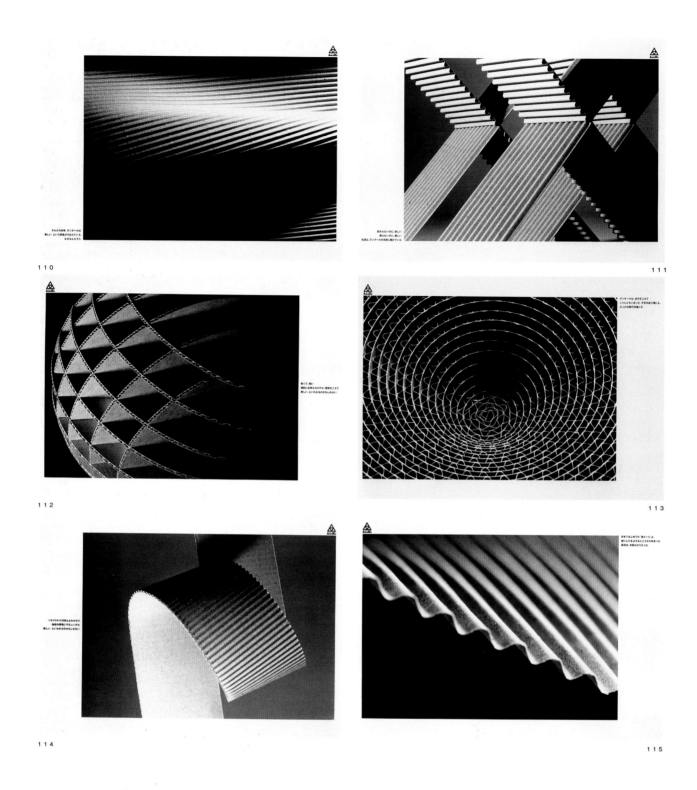

110

111

112

113

114

115

■ **110-115** Art Director: DAISUKE NAKATSUKA Designer: YASUHIKO MATSUMOTO Photographer: KATSUO HANZAWA Stylist: DAISUKE NAKATSUKA Copywriter: HIDEO OKANO Agency: NAKATSUKA DAISUKE INC. Client: RENGO CO., LTD. ■ **110-115** EXAMPLES FROM A SERIES OF POSTERS FOR A BRAND OF CORRUGATED CARDBOARD. THE MESSAGE IS THAT IT IS BEAUTIFUL, LIGHT AND STRONG, ALWAYS TRUE TO ITS FUNCTION AND HARMLESS TO THE ENVIRONMENT. ● **110-115** AUS EINER PLAKAT-SERIE, DIE WELLKARTON GEWIDMET IST. DIE BOTSCHAFT IST, DASS WELLKARTON SCHÖN IST, LEICHT UND STARK, FUNKTIONS-TÜCHTIG SOWIE UMWELTFREUNDLICH. ▲ **110-115** EXEMPLES D'UNE SÉRIE D'AFFICHES CONSACRÉES AU CARTON ONDULÉ OU L'ON VANTE LA BEAUTÉ DE CE SUPPORT, LÉGER ET ROBUSTE, FONCTIONNEL ET RESPECTUEUX DE L'ENVIRONNEMENT. (USA)

116

117

■ 116 ART DIRECTOR/DESIGNER: TODD WATERBURY PHOTOGRAPHER: GEORGE MARKS/BLACKBOX AGENCY: THE DUFFY DESIGN GROUP
CLIENT: FOX RIVER PAPER COMPANY ■ 116 PHOTOGRAPHY AND ILLUSTRATION ON RECYCLED PAPER BY THE FOX RIVER PAPER
COMPANY. THE PRODUCT INFORMATION, IN THE FORM OF A NEWSPAPER CUTTING, IS ONE OF THE MAIN DESIGN ELEMENTS. ● 116
PHOTOGRAPHIE UND ILLUSTRATION AUF RECYCLING-PAPIER DER FOX RIVER PAPER COMPANY. DIE PRODUKTINFORMATION AUF
DEM ZEITUNGSAUSSCHNITT WIRD ZU EINEM WICHTIGEN GESTALTERISCHEN ELEMENT. ▲ 116 PHOTOGRAPHIE ET ILLUSTRATION
SUR PAPIER RECYCLÉ. L'INFORMATION CONCERNANT LE PRODUIT CONSTITUE UN ÉLÉMENT DÉTERMINANT DU DESIGN. (USA)

■ 117 ART DIRECTOR/COPYWRITER: REX PETEET DESIGNERS: REX PETEET, JULIA ALBANESI PHOTOGRAPHER: ELLE SCHUSTER AGENCY:
SIBLEY/PETEET CLIENT: JAMES RIVER PAPER CO. ■ 117 THIS POSTER IS MEANT TO GET CUSTOMERS TO REQUEST A COPY OF A
GUIDE TO ALL JAMES RIVER PRINTING PAPERS. THE SHARDS THAT MAKE UP THE PORTRAIT OF VENUS ARE SAMPLES FROM
VARIOUS SECTIONS OF THE BOOK. ● 117 DIESES PLAKAT IST EINE AUFFORDERUNG, DAS DRUCKPAPIERMUSTERBUCH VON
JAMES RIVER ZU BESTELLEN. DIE EINZELNEN TEILE DES PORTRÄTS DER VENUS GEHÖREN ZU DEN VERSCHIEDENEN KAPITELN
DES BUCHES. ▲ 117 CETTE AFFICHE A ÉTÉ CONÇUE POUR INCITER LE PUBLIC À ACHETER LE CATALOGUE D'ÉCHANTILLONS DE
PAPIER JAMES RIVER. LES DÉTAILS DU PORTRAIT DE VÉNUS ILLUSTRENT LES DIVERS CHAPITRES DE CE CATALOGUE. (USA)

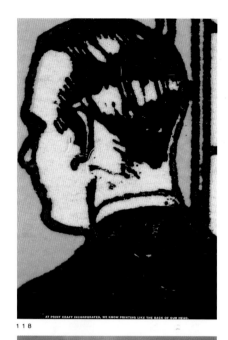

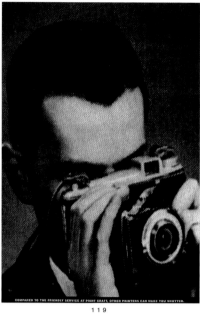

118

119

120

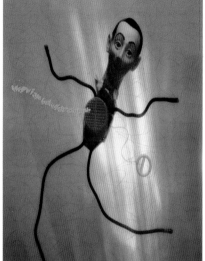

GRAPHIC ADS IS HAVING AN IDENTITY CRISIS.

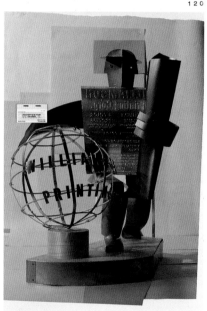

121

122

123

■ 118-120 ART DIRECTORS/DESIGNERS: CHARLES ANDERSON, HALEY JOHNSON, DANIEL OLSON COPYWRITER: LISA PEMRICK AGENCY: C.S. ANDERSON DESIGN CO. CLIENT: PRINT CRAFT, INC. ■ 118-120 FROM A SERIES OF POSTERS USING GIANT HEADS TO DEMONSTRATE THE QUALITY OF THE CLIENT'S PRINTING. ● 118-120 AUS EINER PLAKATSERIE MIT RIESIGEN KÖPFEN FÜR EINE DRUCKEREI. ▲ 118-120 D'UNE SÉRIE D'AFFICHES ORNÉES DE VISAGES EN GROS-PLAN POUR UNE IMPRIMERIE. (USA)

■ 121 ART DIRECTOR/DESIGNER: RICK VALICENTI PHOTOGRAPHERS: CORINNE PFISTER, MICHAEL PAPPAS AGENCY: THIRST ■ 121 THIS POSTER WAS USED AT AN OPEN HOUSE TO SHOW OFF NORTH STAR PRINTING'S NEW EIGHT-COLOR PRESS. ● 121 NORTH STAR PRINTING DEMONSTRIERTE EINE NEUE ACHTFARBEN-DRUCKPRESSE BEI EINEM OPEN-HOUSE-ANLASS MIT DEM DRUCK DIESES PLAKATES. ▲ 121 NORTH STAR PRINTING AVAIT ORGANISÉ UNE DÉMONSTRATION D'UNE NOUVELLE PRESSE À HUIT COULEURS AU COURS D'UNE OPÉRATION PORTES OUVERTES, DONT LES CAPACITÉS TECHNIQUES SONT ILLUSTRÉES PAR CETTE AFFICHE. (USA)

■ 122 ART DIRECTOR/DESIGNER: JERRY SULLIVAN PHOTOGRAPHER: BILL MAYER AGENCY: SULLIVAN HAAS COYLE CLIENT: GRAPHIC ADS ■ 122 A POSTER FOR GRAPHIC ADS, CALLING THE PRINTER "EXTRAORDINARY" AND A "RELIABLE SOURCE FOR AD PREPARA- TIONS." ● 122 «GRAPHIC ADS HAT EINE IDENTITÄTSKRISE.» WEIL DIE EINEN SIE FÜR EINE «AUSSERGEWÖHNLICHE DRUCKEREI»

124

HALTEN, DIE ANDEREN FÜR «ZUVERLÄSSIGE ANZEIGENGESTALTER.» SIE SIND BEIDES. ▲ 122 «GRAPHIC ADS A UNE CRISE D'IDEN-
TITÉ.» CETTE IMPRIMERIE EST CONSIDÉRÉE COMME «EXCEPTIONNELLE» PAR LES UNS ET «SÉRIEUSE» PAR LES AUTRES. (USA)

■ 123 ART DIRECTORS/DESIGNERS: SHARON WERNER, TODD WATERBURY PHOTOGRAPHER: GEOF KERN AGENCY: THE DUFFY DESIGN
GROUP CLIENT: WILLIAMSON PRINTING CO. ■ 123 POSTER PROMOTING WILLIAMSON PRINTING'S TECHNIQUE FOR COMBINING
METALLIC INK WITH FOUR-COLOR PROCESS PRINTING. ● 123 DIE TECHNIK DER VERBINDUNG VON METALLFARBEN MIT VIERFAR-
BENDRUCK IST GEGENSTAND DIESES PLAKATES EINER DRUCKEREI. ▲ 123 CETTE AFFICHE A POUR SUJET LA TECHNIQUE
PERMETTANT DE COMBINER LES COULEURS MÉTALLIQUES ET L'IMPRESSION EN QUADRICHROMIE, UN PROCÉDÉ BREVETÉ. (USA)

■ 124 ART DIRECTOR/DESIGNER: JAMES STANTON PHOTOGRAPHER: TELEPHOTO/INDEX STOCK COPYWRITER: JAMES STANTON AGENCY:
HILL AND KNOWLTON CLIENT: S.D. SCOTT ■ 124 "THE HOTTEST DAYS IN THE HOTTEST MONTH IN NEW YORK," A POSTER PRO-
MOTION OF A PRINTER. ● 124 «DIE HEISSESTEN TAGE IM HEISSESTEN MONAT IN NEW YORK,» WERBUNG FÜR EINEN DRUCKER.
▲ 124 «LES JOURNÉES LES PLUS TORRIDES DU MOIS LE PLUS CHAUD À NEW YORK,» PUBLICITÉ D'UN IMPRIMEUR. (USA)

When it comes to typography, which would you rather have?
The undying gratitude of your company comptroller?
Or one of these?

ONE SHOW AWARD

The next time you come up with a headline you love, call Bill Burk at 1-800-222-6798. We can't guarantee your ledger books will win awards. But there's a good chance your ad will. Great Faces

■ **125** ART DIRECTOR/DESIGNER: SUE CROLICK PHOTOGRAPHER: KERRY PETERSON COPYWRITER: TOM MCELLIGOTT AGENCY: SUE CROLICK ADVERTISING + DESIGN CLIENT: GREAT FACES TYPOGRAPHY ■ **125** GREAT FACES TYPOGRAPHY TELLS ART DIRECTORS THAT ALTHOUGH ITS HAND-SET HEADLINES CAN BE MORE EXPENSIVE, THEY'RE WORTH IT. ● **125** «WAS MÖCHTEN SIE LIEBER, WENN ES UM TYPOGRAPHIE GEHT: DIE UNENDLICHE DANKBARKEIT IHRER BUCHHALTUNG ODER EINEN VON DIESEN?» GREAT FACES TYPOGRAPHY ERINNERT ART DIRECTORS MIT DIESEM PLAKAT, DASS DIE HANDGESETZTEN HEADLINES DER FIRMA ZWAR ETWAS TEURER SEIN KÖNNEN, ES ABER WERT SEIEN, WEIL MAN DAMIT PREISE GEWINNT. ▲ **125** «QU'EST-CE QUE VOUS PRÉFÉRERIEZ QUAND IL EST QUESTION DE TYPOGRAPHIE? LA GRATITUDE ÉTERNELLE DE VOTRE COMPTABLE? OU UN DE CEUX-LÀ?» AVEC CETTE AFFICHE, GREAT FACES TYPOGRAPHY VEUT RAPPELER AUX DIRECTEURS ARTISTIQUES QUE LES TITRES COMPOSÉS À LA MAIN PAR CETTE FIRME SONT SANS DOUTE CHERS, MAIS QU'ILS PERMETTENT DE REMPORTER DES PRIX. (USA)

■ **126** ART DIRECTOR/DESIGNER/ILLUSTRATOR: JENNIFER MORLA AGENCY: MORLA DESIGN CLIENT: MERCURY TYPOGRAPHY ■ **126** THIS POSTER FOR A TYPOGRAPHER AND A SILK-SCREEN HOUSE WAS DESIGNED TO SHOW OFF THE FUTURA TYPEFACE, INCLUDING ITS HISTORY AND ARCHITECTURAL USE. A VERTICAL FORMAT WAS USED TO REINFORCE THE ARCHITECTURAL SENSE OF HEIGHT. ● **126** DIESES PLAKAT FÜR EINEN TYPOGRAPHEN UND EINEN SIEBDRUCKER IST DER FUTURA, IHRER GESCHICHTE UND DER ANWENDUNG IN DER ARCHITEKTUR GEWIDMET. DAS HOCHFORMAT UNTERSTREICHT DEN ARCHITEKTONISCHEN ASPEKT. ▲ **126** CETTE AFFICHE POUR UN TYPOGRAPHE ET UN ATELIER DE SÉRIGRAPHIE EST CONSACRÉE À LA FUTURA, À SON HISTOIRE ET À SES APPLICATIONS DANS L'ARCHITECTURE. LE FORMAT OBLONG SOULIGNE LE CARACTERE ARCHITECTONIQUE. (USA)

127

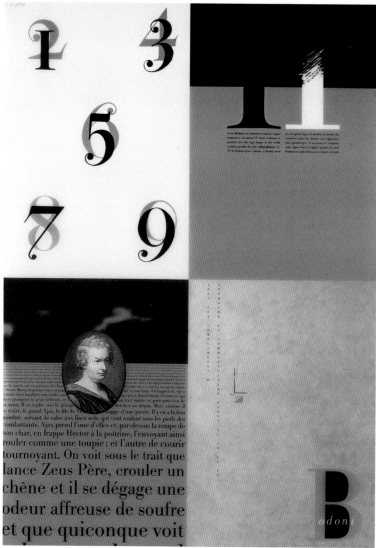

128

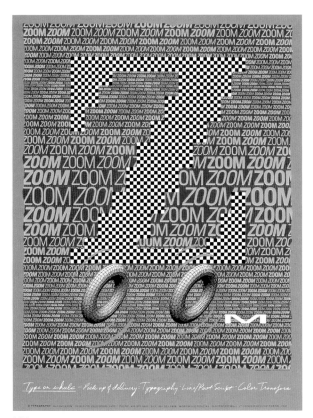

129

130

131

132

■ **131-133** ART DIRECTOR: FRANCES NEWELL DESIGNER: MARK DIAPER AGENCY: NEWELL AND SORRELL CLIENT: WATERSTONE'S ■
131-133 EXAMPLES FROM A SERIES OF PROMOTIONAL POSTERS FOR A CHAIN OF BOOKSTORES. THE THEMES OF THE POSTERS
SHOWN HERE ARE LITERATURE, MODERN ART AND CHRISTMAS. ● **131-133** BEISPIELE AUS EINER PLAKATWERBEKAMPAGNE FÜR
DIE ENGLISCHE BUCHHANDLUNGSKETTE WATERSTONE'S. DIE THEMEN DER HIER GEZEIGTEN PLAKATE SIND LITERATUR, MODER-
NE KUNST UND WEIHNACHTEN. ▲ **131-133** EXEMPLES D'UNE SÉRIE D'AFFICHES PROMOTIONNELLES POUR LA CHAINE DE LIBRAI-
RIES WATERSTONE'S. LES SUJETS DES AFFICHES PRÉSENTÉES ICI SONT LA LITTÉRATURE, L'ART MODERNE ET NOEL. (GBR)

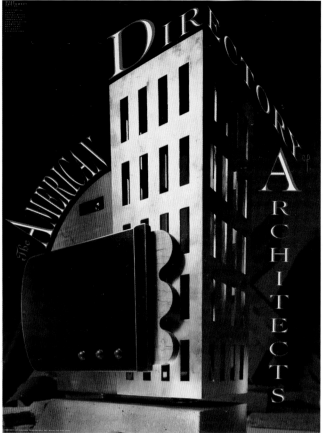

134

135

■ (THIS SPREAD) **134** ART DIRECTOR/DESIGNER: GABOR PALOTAI COPYWRITER: MARIE WALLERSTEDT AGENCY: GABOR PALOTAI DESIGN CLIENT: THE ADVERTISING ASSOCIATION OF SWEDEN ■ **134** THIS POSTER PROMOTES A BOOK ON SWEDISH ADVERTIS-ING AGENCIES. THE LETTER "R" STANDS FOR THE WORD "REKLAM"—SWEDISH FOR "ADVERTISING." ● (DIESE DOPPELSEITE) **134** FÜR EIN BUCH ÜBER SCHWEDISCHE WERBEAGENTUREN. DAS «R» STEHT FÜR «REKLAME.» ▲ (CETTE DOUBLE PAGE) **134** LE «R» SUR CETTE AFFICHE POUR UN LIVRE SUR LES AGENCES DE PUBLICITÉ SUÉDOISES EST L'INITIALE DU MOT «RÉCLAME.» (SWE)

■ (THIS SPREAD) **135** ART DIRECTORS: JOEL FULLER, TOM STERLING DESIGNER: TOM STERLING PHOTOGRAPHER: JOSÉ MOLINA STYLIST: TOM STERLING COPYWRITERS: JOEL FULLER, PHILIP SMITH AGENCY: PINKHAUS DESIGN CORP. CLIENT: PINKHAUS DESIGN CORP. ■ **135** POSTER PROMOTION FOR THE WEST/SOUTHWEST EDITION OF THE AMERICAN DIRECTORY OF ARCHITECTS, SENT TO BOOKSTORES. ● (DIESE DOPPELSEITE) **135** AN BUCHHÄNDLER ADRESSIERTES PLAKAT FÜR EIN HANDBUCH ÜBER ARCHI-TEKTEN. ▲ (CETTE DOUBLE PAGE) **135** CETTE AFFICHE ANNONCE LA PARUTION D'UN OUVRAGE SUR L'ARCHITECTURE .(USA)

■ (THIS SPREAD) **136-138** ART DIRECTOR: ANDREI SHELUTTO DESIGNER/ILLUSTRATOR: JELENA KITAJEVA PUBLISHER: BELARUS PUB-LISHING HOUSE ■ **136-138** THE THEME OF THESE POSTERS IS SOVIET INDUSTRIAL DESIGN BETWEEN 1920 AND 1930: THE FIRST SOVIET AIRPLANE, THE AK-1 (1924), THE FIRST SOVIET RACING CAR (1937) AND THE FIRST FREIGHT-TRAIN ENGINE (1921). ● (DIESE DOPPELSEITE) **136-138** SOWJETISCHES INDUSTRIEDESIGN ZWISCHEN 1920 UND 1930: DAS ERSTE SOWJETISCHE FLUG-ZEUG AK-1 1924; DAS ERSTE RENNAUTO, 1937; DIE ERSTE GÜTERZUG-LOKOMOTIVE, 1921. ▲ (CETTE DOUBLE PAGE) **136-138** LE DESIGN INDUSTRIEL SOVIÉTIQUE ENTRE 1920 ET 1930 EST LE SUJET DE CETTE SÉRIE D'AFFICHES: LE PREMIER AVION SOVIÉTIQUE DE 1924; LA PREMIERE VOITURE DE COURSES, DE 1937; LE PREMIER TRAIN DE MARCHANDISES, DE 1921. (WRU)

■ (FOLLOWING SPREAD) **139, 140** ART DIRECTOR/PHOTOGRAPHER: WILLIAM DEMICHELE DESIGNER: CYNTHIA MILLER AGENCY: DE MICHELE DESIGNS CLIENT: PROTEUS PRESS ■ **139, 140** TWO OF THE TATTOOED WOMEN SHOWN IN THE BOOK BEING ADVERTISED SERVE AS EYE-CATCHERS FOR THESE POSTERS. ● (FOLGENDE DOPPELSEITE) **139, 140** «DIE ILLUSTRIERTE FRAU,» WERBUNG FÜR EIN BUCH. ▲ (DOUBLE PAGE SUIVANTE) **139, 140** «LA FEMME ILLUSTRÉE,» AFFICHES POUR UN LIVRE. (USA)

136

137

138

THE ILLUSTRATED WOMAN

A BOOK BY PROTEUS PRESS
PHOTOGRAPHS BY WILLIAM DEMICHELE

©1991 PROTEUS PRESS INC., ALBANY, NEW YORK • COLLECTOR: ANGEL, LOS ANGELES, CALIFORNIA • TATTOO ARTIST: BOB ROBERTS

139

THE ILLUSTRATED WOMAN

A BOOK BY PROTEUS PRESS
PHOTOGRAPHS BY WILLIAM DEMICHELE

©1991 PROTEUS PRESS INC., ALBANY, N.Y. • COLLECTOR: ISOBEL HITCHCOCK 1991 BEST TATTOOED FEMALE • TATTOO ARTIST: BILL HANNONG

140

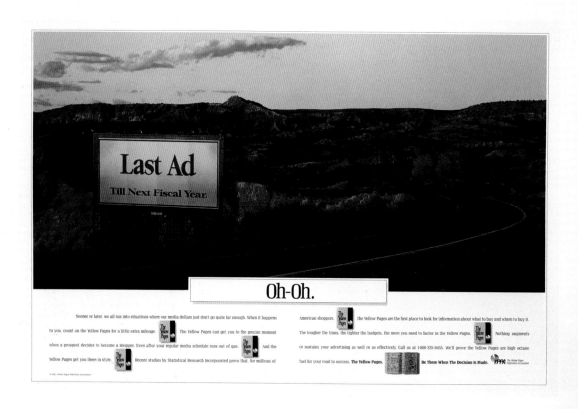

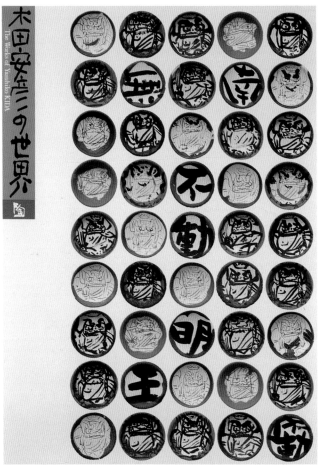

143

144

■ **141** ART DIRECTOR: BILL ZABOWSKI PHOTOGRAPHER: JIM ARNDT COPYWRITER: PETE SMITH AGENCY: MARTIN/WILLIAMS, INC. CLIENT: YELLOW PAGES PUBLISHERS ASSOCIATION ■ **141** THE MESSAGE OF THIS POSTER IS THAT EVEN IF YOUR MEDIA DOLLARS DON'T GET YOU FAR, YOU CAN COUNT ON THE YELLOW PAGES TO PROVIDE SOME EXTRA MILEAGE. ● **141** DIE BOTSCHAFT DIESES PLAKATES FÜR EIN BRANCHENBUCH LAUTET: WENN DAS MEDIABUDGET NICHT AUSREICHT, HILFT DAS BRANCHENBUCH QUASI ÜBER DIE LETZTEN KILOMETER. ▲ **141** CETTE AFFICHE POUR UN ANNUAIRE PAR BRANCHES A POUR MESSAGE: QUAND LE BUDGET MÉDIAS NE SUFFIT PAS, L'ANNUAIRE PAR BRANCHES PEUT VOUS AIDER POUR LES DERNIERS KILOMETRES. (USA)

■ **142** ART DIRECTOR/ILLUSTRATOR: YASUHIKO KIDA DESIGNERS: YASUHIKO KIDA, TSUYOSHI SUGINO, HISAYO SATAKE ■ **142** IMAGE POSTER FOR A BOOK ON THE WORK OF THE JAPANESE ARTIST YASUHIKO KIDA. ● **142** WERBUNG FÜR EIN BUCH ÜBER DIE ARBEIT DES KÜNSTLERS YASUHIKO KIDA. ▲ **142** PUBLICTIÉ POUR UN LIVRE SUR LES CRÉATIONS DE L'ARTISTE YASUHIKO KIDA. (JPN)

■ **143, 144** ART DIRECTORS/DESIGNERS: GARY GOLDSMITH, HENRIETTE LIENKE PHOTOGRAPHER: ROBERT AMMIRATI COPYWRITER: DEAN HACOHEN AGENCY: GOLDSMITH/JEFFREY CLIENT: NYNEX INFORMATION RESOURCES ■ **143, 144** THESE POSTERS WERE SENT TO THE NYNEX SALES FORCE, WHICH SELLS ADS FOR BOTH THE CONSUMER AND BUSINESS-TO-BUSINESS DIRECTORIES. AT THE TIME OF THE PROMOTION, THE COVER OF THE CONSUMER BOOK WAS YELLOW AND THE BUSINESS-TO-BUSINESS BOOK WAS BROWN. ● **143, 144** AN DIE NYNEX-AUSSENDIENSTMITARBEITER GERICHTETE PLAKATE. ES GEHT UM ANZEIGENAKQUISITION FÜR DIE BEIDEN BRANCHENVERZEICHNISSE «CONSUMER YELLOW PAGE» UND «BUSINESS TO BUSINESS DIRECTORY.» DER UM- SCHLAG DES EINEN VERZEICHNISSES IST GELB, DER DES ANDEREN BRAUN. ▲ **143, 144** AFFICHES ADRESSÉES AUX SERVICES DE VENTE DE NYNEX, QUI DISTRIBUE LES PAGES JAUNES DU CONSOMMATEUR ET UN ANNUAIRE DE LA PUBLICITÉ. AU MOMENT DE CETTE ACTION PROMOTIONNELLE, LA COUVERTURE DU PREMIER LIVRE ÉTAIT JAUNE ET CELLE DU SECOND BRUN. (USA)

145

146

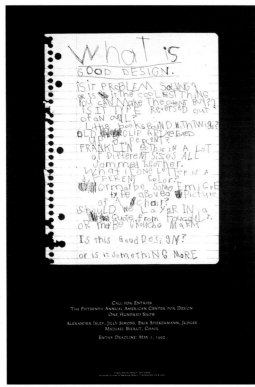

148

149

■ **148, 149** ART DIRECTORS: MICHAEL BIERUT 148, COLIN FORBES 149 DESIGNERS: MICHAEL BIERUT 148, JOHN KLOTNIA 149
PHOTOGRAPHER: BILL WHITEHURST 149 HAND-LETTERING: ELIZABETH BIERUT 148 COPYWRITER: SARAH HAUN AGENCY: PENTAGRAM
DESIGN ■ **148, 149** CALL-FOR-ENTRIES POSTERS FOR THE CHICAGO 100 SHOW AND FOR THE PENTAGRAM PRIZE 1992. ● **148,**
149 AUFFORDERUNGEN ZUR TEILNAHME AN WETTBEWERBEN, DER CHICAGO 100 SHOW UND DEM PENTAGRAM-PREIS 1992. ▲
148, 149 AFFICHES INVITANT À PARTICIPER AUX CONCOURS DU CHICAGO 100 SHOW ET DU PRIX PENTAGRAM 1992. (USA)

■ **150** ART DIRECTOR/DESIGNER/ILLUSTRATOR: FRANK VIVA AGENCY: FRANK VIVA DESIGN CLIENT: WIGGINS TEAPE OVERSEAS SALES
LTD. ■ **150** A CALL FOR ENTRIES FOR A COMPETITION SPONSORED BY A BRITISH PAPER MANUFACTURER. THE IMAGE THAT THE
COMPANY WISHED TO PROJECT IN THIS POSTER, WHICH WAS AIMED AT DESIGNERS IN NORTH AMERICA, WAS "OLD-WORLD
BRITISH." ● **150** AN NORDAMERIKANISCHE DESIGNER GERICHTETE EINLADUNG ZUR TEILNAHME AM WETTBEWERB EINES BRITI-
SCHEN PAPIERHERSTELLERS. MIT DEM PLAKAT WOLLTE DIE FIRMA «BRITISCHES, ALTE-WELT-IMAGE» VERMITTELN. ▲ **150** AF-
FICHE DESTINÉE AUX DESIGNERS D'AMÉRIQUE DU NORD, LES INVITANT À PARTICIPER À UN CONCOURS ORGANISÉ PAR UN FA-
BRICANT DE PAPIER ANGLAIS. LA FIRME VOULAIT COMMUNIQUER AU MOYEN DE CETTE AFFICHE UNE IMAGE «TRES BRITISH.» (CAN)

LONDON CALLING

CALLING FOR ENTRIES FROM NORTH AMERICAN DESIGNERS

The challenge: create a brave New World letterhead using the Old World's finest business paper — Conqueror.

The sponsor: Wiggins Teape, Britain's premier manufacturer of fine papers for more than a century.

The prize: a two-week trip for two to London and Paris: exhibition of the winning work in both cities.

The deadline: March 31, 1992.

conqueror

150

■ 151 Art Director: CHARLES ANDERSON Designers: CHARLES ANDERSON, TODD HAUSWIRTH, DANIEL OLSON Copywriter: LISA PEMRICK Agency: C.S. ANDERSON DESIGN COMPANY Client: AIGA NATIONAL ■ 151 POSTER PROMOTING THE AIGA NATIONAL T-SHIRT CONTEST. IT FEATURES AN ENLARGEMENT OF THE INSIDE PORTION OF THE CALL FOR ENTRIES. ● 151 ANKÜNDIGUNG EINES T-SHIRT-WETTBEWERBS. ES WURDE MIT EINER VERGRÖSSERUNG AUS DER EINLADUNGSKARTE GEARBEITET. ▲ 151 AN-NONCE D'UN CONCOURS DE T-SHIRTS ORGANISÉ PAR L'AIGA. IL S'AGIT D'UN AGRANDISSEMENT DE LA CARTE D'INVITATION. (USA)

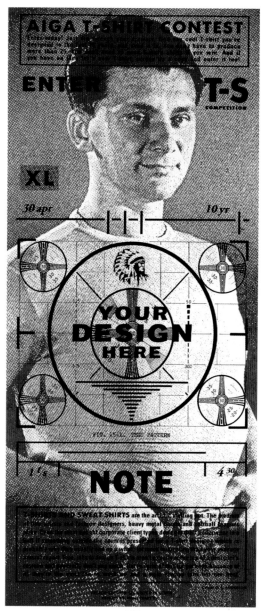

151

■ 152 Art Director/Designer: FRED WOODWARD Illustrator: TERRY ALLEN Client: SOCIETY OF PUBLICATION DESIGNERS ■ 152 "HOW DOES YOUR WORK MEASURE UP?"—A CALL-FOR-ENTRIES POSTER FOR THE SOCIETY OF PUBLICATION DESIGNERS. ● 152 FÜR EINEN WETTBEWERB DER SOCIETY OF PUBLICATION DESIGNERS: NEHMEN SIE MASS; SCHÄTZEN SIE IHRE ARBEIT EIN. ▲ 152 INVITATION À UN CONCOURS DE LA SOCIETY OF PUBLICATION DESIGNERS SUR LE MOTTO «MESUREZ VOTRE TRAVAIL.» (USA)

HOW DOES YOUR WORK MEASURE UP?

ociety of

esigners

ublication

CALL FOR ENTRIES

ENTER

1/16/91

152

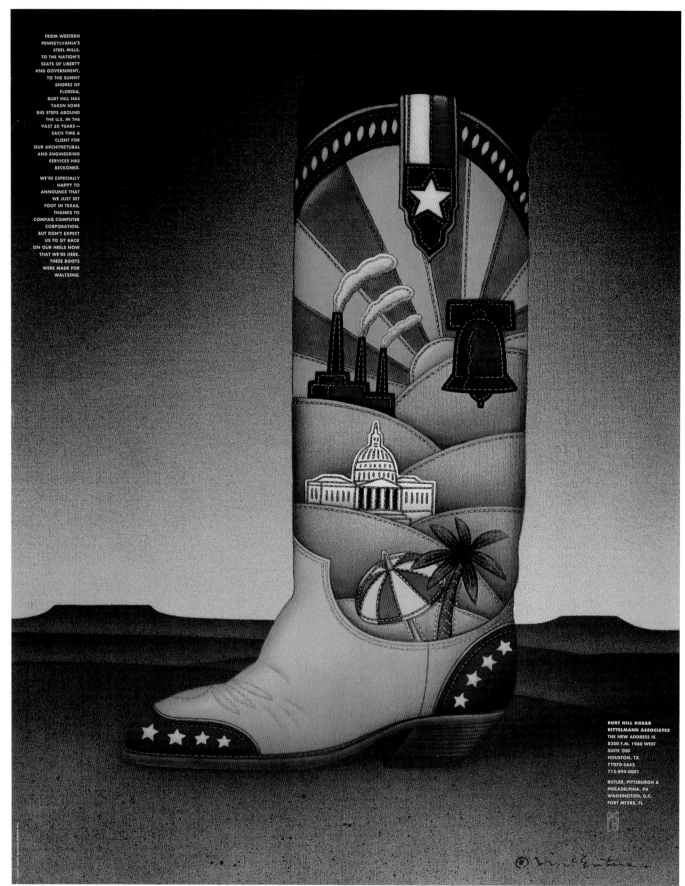

FROM WESTERN
PENNSYLVANIA'S
STEEL MILLS,
TO THE NATION'S
SEATS OF LIBERTY
AND GOVERNMENT,
TO THE SUNNY
SHORES OF
FLORIDA,
BURT HILL HAS
TAKEN SOME
BIG STEPS AROUND
THE U.S. IN THE
PAST 50 YEARS—
EACH TIME A
CLIENT FOR
OUR ARCHITECTURAL
AND ENGINEERING
SERVICES HAS
BECKONED.

WE'RE ESPECIALLY
HAPPY TO
ANNOUNCE THAT
WE JUST SET
FOOT IN TEXAS,
THANKS TO
COMPAQ COMPUTER
CORPORATION.
BUT DON'T EXPECT
US TO SIT BACK
ON OUR HEELS NOW
THAT WE'RE HERE.
THESE BOOTS
WERE MADE FOR
WALTZING.

BURT HILL KOSAR
RITTELMANN ASSOCIATES
THE NEW ADDRESS IS
8300 F.M. 1960 WEST
SUITE 200
HOUSTON, TX
77070-5643
713-894-0001

BUTLER, PITTSBURGH &
PHILADELPHIA, PA
WASHINGTON, D.C.
FORT MYERS, FL

153

154

■ **153** Art Director: LOWELL WILLIAMS Designer: LOWELL WILLIAMS Illustrator: LARRY MCENTIRE Agency: PENTAGRAM DESIGN Client: BURT HILL KOSAR RITTELMANN ASSOC. ■ **153** POSTER FOR AN ARCHITECTURAL AND ENGINEERING FIRM THAT HAS BEEN IN EXISTENCE FOR MORE THAN 50 YEARS, AND HAS JUST SET FOOT IN TEXAS. ● **153** PLAKATFÜR EINE ARCHITEKTUR- UND BAUINGENIEUR-FIRMA, DIE SEIT ÜBER 50 JAHREN IM GESCHÄFT IST UND NUN AUCH IN TEXAS FUSS GEFASST HAT. ▲ **153** PUBLICITÉ POUR UN STUDIO D'ARCHITECTES ET D'INGÉNIEURS DU BATIMENT QUI EXISTE DEPUIS PLUS DE 50 ANS. APRES AVOIR EXERCÉ SON ACTIVITÉ DANS PLUSIEURS RÉGIONS DES ETATS-UNIS, CETTE FIRME S'EST IMPLANTÉE AU TEXAS. (USA)

■ **154** Designer: JUDY VENONSKY Photographer/Client: TONY WARD ■ **154** THIS POSTER, PROMOTING TONY WARD PHOTO-GRAPHY, TARGETS DESIGNERS AND ART DIRECTORS IN THE PHILADELPHIA AREA. ● **154** AN DESIGNER UND ART DIRECTOREN IM RAUM PHILADELPHIA GERICHTETES PLAKAT, DAS FÜR EINEN PHOTOGRAPHEN WIRBT. ▲ **154** PROMOTION DU PHOTOGRAPHE TONY WARD DESTINÉE AUX DESIGNERS ET DIRECTEURS ARTISTIQUES TRAVAILLANT DANS LA RÉGION DE PHILADELPHIE. (USA)

155

156

157

158

Design:Vignelli
NewYork

Design:Vignelli,
New York
Die Neue Sammlung
31.1. bis 5.4.1992
Dienstag bis Sonntag
10 bis 17 Uhr

159

■ **155-158** ART DIRECTOR/DESIGNER/ILLUSTRATOR: MASAKAZU TANABE AGENCY/CLIENT: MEDIA CO., LTD. ■ **155-158** FROM A SERIES OF POSTERS FOR THE JAPANESE DESIGN FIRM MEDIA CO. ● **155-158** AUS EINER SERIE VON PLAKATEN FÜR DIE MEDIA CO., EINE JAPANISCHE DESIGN-FIRMA. ▲ **155-158** D'UNE SÉRIE D'AFFICHES POUR UNE FIRME DE DESIGN JAPONAISE, MEDIA CO. (JPN)

■ **159** DESIGNER: PIERRE MENDELL CLIENT: DIE NEUE SAMMLUNG ■ **159** POSTER ANNOUNCING AN EXHIBITION OF THE WORK OF THE DESIGN COMPANY VIGNELLI ASSOCIATES AT THE MUSEUM DIE NEUE SAMMLUNG IN MUNICH. ● **159** ANKÜNDIGUNG EINER AUSSTELLUNG DER ARBEITEN DER DESIGN-FIRMA VIGNELLI ASSOCIATES IM MÜNCHNER MUSEUM DIE NEUE SAMMLUNG. ▲ **159** AFFICHE POUR EXPOSITION DE LA FIRME DE DESIGN VIGNELLI ASSOCIATES, AU MUSÉE DIE NEUE SAMMLUNG À MUNICH. (GER)

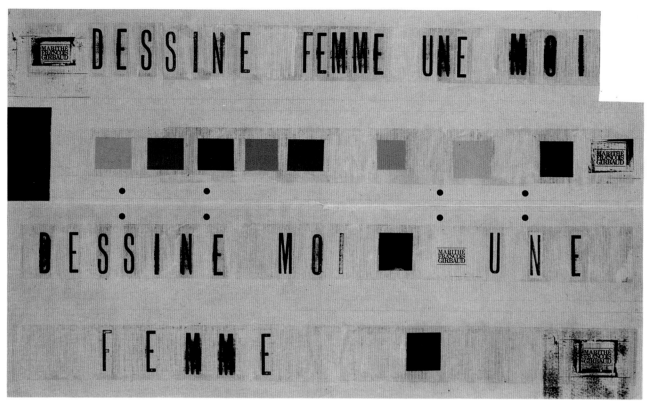

160

It seems like yesterday we were in college, figuring how we were to deal with the next week's exams, and in the middle of all that, contemplating the larger questions at hand. Where will we go? What will become of us? Will we succeed? And if we suceed, will we know when it happens? It's funny how things work out, you know. Now we contemplate system crashes, profit margins, the condensing of time. It has been a whirlwind period. The seed was planted amidst the fertile soil of Iowa over ten years ago. John Swieter left school and began working through the channels of studios and agencies across that fair state. After a few years and a few reality checks along the way, he packed his bags and headed for Dallas. We call it Big D. He set the gears in motion. The awards started coming in, and our clients kept coming back. We flourished because of our hard work. Now, after six years of mechanicals, six hundred press checks and six thousand broken exacto blades we are still contemplating the same larger questions. Where will we go? What will become of us? Will we succeed? Our clients are growing, we're growing, the world is growing and hopefully we are all moving in the right direction. Which makes us realize, that as human beings, we only have one choice. Create or die.

161

162

■ **160** ART DIRECTOR/DESIGNER: BENITA RAPHAN AGENCY: BENITA RAPHAN DESIGN CLIENT: MARITHÉ & FRANÇOIS GIRBAUD ■ **160** "DRAW A WOMAN FOR ME" (AN ALLUSION TO THE LINE "DRAW A SHEEP FOR ME," FROM SAINT-EXUPÉRY'S *THE LITTLE PRINCE*)— A POSTER FOR A DESIGN STUDIO. ● **160** «ZEICHNE MIR EINE FRAU» (EINE ANSPIELUNG AUF DAS «ZEICHNE MIR EIN SCHAF» IN *DER KLEINE PRINZ*). ▲ **160** AFFICHE DONT LE SLOGAN FAIT ALLUSION AU «DESSINE-MOI UN MOUTON» DU *PETIT PRINCE*. (FRA)

■ **161** ART DIRECTOR: JOHN SWIETER DESIGNERS: JOHN SWIETER, JIM VOGEL, PAUL MUNSTERMAN AGENCY/CLIENT: SWIETER DESIGN ■ **161** A SELF-PROMOTIONAL POSTER FOR A DESIGN STUDIO. IT TELLS OF THE DEVELOPMENT OF THE COMPANY AND STATES THAT HUMAN BEINGS MUST EITHER CREATE OR DIE. ● **161** WERBUNG EINES DESIGN-STUDIOS. IM TEXT GEHT ES UM DIE ENTWICKLUNG DES DESIGNERS BZW. DER FIRMA. DIE SCHLUSSFOLGERUNG: DER MENSCH MUSS KREATIV SEIN ODER STER- BEN. ▲ **161** AFFICHE ÉDITÉE CHAQUE ANNÉE PAR UN STUDIO DE DESIGN. LE TEXTE ÉVOQUE LE DÉVELOPPEMENT DE LA FIRME DEPUIS SES DÉBUTS ET LES PERSPECTIVES QUI S'OFFRENT DANS LA CONJONCTURE ACTUELLE: «CRÉER OU MOURIR.» (USA)

■ **162** ART DIRECTOR: ANDY EWAN DESIGNERS: ANDY EWAN, NICOLA PENNY, LYNNE JODDRELL PHOTOGRAPHER: NICOLA PENNY AGENCY/CLIENT: THE YELLOW PENCIL COMPANY ■ **162** "THE SMALLEST SEED IS BETTER THAN THE GREATEST INTENTION." A POSTER PROMOTION FOR THE YELLOW PENCIL COMPANY, USING COLOR AND EXAGGERATION IN ORDER TO BE NOTICED AND REMEMBERED. ● **162** «DER KLEINSTE SAMEN IST BESSER ALS DIE GRÖSSTE ABSICHT.» EIGENWERBUNG FÜR DAS DESIGN-STU- DIO THE YELLOW PENCIL COMPANY. ▲ **162** «LE POTIRON.» AFFICHE AUTOPROMOTIONNELLE D'UN STUDIO DE DESIGN GRAPHI- QUE: LES COULEURS DU LÉGUME ONT ÉTÉ TRANSFORMÉES VOLONTAIREMENT, LE JAUNE ÉVOQUANT LE NOM DE LA FIRME. (GBR)

163

164

■ 163-165 ART DIRECTOR/DESIGNER: TADANORI ITAKURA PHOTOGRAPHER: HIROTO ISHIWATA 163, 164 AGENCY: ITAKURA DESIGN INSTITUTE INC. CLIENT: SAKURAI GRAPHIC SYSTEMS CORPORATION ■ 163-165 EXAMPLES OF POSTERS PROMOTING A PRINTER AND ANNOUNCING AN EXHIBITION. TADANORI ITAKURA'S WORK DEMONSTRATES THE PRINTER'S CAPACITY FOR OFFSET AND SCREEN PRINTING. ● 163-165 AUS EINER SERIE VON PLAKATEN FÜR EINEN DRUCKER, DIE GLEICHZEITIG AUF EINE AUS-STELLUNG DER ARBEITEN VON TADANORI HINWEISEN UND DIE DRUCKQUALITÄT IM OFFSET- UND SIEBDRUCKBEREICH DEMON-STRIEREN. ▲ 163-165 AFFICHES PROMOTIONNELLES D'UN IMPRIMEUR SPÉCIALISÉ DANS L'OFFSET ET LES SYSTEMES DE TRAMES: ELLES ONT ÉTÉ RÉALISÉES À L'OCCASION D'UNE EXPOSITION PRÉSENTANT LES CRÉATIONS DE TADANORI ITAKURA. (JPN)

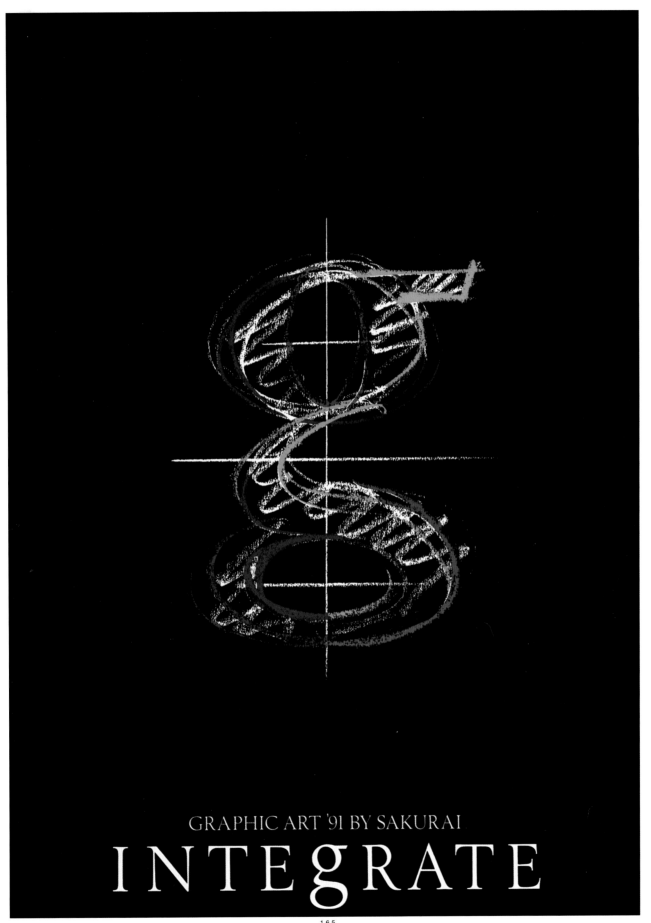

GRAPHIC ART '91 BY SAKURAI

INTEGRATE

165

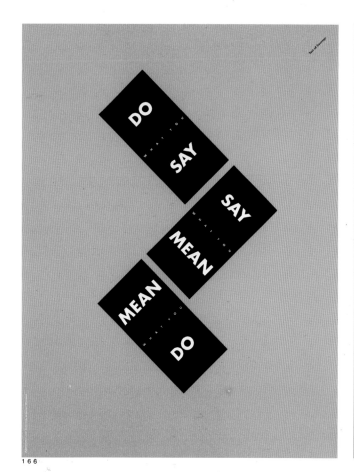

166

167

■ 166 ART DIRECTOR/DESIGNER/COPYWRITER: GERMAR WAMBACH AGENCY: WAMBACH CLIENT: PLAKATION/DETLEF BEHR & GERMAR WAMBACH ■ 166 "DO WHAT YOU SAY. SAY WHAT YOU THINK. THINK ABOUT WHAT YOU DO." A NEW YEAR'S POSTER FOR A GRAPHIC DESIGNER. ● 166 «TU' WAS DU SAGST. SAG' WAS DU DENKST. DENK' WAS DU TUST.» NEUJAHRSPLAKAT EINES GRA- PHIKERS. ▲ 166 «FAIS CE QUE TU DIS. DIS CE QUE TU PENSES. PENSE CE QUE TU FAIS.» AFFICHE PUBLIÉE AU NOUVEL AN. (GER)

■ 167 DESIGNER: THOMAS DI PAOLO ■ 167 A SELF-PROMOTIONAL POSTER BY A GERMAN GRAPHIC DESIGNER. ● 167 EIGENWER- BUNG FÜR EINEN GRAPHIK-DESIGNER. ▲ 167 AFFICHE AUTOPROMOTIONNELLE D'UN DESIGNER GRAPHIQUE ALLEMAND. (GER)

■ 168 ART DIRECTOR: DON ROOD DESIGNER: DON ROOD PHOTOGRAPHER: JON DESHLER AGENCY: DON ROOD DESIGN CLIENT: ZIBA DESIGN ■ 168 POSTER FOR AN INDUSTRIAL-DESIGN FIRM THAT DOES PRELIMINARY STUDIES IN STYROFOAM. ● 168 PLAKAT- WERBUNG FÜR EINE INDUSTRIE-DESIGNFIRMA, DIE ERSTE MODELLE IN STYROPOR HERSTELLT. ▲ 168 AFFICHE PUBLICITAIRE POUR UNE FIRME DE DESIGN INDUSTRIEL QUI RÉALISE SES ÉTUDES PRÉLIMINAIRES DE MODELES EN STYROPORE. (USA)

168

NINAONA
JOTO

169

Bieber

170

CHRISTOPHER GREEN

508 · 778 · 0118

171

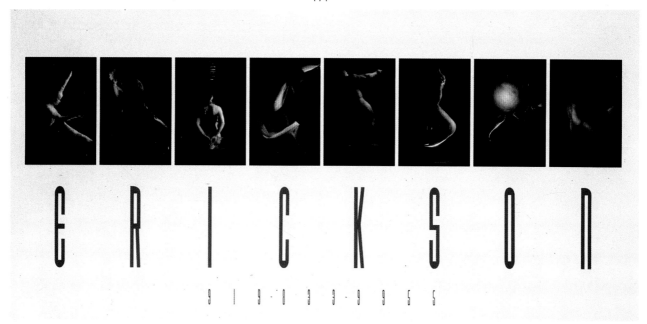

ERICKSON

919 · 833 · 9955

173

■ **171, 172** DESIGNER: TOM SIMONS PHOTOGRAPHER/CLIENT: CHRISTOPHER GREEN ■ **171, 172** THESE PROMOTIONAL POSTERS FOR CHRISTOPHER GREEN ARE ACTUAL PHOTOGRAPHIC PRINTS. THE POSTERS WERE DESIGNED SO THAT GREEN, A PHOTOGRA- PHER, COULD PRODUCE THEM HIMSELF IN THE LAB. ● **171, 172** DIESE PLAKATE FÜR DEN PHOTOGRAPHEN CHRISTOPHER GREEN KONNTEN VON IHM SELBST IM LABOR HERGESTELLT WERDEN: ES SIND PHOTOABZÜGE. ▲ **171, 172** DEUX AFFICHES AUTOPRO- MOTIONNELLES DU PHOTOGRAPHE CHRISTOPHER GREEN, QU'IL A LUI-MÊME RÉALISÉES DIRECTEMENT EN LABORATOIRE. (USA)

■ **173** ART DIRECTOR: LARRY BENNETT DESIGNER: LARRY BENNETT PHOTOGRAPHER: JIM ERICKSON CLIENT: JIM ERICKSON PHOTOGRAPHY ■ **173** IN THIS PROMOTIONAL POSTER FOR JIM ERICKSON, A PHOTOGRAPHER, THE POSES OF THE SUBJECTS SPELL OUT "ERICKSON.". ● **173** EIGENWERBUNG FÜR DEN PHOTOGRAPHEN JIM ERICKSON. DIE EINZELNEN BUCHSTABEN DES

CHRISTOPHER GREEN

172

R E I D

174

NAMEN «ERICKSON» WERDEN DURCH DIE POSEN DER MODELLE DARGESTELLT. ▲ 173 AFFICHE AUTOPROMOTIONNELLE DU PHOTOGRAPHE JIM ERICKSON. LES MODELES REPRÉSENTÉS ICI MIMENT CHACUN UNE LETTRE DU MOT «ERICKSON.» (USA)

■ 174 Art Director: KEN REID Designer: BETSY REID Photographer: KEN REID Client: KEN REID PRINT/FILM ■ 174 "MAKE YOUR SPOTS JUMP." A POSTER ANNOUNCING THE PHOTOGRAPHER'S DEBUT AS A FILM DIRECTOR. ● 174 «LASSEN SIE IHRE SPOTS SPRINGEN.» DIESES EIGENWERBUNGSPLAKAT INFORMIERT ÜBER DAS DEBUT DES PHOTOGRAPHEN KEN REID ALS FILM-REGISSEUR. ▲ 174 «FAITES SAUTER VOS SPOTS.» AFFICHE AUTOPROMOTIONNELLE RÉALISÉE CONJOINTEMENT À UN SPOT TV SUR LE MEME SUJET. LE PHOTOGRAPHE KEN REID DÉSIRAIT AINSI ANNONCER SES DÉBUTS COMME METTEUR EN SCENE. (USA)

■ **175-177** ᴀʀᴛ ᴅɪʀᴇᴄᴛᴏʀ: PETER HESSLER ᴘʜᴏᴛᴏɢʀᴀᴘʜᴇʀ: GÜNTER PFANNMÜLLER ᴀɢᴇɴᴄʏ: BEITHAN, HESSLER, MÄTTIG ᴄʟɪᴇɴᴛ: STUDIO PFANNMÜLLER ■ **175-177** FROM A SERIES OF SELF-PROMOTIONAL POSTERS FOR THE PFANNMÜLLER PHOTO STUDIO. ● **175-177** BEISPIELE AUS EINER REIHE VON EIGENWERBUNGSPLAKATEN DES PHOTOSTUDIOS PFANNMÜLLER. ▲ **175-177** CES AFFICHES AUTOPROMOTIONNELLES DU STUDIO DE PHOTOGRAPHIE PFANNMÜLLER ÉTAIENT RÉUNIES DANS UN DOSSIER. (GER)

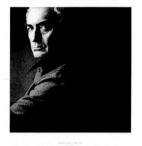  

175   176   177

■ **178** ᴀʀᴛ ᴅɪʀᴇᴄᴛᴏʀ: PHILIP BEKKER ᴅᴇꜱɪɢɴᴇʀ: RICK ANWYL ᴘʜᴏᴛᴏɢʀᴀᴘʜᴇʀ: PHILIP BEKKER ꜱᴛʏʟɪꜱᴛ: PHILIP BEKKER ᴀɢᴇɴᴄʏ: RICHARD ANWYL LTD. ᴄʟɪᴇɴᴛꜱ: BEKKER PHOTOGRAPHY/METEOR PHOTOGRAPHY ■ **178** A SELF-PROMOTION FOR THE PHOTOGRAPHER, PHILIP BEKKER, USING 8X10" POLAROID TRANSFER FILM. ● **178** EIGENWERBUNGSPLAKAT DES PHOTOGRAPHEN PHILIP BEKKER, AUFGENOMMEN MIT EINEM 8X10" POLAROID-TRANSFER-FILM. ▲ **178** AFFICHE AUTOPROMOTIONNELLE D'UN PHOTOGRAPHE ET D'UN LABORATOIRE DE DÉVELOPPEMENT, RÉALISÉE AU MOYEN D'UN FILM 8X10 POLAROID TRANSFER. (USA)

METEOR PHOTO ▼ 847, 1450 STREET N.W. ▼ ATLANTA, GEORGIA 303... ▼ 4040-892-1444 ▼ PHOTOGRAPHY: PHILIP BEKKER FOR BRAD SKINNER ▼ DESIGN: RICHARD PINN-LOD

PHILIP BEKKER

METEOR PHOTO

178

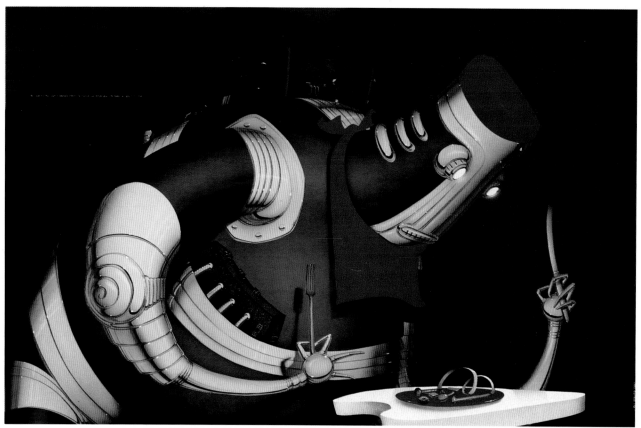

179

180

■ 179, 180 ART DIRECTOR: ALAN LIDJI DESIGNER: ALAN LIDJI ILLUSTRATOR: BILL MAYER AGENCY: LIDJI DESIGN CLIENT: BILL MAYER
■ 179, 180 "ROBOT" AND "BOOKWORM," TWO SELF-PROMOTIONAL POSTERS FOR THE ILLUSTRATOR BILL MAYER. ● 179, 180
«ROBOTER» UND «BÜCHERWURM,» ZWEI EIGENWERBUNGSPLAKATE DES AMERIKANISCHEN ILLUSTRATORS BILL MAYER. ▲ 179,
180 «ROBOT» ET «TEIGNE DES LIVRES.» DEUX AFFICHES AUTOPROMOTIONNELLES DE L'ILLUSTRATEUR BILL MAYER. (USA)

CULTURE

KULTURE

CULTURE

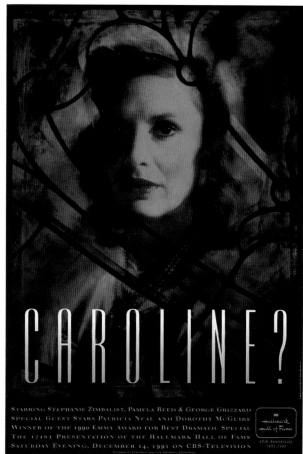

183

184

■ (PREVIOUS SPREAD) 181 ART DIRECTOR: JOHN MULLER DESIGNERS: JOHN MULLER, SCOTT CHAPMAN ILLUSTRATOR: MARK ENGLISH COPYWRITER: ELLEN HOCH AGENCY: MULLER + CO. CLIENT: HALLMARK, INC. ■ 181 FOR A TELEVISION MOVIE. ● (VORANGEHENDE DOPPELSEITE) 181 FÜR EINEN FERNSEHFILM. ▲ (DOUBLE PAGE PRÉCÉDENTE) 181 AFFICHE POUR UN FILM TÉLÉVISÉ. (USA)

■ (PREVIOUS SPREAD) 182 ART DIRECTOR: JOHN MCTAGUE ILLUSTRATOR: JOHN MATTOS CLIENT: DISNEY PICTURES ■ 182 A 1930-ISH RENDERING OF *THE ROCKETEER*. ● (VORANGEHENDE DOPPELSEITE) 182 INTERPRETATION VON *THE ROCKETEER* IM STIL DER 30ER JAHRE. ▲ (DOUBLE PAGE PRÉCÉDENTE) 182 INTERPRÉTATION DE *THE ROCKETEER* DANS LE STYLE DES ANNÉES 30. (USA)

■ (THIS SPREAD) 183 ART DIRECTOR: JOHN MULLER DESIGNERS: JOHN MULLER, SCOTT CHAPMAN PHOTOGRAPHER: MICHAEL REGNIER COPYWRITER: JAN PARKINSON AGENCY: MULLER + CO CLIENT: HALLMARK, INC. ■ 183 A POSTER FOR AN UPCOMING TELE- VISION MOVIE. ● (DIESE DOPPELSEITE) 183 INFORMATION ÜBER EINEN TV-FILM, DER IM RAHMEN EINER SPEZIELLEN REIHE GE- ZEIGT WIRD. ▲ (CETTE DOUBLE PAGE) 183 AFFICHE INFORMANT SUR UN FILM QUI DOIT ETRE DIFFUSÉ À LA TÉLÉVISION. (USA)

■ (THIS SPREAD) 184 ART DIRECTOR: ANNA BERKENBUSCH DESIGNERS: ANNA BERKENBUSCH, KATRIN SCHEK AGENCY: ANNA BER- KENBUSCH DESIGN CLIENT: IMPULS FILM ■ 184 ANNOUNCEMENT OF THE FILM *WITH YOUR BELOVED ONES*. ● (DIESE DOP- PELSEITE) 184 FILMPLAKAT. ▲ (CETTE DOUBLE PAGE) 184 ANNONCE DU FILM *DANS LE CERCLE DE SES PROCHES*. (GER)

■ (THIS SPREAD) 185-188 ART DIRECTORS: FRAN MICHELMAN 185, 186, LINDA STILLMAN 187, SEYMOUR CHWAST 188 DESIGNERS: PAUL DAVIS 185, SEYMOUR CHWAST 186, 188, CONNIE CIRCOSTA 187 ILLUSTRATORS: PAUL DAVIS 185, RICHARD MANTEL 186, ROBERT ANDREW PARKER 187, SEYMOUR CHWAST 188 AGENCIES: PAUL DAVIS STUDIO 185, STILLMAN DESIGN ASSOCIATES 187, THE PUSHPIN GROUP 188 CLIENT: MOBIL CORPORATION ■ 185-188 POSTERS ANNOUNCING MOBIL MASTERPIECE TV PRESENTATIONS OF MOVIES. ● (DIESE DOPPELSEITE) 185-188 ANKÜNDIGUNGEN VERSCHIEDENER, AM FERNSEHEN AUSGE- STRAHLTER FILME. ▲ (CETTE DOUBLE PAGE) 185-188 AFFICHES ANNONÇANT DIVERS FILMS DIFFUSÉS À LA TÉLÉVISION. (USA)

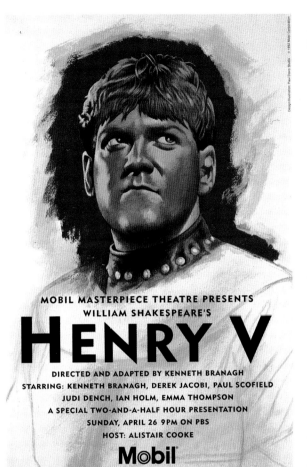

185

186

187

188

189

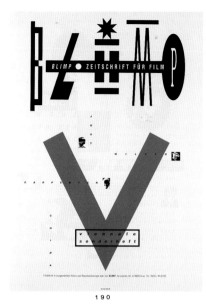

190

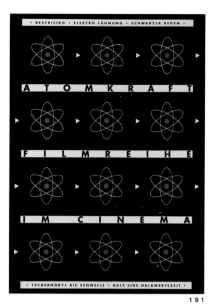

191

192

193

194

■ **189** ART DIRECTOR: ADOLFO ALAYON DESIGNER: ADOLFO ALAYON PHOTOGRAPHER: ALFREDO ALLAIS AGENCY: LAGOVEN S.A./IN-HOUSE CLIENT: LAGOVEN S.A. ■ 189 POSTER FOR A DOCUMENTARY FILM AND VIDEO FESTIVAL. ● 189 PLAKAT FÜR EIN DOKUMENTARFILM- UND VIDEO-FESTIVAL. ▲ 189 AFFICHE POUR UN FESTIVAL DU FILM DOCUMENTAIRE ET DE LA VIDÉO. (VEN)

■ **190** DESIGNERS: KARL ULBL, DIETMAR JAKELY COPYWRITER: BOGDAN GRBIC AGENCY: ULBL+JAKELY CLIENT: BLIMP ■ 190 POSTER FOR A VIENNA FILM FESTIVAL AND THE MAGAZINE *BLIMP*. ● 190 PLAKAT FÜR DAS WIENER FILMFESTIVAL UND DIE FILMZEITSCHRIFT *BLIMP*. ▲ 190 PUBLICITÉ POUR UN FESTIVAL CINÉMATOGRAPHIQUE ET LA REVUE DE CINÉMA *BLIMP*. (AUT)

■ **191** ART DIRECTOR/DESIGNER: SASCHA LOBE AGENCY: ATELIER PETER KRAUS CLIENT: CINEMA ■ 191 THIS POSTER HAD TO BE IMPARTIAL; THE ANNOUNCED FILM SERIES ON NUCLEAR POWER SERVED AS A BASIS FOR DISCUSSION. ● 191 FÜR EINE FILMREIHE ZUM THEMA ATOMKRAFT. ▲ 191 AFFICHE POUR UNE SÉRIE DE FILMS SUR LE THEME DE L'ÉNERGIE ATOMIQUE. (GER)

■ **192** DESIGNER: RUEDI BAUR AGENCY: INTEGRAL CONCEPT CLIENT: CENTRE DE RECHERCHE ET D'ACTION CULTURELLE (CRAC) ■ 192 *BETRAYING*—FILM POSTER. ● 192 *DER BETRUG*, FILMANKÜNDIGUNG. ▲ 192 AFFICHE ANNONÇANT UN FILM. (FRA)

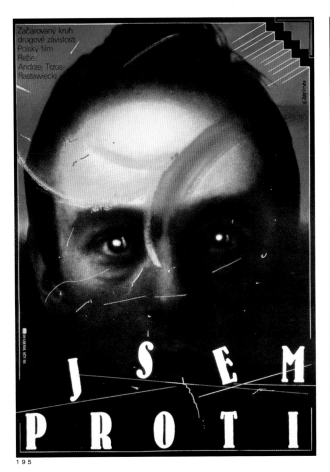

195

196

■ 193 ART DIRECTOR/DESIGNER: JENNIFER STERLING PHOTOGRAPHER: GALLEN MEI AGENCY: COJOTO DESIGN CLIENT: FILM SOCIETY ■
193 POSTER FOR A FILM FESTIVAL. THE FILM LEAD WAS LAYERED IN WITH A MOVIE FIGURE IN THE BACKGROUND. ● 193 FÜR
EIN FILM-FESTIVAL. ▲ 193 AFFICHE POUR UN FESTIVAL DE CINÉMA. A L'ARRIERE-PLAN DU TITRE, LE HÉROS D'UN FILM. (USA)

■ 194 ART DIRECTOR/DESIGNER: RALPH SCHRAIVOGEL CLIENT: PRÄSIDIALABTEILUNG DER STADT ZÜRICH ■ 194 TWO-COLOR SILK-
SCREEN POSTER FOR A SPECIAL AFRICAN FILM WEEK. ● 194 ZWEIFARBENSIEBDRUCK AUF PACKPAPIER, FÜR AFRIKANISCHE
FILMTAGE. ▲ 194 SÉRIGRAPHIE EN DEUX COULEURS SUR PAPIER D'EMBALLAGE, POUR DES JOURNÉES DU CINÉMA AFRICAIN. (SWI)

■ 195 ART DIRECTOR: JAN SOLPERA DESIGNER: JAN SOLPERA AGENCY: TYPO & ■ 195 FILM POSTER. ● 195 FILMPLAKAT ▲ 195
AFFICHE DE FILM. (CFR)

■ 196 ART DIRECTOR: BERNARD BAISSAIT DESIGNER: ANNE DURANTON AGENCY: COMPAGNIE BERNARD BAISSAIT CLIENTS: MINIS-
TERE DE LA CULTURE, CENTRE NATIONAL DE LA CINÉMATOGRAPHIE ■ 196 POSTER ANNOUNCING SPECIAL SHOWINGS OF OLD
FILMS. ● 196 ANKÜNDIGUNG VON VORFÜHRUNGEN ALTER FILME. ▲ 196 ANNONCE DE LA PROJECTION DE VIEUX FILMS. (FRA)

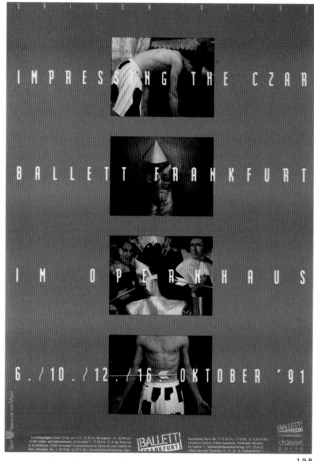

197

198

■ **197, 198** ART DIRECTOR: MICHAEL HOFFMEYER PHOTOGRAPHERS: DOMINIK MENTZOS 197, WILLIAM FORSYTHE 198 AGENCY: M.A.D. CLIENT: BALLETT FRANKFURT ■ **197, 198** POSTERS ANNOUNCING BALLET PERFORMANCES IN FRANKFURT. ● **197, 198** PLAKATE FÜR AUFFÜHRUNGEN DES BALLETTS FRANKFURT. ▲ **197, 198** AFFICHES ANNONÇANT UN SPECTACLE DE DANSE À FRANCFORT. (GER)

■ **199** ART DIRECTOR: PIERRE DAVID DESIGNER: PIERRE DAVID PHOTOGRAPHER: SUZANNE LANGEVIN CLIENT: LES BALLETS JAZZ DE MONTRÉAL ■ **199** POSTER ANNOUNCING THE 20TH-ANNIVERSARY TOUR OF LES BALLETS JAZZ DE MONTREAL. ● **199** PLAKAT-ANKÜNDIGUNG EINER TOURNEE VON LES BALLETS JAZZ DE MONTREAL ZUM 20JÄHRIGEN BESTEHEN DES BALLETTS. ▲ **199** AN-NONCE DU SPECTACLE D'UNE COMPAGNIE DE DANSE PUBLIÉE À L'OCCASION DU 20E ANNIVERSAIRE DE SA FONDATION. (CAN)

199

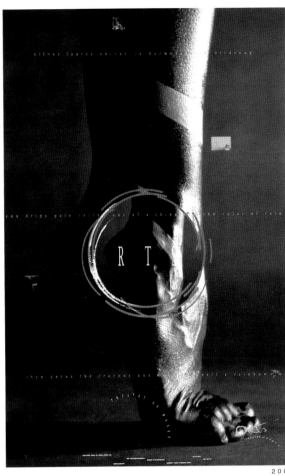

200

■ 200 ART DIRECTORS: JACKSON BOELTS, ERIC BOELTS DESIGNERS: JACKSON BOELTS, ERIC BOELTS PHOTOGRAPHERS: ERIC BOELTS, HERB STRATFORD AGENCY: BOELTS BROS. DESIGN CLIENT: ORTS ■ 200 POSTER FROM A SERIES PRESENTING AN AVANT-GARDE DANCE GROUP. ● 200 BEISPIEL AUS EINER REIHE VON PLAKATEN, MIT DENEN EINE MODERNE, VIELSEITIGE BALLETT-TRUPPE PRÄSENTIERT WIRD. ▲ 200 D'UNE SÉRIE D'AFFICHES D'UNE COMPAGNIE DE DANSE D'AVANT-GARDE. (USA)

201

202

■ **201** ART DIRECTOR/DESIGNER: NIKLAUS TROXLER ILLUSTRATOR: NIKLAUS TROXLER AGENCY: NIKLAUS TROXLER GRAFIK-STUDIO CLIENT: KLEINTHEATER LUZERN ■ **201** POSTER CELEBRATING THE 25TH ANNIVERSARY OF A THEATER. ● **201** PLAKAT ZUM 25JÄH-RIGEN BESTEHEN DES KLEINTHEATERS LUZERN. ▲ **201** AFFICHE CRÉÉE POUR LES 25 ANS D'UN THÉÂTRE DE LUCERNE. (SWI)

■ **202** CREATIVE DIRECTOR: RUEDI WYLER ART DIRECTOR: MARKUS CAVEGN PHOTOGRAPHER: JULIEN VONIER AGENCY: RUEDI WYLER WERBUNG CLIENT: PRÄSIDIALABTEILUNG DER STADT ZÜRICH ■ **202** ANNOUNCEMENT OF AN INTERNATIONAL THEATER FESTIVAL. ● **202** ANKÜNDIGUNG DES ZÜRCHER THEATERSPEKTAKELS. ▲ **202** POUR UN FESTIVAL INTERNATIONAL DE THÉÂTRE. (SWI)

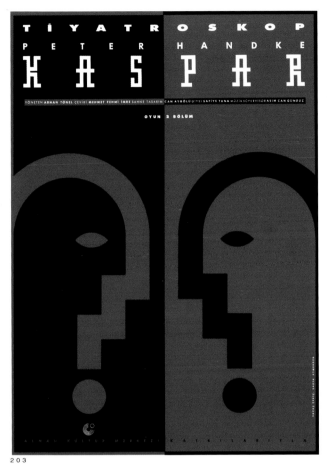

203

204

■ 203 ART DIRECTORS: SAVAS CEKIC, SAHIN AYMERGEN DESIGNERS: SAVAS CEKIC, SAHIN AYMERGEN AGENCY: VALÖR DESIGN PRO-
MOTION AGENCY CLIENT: GOETHE INSTITUT ■ 203 POSTER FOR THE PERFORMANCE OF A PLAY BY PETER HANDKE, AN AUSTRIAN
PLAYWRIGHT, IN A TURKISH THEATER. ● 203 FÜR DIE AUFFÜHRUNG EINES THEATERSTÜCKES VON PETER HANDKE IN EINEM TÜR-
KISCHEN THEATER. ▲ 203 AFFICHE ANNONÇANT LA REPRÉSENTATION D'UNE PIECE DE PETER HANDKE DANS UN THÉÂTRE. (TUR)

■ 204 DESIGNER: EUGEN BACHMANN-GEISER ILLUSTRATOR: JOHANNES GRÜTZKE CLIENT: NEUE SCHAUSPIEL AG ■ 204 THE
BEAUTIFUL STRANGER—ANNOUNCEMENT OF A PLAY BY KLAUS POHL AT THE ZÜRICH MUNICIPAL THEATRE. ● 204 PLAKAT-
ANKÜNDIGUNG DER INSZENIERUNG EINES STÜCKES VON KLAUS POHL AM ZÜRCHER SCHAUSPIELHAUS. ▲ 204 AFFICHE DE LA
PIECE «LA BELLE ÉTRANGERE» DE KLAUS POHL, REPRÉSENTÉE AU THÉÂTRE MUNICIPAL DE LA VILLE DE ZURICH. (SWI)

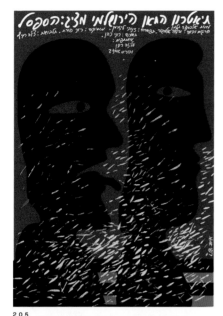

205

206

207

208

209

210

211

212

213

214

■ 205 DESIGNER: RAPHIE ETGAR CLIENT: THE KHAN THEATRE ■ 205 *THE BENCH.* THIS PLAY IS ABOUT TWO STRANGERS WHO MEET IN A PARK. ● 205 *DIE BANK*—DAS STÜCK HANDELT VON ZWEI FREMDEN, DIE SICH IN EINEM PARK BEGEGNEN. ▲ 205 ANNONCE D'UNE PIECE INTITULÉE *LE BANC*—ELLE PARLE DE LA RENCONTRE DE DEUX INCONNUS DANS UN PARC. (ISR)

■ 206 ART DIRECTOR/DESIGNER/ILLUSTRATOR: PETER GOOD PHOTOGRAPHER: JIM COON COPYWRITER: STEVE CAMPO AGENCY: PETER GOOD GRAPHIC DESIGN CLIENT: THEATERWORKS ■ 206 POSTER ANNOUNCING THE SEASON'S PLAYS. ● 206 ANKÜNDIGUNG VON FÜNF AUFFÜHRUNGEN. ▲ 206 ANNONCE DES CINQ REPRÉSENTATIONS THÉÁTRALES DE LA SAISON DANS UN THÉÂTRE. (USA)

■ 207 ART DIRECTOR/DESIGNER/ILLUSTRATOR/COPYWRITER/AGENCY/CLIENT: ESMAIL SHISHEHGARAN ■ 207 NARCOTICS AND DRUGS— ANNOUNCEMENT OF A PLAY ABOUT THE PROBLEMS OF IRAN'S YOUNG GENERATION. ● 207 BETÄUBUNGSMITTEL UND DROGEN— EIN THEATERSTÜCK ÜBER DIE PROBLEME DER JUGEND IM IRAN. ▲ 207 SUR LE THEME NARCOTIQUES ET DROGUES. (IRA)

■ 208, 210 ART DIRECTOR: SABINE KRANZ ILLUSTRATOR: SABINE KRANZ CLIENT: GESAMTHOCHSCHULE KASSEL ■ 208, 210 EXAMPLES FROM A SERIES OF POSTERS DESIGNED BY A STUDENT FOR PERFORMANCES OF WAGNER'S RING CYCLE. ● 208, 210 AUS EINER SERIE VON PLAKATEN EINER STUDENTIN FÜR AUFFÜHRUNGEN DES NIBELUNGENZYKLUS VON RICHARD WAGNER. ▲ 208, 210 D'UNE SÉRIE D'AFFICHES ANNONÇANT LA REPRÉSENTATION DU CYCLE DES NIBELUNGEN DE RICHARD WAGNER. (GER)

■ 209, 211, 213 ART DIRECTOR/DESIGNER/ILLUSTRATOR/STYLIST: FERENC BARAT PHOTOGRAPHER: LASZLO DORMAN 209, 213 CLIENT: NOVOSADSKO POZORISTE ■ 209, 211, 213 SILK-SCREEN POSTERS FOR *LYSISTRATA, MOTHER COURAGE* AND *SORROWFUL SUNDAY*, A PLAY ABOUT A HUNGARIAN COMPOSER. ● 209, 211, 213 SIEBDRUCKPLAKATE: *LYSISTRATA, MUTTER COURAGE* UND *DUNKLER SONNTAG*, ÜBER DAS LEBEN DES UNGARISCHEN KOMPONISTEN SEREZ REZSÖ. ▲ 209, 211, 213 SÉRIGRAPHIES POUR *LYSISTRATA, MERE COURAGE* ET *SOMBRE DIMANCHE*, SUR LA VIE TRAGIQUE D'UN COMPOSITEUR HONGROIS. (YUG)

■ 212 ART DIRECTOR/DESIGNER/ILLUSTRATOR/AGENCY: JIRI JANDA ■ 212 FOR AN EXHIBITION TITLED "WOMAN—MOVEMENT—TIME." ● 212 FÜR DIE AUSSTELLUNG «FRAU—BEWEGUNG—ZEIT.» ▲ 212 ANNONCE DE L'EXPOSITION «FEMME—MOUVEMENT—TEMPS.» (CFR)

■ 214 AGENCY: MIROSLAV MICHALKO CLIENT: THEATRE "Y" ■ 214 POSTER FOR A PRESENTATION OF SHAKESPEARE'S *OTHELLO.* ● 214 FÜR EINE AUFFÜHRUNG VON SHAKESPEARES *OTHELLO.* ▲ 214 POUR UNE REPRÉSENTATION D'*OTHELLO* DE SHAKESPEARE. (CFR)

216

215

217

218

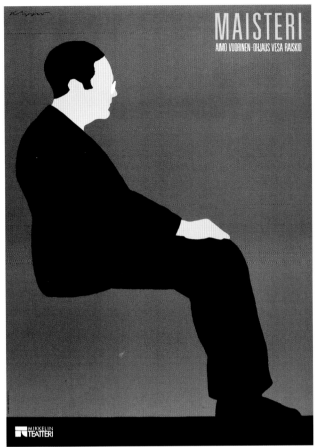

219

220

■ **215** DESIGNER: HANNA KOLLER CLIENT: MUSEUM FÜR GESTALTUNG ZÜRICH ■ 215 "ADVERTISING IS FOR ALL," A POSTER WITH A TRADITIONAL SWISS FONDUE COOKING IN THE BACKGROUND, FOR AN EXHIBITION IN THE DESIGN MUSEUM OF ZÜRICH. ● 215 FÜR EINE AUSSTELLUNG ÜBER WERBUNG. ▲ 215 POUR UNE EXPOSITION INTITULÉE: «LA PUBLICITÉ EST LÀ POUR TOUS.» (SWI)

■ **216** ART DIRECTOR/DESIGNER/ILLUSTRATOR: JOZE DOMJAN CLIENT: SLOVEN NATIONAL THEATER ■ 216 POSTER FOR A THEATER PERFORMANCE IN SLOVENIA. ● 216 FÜR EINE THEATERAUFFÜHRUNG IN SLOWENIEN. ▲ 216 POUR UNE PIECE DE THÉÂTRE. (SLO)

■ **217** ILLUSTRATOR: SABINE KRANZ CLIENT: GESAMTHOCHSCHULE KASSEL ■ 217 SILK-SCREEN FROM A SERIES OF OPERA POST-ERS, DESIGNED BY A STUDENT. ● 217 SIEBDRUCKPLAKAT EINER STUDENTIN IM RAHMEN DER SERIE »OPERNPLAKATE EINER SPIELZEIT,« EINEM PROJEKT DER GESAMTHOCHSCHULE KASSEL. ▲ 217 SÉRIGRAPHIE POUR UN CYCLE D'OPÉRAS. (GER)

■ .218 DESIGNER: RAPHIE ETGAR CLIENT: MAXIM-GORKI THEATER ■ 218 POSTER FOR A PERFORMANCE BY THE ISRAELI MOON-LIGHT THEATER IN BERLIN. ● 218 ANKÜNDIGUNG EINER AUFFÜHRUNG DES MOONLIGHT THEATERS AUS ISRAEL IN BERLIN. ▲ 218 ANNONCE D'UNE REPRÉSENTATION À BERLIN D'UN THÉÂTRE ISRAÉLIEN DONT LE NOM SIGNIFIE «CLAIR DE LUNE.» (GER)

■ **219, 220** ART DIRECTOR/DESIGNER: KARI PIIPPO AGENCY: KARI PIIPPO OY CLIENT: MIKKELIN TEATTERI ■ 219, 220 POSTERS FOR TWO PERFORMANCES AT A FINNISH THEATER: *MASTER* AND *ANNIE GET YOUR GUN*. ● 219, 220 PLAKATE FÜR ZWEI AUFFÜHRUN-GEN AN EINEM FINNISCHEN THEATER. ▲ 219, 220 DEUX AFFICHES DE THÉÂTRE: *MAITRE* ET *ANNIE GET YOUR GUN*. (FIN)

HOMBURGER MEISTERKONZERTE

Verkehrsverein e.V.
in Verbindung
mit dem
Kulturamt der
Stadt Homburg

Vorverkauf im
Städtischen Kultur-
und Verkehrsamt,
Rathaus, Am Forum,
Tel. (0 68 41) 20 66
Serviceschalter
Saarbrücker Zeitung,
Saarbrücken,
»Der Musikus«,
Karlsbergstr. 9,
Homburg,
Volksbank Homburg,
Gardinenstudio
Lambert, Bexbach

221

222

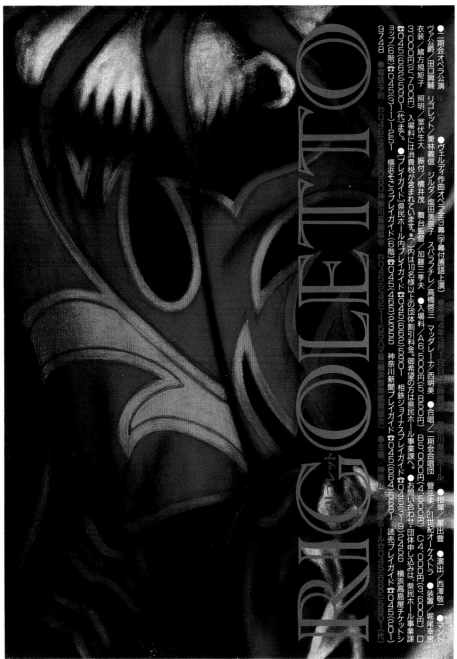

223

■ **221** ART DIRECTOR: GILBERT E. BAIER DESIGNER: BERNHARD HOFFMANN ILLUSTRATOR: BERNHARD HOFFMANN AGENCY: FORMART
WERBEAGENTUR GMBH CLIENT: KULTURAMT STADT HOMBURG ■ **221** POSTER ANNOUNCING A SERIES OF CONCERTS. THE BOW
TIE SERVES AS A SYMBOL OF THE RELATIONSHIP BETWEEN THE MUSICIANS AND THE PUBLIC. ● **221** PLAKAT FÜR EINE KON-
ZERTREIHE, FÜR DIE DIE BEZEICHNUNG «HOMBURGER MEISTERKONZERTE» ZUM MARKENZEICHEN WERDEN SOLL. DIE FLIEGE
DIENT ALS SYMBOL DER VERBINDUNG ZWISCHEN DEN MUSIKERN UND DEM PUBLIKUM. ▲ **221** ANNONCE D'UN CYCLE DE CON-
CERTS D'UNE QUALITÉ EXCEPTIONNELLE. LE PAPILLON SYMBOLISE LA RELATION ENTRE LES MUSICIENS ET LE PUBLIC. (GER)

■ **222** ART DIRECTORS: NANCY DONALD, MARK RYDEN ILLUSTRATOR: MARK RYDEN CLIENT: SONY MUSIC ■ **222** PROMOTIONAL
POSTER FOR MICHAEL JACKSON'S ALBUM *DANGEROUS*. THE SAME ILLUSTRATION WAS USED ON THE ALBUM COVER. ● **222**
PLAKAT FÜR MICHAEL JACKSON MIT DER GEISTERBAHNILLUSTRATION SEINER LP *DANGEROUS*. ▲ **222** POUR LA PROMOTION DE
L'ALBUM DE MICHAEL JACKSON, *DANGEROUS*. L'ILLUSTRATION DU TRAIN FANTÔME FIGURE AUSSI SUR LA POCHETTE. (USA)

■ **223** ART DIRECTOR: TAKAYUKI ITOH DESIGNER: MASAYUKI TSUKAMOTO ILLUSTRATOR: TAKAYUKI ITOH AGENCY: TAKAYUKI ITOH
DESIGN OFFICE CO., LTD. ■ **223** POSTER ANNOUNCING THE PERFORMANCE OF A VERDI OPERA IN JAPAN. ● **223** PLAKATANKÜN-
DIGUNG EINER VERDI-AUFFÜHRUNG IN JAPAN. ▲ **223** POUR UNE REPRÉSENTATION DE L'OPÉRA DE VERDI AU JAPON. (JPN)

Jubiläumskonzert 25 Jahre Jazz in Willisau
Fr 5. April 20 h, Mohren: Horace Tapscott Quartet, Maceo Parker Roots Revisted

224

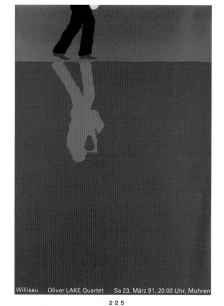

Willisau   Oliver LAKE Quartet   Sa 23. März 91, 20.00 Uhr, Mohren

225

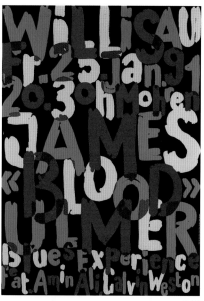

226

HIER SPIELT DIE MUSIK!

INTERNATIONALES MUSIKFESTIVAL
ARNOLD SCHÖNBERG UND
NEUE MUSIK AUS DEUTSCHLAND,
ÖSTERREICH UND DER SCHWEIZ.
DUISBURG 13. SEPT 92 – 8. JUNI 93
INFORMATIONEN: FESTIVALBÜRO, NECKARSTR. I.
4100 DU I, TEL.: 0203/30 09 124, FAX: 0203/30 09 200

227

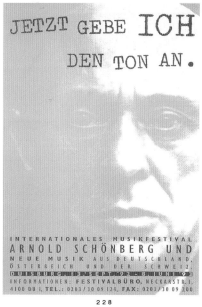

JETZT GEBE ICH DEN TON AN.

INTERNATIONALES MUSIKFESTIVAL
ARNOLD SCHÖNBERG UND
NEUE MUSIK AUS DEUTSCHLAND,
ÖSTERREICH UND DER SCHWEIZ.
DUISBURG 13. SEPT 92 – 8. JUNI 93
INFORMATIONEN: FESTIVALBÜRO, NECKARSTR. I.
4100 DU I, TEL.: 0203/30 09 124, FAX: 0203/30 09 200

228

INTERNATIONALES MUSIKFESTIVAL
ARNOLD SCHÖNBERG UND
NEUE MUSIK AUS DEUTSCHLAND,
ÖSTERREICH UND DER SCHWEIZ.
DUISBURG 13. SEPT 92 – 8. JUNI 93
INFORMATIONEN: FESTIVALBÜRO, NECKARSTR. I.
4100 DU I, TEL.: 0203/30 09 124, FAX: 0203/30 09 200

229

ОПЕРА
ГАСТРОЛИ АНГЛИЙСКОЙ НАЦИОНАЛЬНОЙ ОПЕРЫ
ENGLISH NATIONAL OPERA TOUR IN USSR
НА РУССКОЙ СЦЕНЕ

230

toad the wet sprocket f e a r

231

Just for the record...
BARBRA STREISAND
A 30 Year Celebration

232

233

■ **224-226** ART DIRECTOR/DESIGNER/ILLUSTRATOR/AGENCY: NIKLAUS TROXLER GRAFIK-STUDIO CLIENT: JAZZ IN WILLISAU ■ **224-226** FROM A SERIES OF POSTERS FOR A JAZZ FESTIVAL: 25 YEARS OF THE FESTIVAL, A CONCERT BY THE OLIVER LAKE QUARTET, AND JAMES BLUES ULMER—BLUES EXPERIENCE. ● **224-226** FÜR DAS JAZZ FESTIVAL IN WILLISAU. ▲ **224-226** POUR LE FESTIVAL DE JAZZ DE WILLISAU: LES 25 ANS DU FESTIVAL, OLIVER LAKE QUARTET, JAMES BLUES ULMER—BLUES EXPERIENCE. (SWI)

■ **227-229** DESIGNER: NINJA VON OERTZEN CLIENT: STADT DUISBURG ■ **227-229** A SERIES OF POSTERS AIMED AT YOUNG PEOPLE, DESIGNED AS AN ALTERNATIVE TO THE OFFICIAL POSTERS FOR THE MUSIC FESTIVAL OF THE CITY OF DUISBURG. ● **227-229** DIESE PLAKATESERIE, EINE ALTERNATIVE ZUR OFFIZIELLEN KAMPAGNE DER STADT DUISBURG RICHTET SICH AN DAS JUNGE PUBLIKUM. ▲ **227-229** SÉRIE D'AFFICHES ALTERNATIVES S'ADRESSANT À UN PUBLIC JEUNE, ANNONÇANT LE FESTIVAL DE MUSIQUE DE LA VILLE DE DUISBURG SUR LE THEME: «ARNOLD SCHÖNBERG ET LA NOUVELLE MUSIQUE ALLEMANDE.» (GER)

■ **230** ART DIRECTOR: JULIAN MORTON DESIGNER/ILLUSTRATOR/COPYWRITER: JELENA KITAJEVA AGENCY: ORIGEN ARTS LIMITED CLIENT: ENGLISH NATIONAL OPERA ■ **230** POSTER FOR A TOUR OF THE ENGLISH NATIONAL OPERA IN RUSSIA. ● **230** FÜR EINE TOURNEE DER ENGLISH NATIONAL OPERA IN RUSSLAND. ▲ **230** AFFICHE ANNONÇANT UNE TOURNÉE DE L'ENGLISH NATIONAL OPERA. (GBR)

■ **231, 232** ART DIRECTORS: MARY MAURER 231, GABRIELLE RAUMBERGER 232 DESIGN DIRECTOR: NANCY DONALD 231 DESIGNER: GABRIELLE RAUMBERGER 232 PHOTOGRAPHER: HANS NELEMAN 231 CLIENT: SONY MUSIC ■ **231, 232** POSTERS PROMOTING NEW ALBUMS BY THE GROUP "TOAD THE WET SPROCKET" AND BARBRA STREISAND. ● **231, 232** WERBUNG FÜR NEUE LANGSPIEL-PLATTEN DER GRUPPE «TOAD THE WET SPROCKET» UND DER SÄNGERIN BARBRA STREISAND. ▲ **231, 232** DEUX AFFICHES DE PRO-MOTION DE DISQUES: POUR LE GROUPE «TOAD THE WET SPROCKET» ET POUR UN NOUVEL ALBUM DE BARBRA STREISAND. (USA)

■ **233** ART DIRECTOR/DESIGNER: MICHAEL BAVIERA PHOTOGRAPHER: JEAN-PIERRE KUHN AGENCY: BBV MICHAEL BAVIERA CLIENT: CAMESI ■ **233** ANNOUNCEMENT OF AN EXHIBITION OF THE WORK OF THE PAINTER CAMESI IN AN ORATORY. ● **233** FÜR EINE AUSSTELLUNGS DES MALERS CAMESI. ▲ **233** ANNONCE D'UNE EXPOSITION DU PEINTRE CAMESI DANS UN ORATOIRE. (SWI)

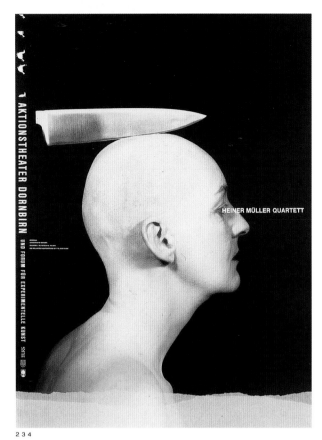

234

235

236

237

The Headless Horseman
of Sleepy Hollow

World Premiere
of Jon Deak's composition
based on Washington Irving's
American Classic.
Mstislav Rostropovich
conducting the
National Symphony Orchestra
and the Manchester String Quartet

Commissioned by the
Merck Company Foundation in 1991
in celebration of the centennial
of Merck & Co., Inc.

Manchester String Quartet:
Hyun-Woo Kim, violin
Jane Bowyer Stewart, violin
Nancy Thomas Bittner, viola
Glenn Garlick, cello

Kennedy Center Concert Hall

January 30 and February 1, 1992
8:30 pm

February 4, 1992
7:00 pm

238

239

■ **234** ART DIRECTOR: SIGI RAMOSER DESIGNER: SIGI RAMOSER PHOTOGRAPHER: HERBERT NEUNER AGENCY: SIGI RAMOSER CLIENT: AKTIONSTHEATER DORNBIRN ■ 234 POSTER FOR A PLAY DEALING WITH A SOCIETY LOSING ITS ABILITY TO COMMUNICATE. ● 234 ANKÜNDIGUNG DER AUFFÜHRUNG EINES STÜCKES VON HEINER MÜLLER: DIE ENDZEIT EINER BEZIEHUNGSFÄHIGEN GESELLSCHAFT. ▲ 234 ANNONCE D'UNE PIECE OU IL EST QUESTION DE LA FIN D'UNE SOCIÉTÉ CAPABLE DE COMMUNIQUER. (AUT)

■ **235** ART DIRECTOR/DESIGNER/ILLUSTRATOR: JOAO MACHADO CLIENT: CAMARA MUNICIPAL DO PORTO ■ 235 ANNOUNCEMENT OF A EUROPEAN JAZZ FESTIVAL. ● 235 FÜR EIN JAZZFESTIVALS IN PORTO. ▲ 235 POUR UN FESTIVAL DE JAZZ À PORTO. (POR)

■ **236** ART DIRECTOR/DESIGNER/ILLUSTRATOR: GÜNTHER KIESER CLIENT: HESSISCHER RUNDFUNK ■ 236 POSTER FOR A JAZZ FESTIVAL IN FRANKFURT. ● 236 ANKÜNDIGUNG EINES JAZ FESTIVALS. ▲ 236 ANNONCE DU FESTIVAL DE JAZZ DE FRANCFORT. (GER)

■ **237** DESIGNER: RAPHIE ETGAR CLIENT: JERUSALEM SYMPHONY ORCHESTRA ■ 237 POSTER FOR THE SEASON-OPENING CONCERT OF THE JERUSALEM SYMPHONY ORCHESTRA. ● 237 FÜR EIN KONZERT, MIT DEM DAS SYMPHONIE ORCHESTER VON JERUSALEM DIE SAISON ERÖFFNET. ▲ 237 POUR UN CONCERT OUVRANT LA SAISON DE L'ORCHESTRE SYMPHONIQUE DE JÉRUSALEM. (ISR)

■ **238** ART DIRECTOR/DESIGNER/ILLUSTRATOR: PETER GOOD AGENCY: PETER GOOD GRAPHIC DESIGN CLIENT: MERCK COMPANY FOUNDATION ■ 238 POSTER ANNOUNCING THE WORLD PREMIERE OF A MUSICAL PERFORMANCE BASED ON A STORY BY WASHINGTON IRVING. ● 238 FÜR DIE WELTURAUFFÜHUNG EINER MUSIKALISCHEN VERSION VON WASHINGTON IRVINGS KLASSIKER. ▲ 238 ANNONCE DE LA PREMIERE DE LA VERSION MUSICALE DE LA CÉLEBRE NOUVELLE DE WASHINGTON IRVING. (USA)

■ **239** ART DIRECTOR/DESIGNER/ILLUSTRATOR: IAN WHITE CLIENT: POLYDOR RECORDS AUSTRALIA ■ 239 A POSTER PROMOTING VAN MORRISON. ● 239 PROMOTION FÜR VAN MORRISON. ▲ 239 AFFICHE PROMOTIONNELLE POUR LE MUSICIEN VAN MORRISON. (AUS)

EDVARD GRIEG 1843–1907

1

Der Komponist, der Norwegen einen festen Platz auf der musikalischen Weltkarte sicherte

"Der norwegische Künstler hat eine herrliche Berufung – ich möchte mit niemandem auf der Welt tauschen!"

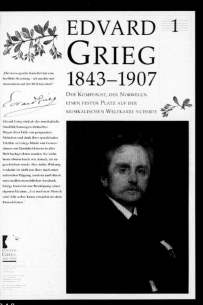

Edvard Grieg wird als das musikalische Sinnbild Norwegens betrachtet. Wegen ihrer Fülle von prägnanten Melodien und dank ihrer sprudelnden Vitalität ist Griegs Musik von Generationen von Musikliebhabern in aller Welt hochgeschätzt worden. Sie wirkt heute ebenso frisch wie damals, als sie geschrieben wurde. Ihre starke Wirkung verdankt sie nicht nur ihrer markanten nationalen Prägung, sondern auch ihrem universellen menschlichen Ausdruck. Griegs Kunst ist eine Bestätigung seines eigenen Maxime: "Erst muß man Mensch sein! Alle wahre Kunst erwächst aus dem Menschlichen."

EDVARD GRIEG 1843–1907

2

DER JUNGE GRIEG

In Griegs Adern floß norwegisches, schottisches und dänisches Blut. Sein Urgroßvater Alexander (1739–1803) wanderte um 1770 aus Schottland aus und ließ sich in Bergen nieder. Als er im Jahre 1779 die norwegische Staatsbürgerschaft erhielt, änderte er die Schreibweise seines Namens von Greig in Grieg. Sein Sohn John (1772–1844) heiratete Maren Regine Haslund (1776–1853), die Tochter eines dänischen Musikers.

3

STUDIENJAHRE IN LEIPZIG

Als Fünfzehnjähriger schrieb sich Grieg im Herbst 1858 als Student am Leipziger Musikkonservatorium ein. Fast vier Jahre lang studierte er Klavier und Komposition unter hervorragenden Künstlern und Pädagogen. Er entwickelte sich zu einem ausgezeichneten Pianisten, und seine Studienberichte und ersten Kompositionen zeugen von einer außerordentlichen Begabung.

4

KÜNSTLERISCHE REIFUNG

Während eines Aufenthalts in Kopenhagen 1863–65 entfaltete Grieg eine umfassende Tätigkeit. Nachdem er seine erste – und einzige – Symphonie komponiert hatte, fühlte er einen starken Drang, seine eigene musikalische Identität zu finden. Unter Einfluß von Ole Bull und Rikard Nordraak lernte er in kurzer Zeit seine ersten bahnbrechenden Werke: die vier Humoresken, die Klaviersonate und die erste Violinsonate, in denen es ihm gelang, eine markante, persönliche Ausdrucksweise mit vollnorwegischen Stilmerkmalen zu vereinen.

5

NINA GRIEG

"Ich liebte ein junges Mädchen mit einer wunderbaren Stimme und einer ebenso wunderbaren Vortragsweise. Dieses Mädchen wurde meine Frau und Lebensgefährtin, und sie ist es bis auf den heutigen Tag. Sie ist – ich darf es wohl sagen – für mich die einzige wahre Interpretin meiner Lieder geblieben. Meine Lieder entstanden mit der Notwendigkeit eines Naturgesetzes und wurden alle für sie geschrieben."

6

DAS KLAVIERKONZERT IN a-MOLL

Edvard Griegs Klavierkonzert steht nebst den zwei Peer-Gynt-Suiten als dasjenige Werk, das mit seinem Namen am engsten verbunden ist. Als eine der bestverstandenen Kompositionen dieser Art in der Spätromantik hat das Konzert seine ursprüngliche Frische bewahrt und besitzt auch heute noch die gleiche Wirkung wie bei der ersten Aufführung 1869. Mit seinen faszinierenden Melodik und seiner feingeschliffenen Harmonik gehört es zu den köstlichsten gespielten Werken seines Genres. In der glanzvollen Solopartie ist das Elegant-Virtuose mit edelster Lyrik vereint.

7

IM BANNE DER SAGAS

In der ersten Hälfte der 1870er Jahre kam Griegs Nationalgefühl aufs neue stark zum Ausdruck. Seine Inspirationsquelle war diesmal der patriotische Dichter Bjørnstjerne Bjørnson (1832–1910), der durch seine spannenden, historischen Dramen Griegs reges Interesse für die altnordischen Sagas weckte. In kurzer Zeit schrieb Grieg mehrere großartige Werke zu Bjørnson-Texten: Das Melodram Bergliot, die Bühnenmusik zum Schauspiel Sigurd Jorsalfar und die zwei ersten Akte einer unvollendeten Oper, Olav Trygvason. Mit breiten, farbenreichen Strichen malte Grieg hier großartige Bilder aus der Geschichte seines Heimatlandes.

8

"PEER GYNT"

Auf Aufforderung des norwegischen Dramatikers Henrik Ibsen (1828–1906) schrieb Grieg 1874–75 die Bühnenmusik für eine Inszenierung von Ibsens dramatischem Gedicht Peer Gynt. Dem Beitrag Griegs, 26 Einzelnummern umfassend, war der Erfolg der Uraufführung in Oslo 1876 maßgeblich zu verdanken. Der internationale Durchbruch dieser Musik kam jedoch erst, nachdem Grieg acht der farbenreichsten Stücke für zwei Orchestersuiten (1888 und 1892) bearbeitet hatte. Diese musikalischen Perlen, die seiner einer ungemein große Popularität erlangten, gehören auch heute noch zu den beliebtesten Werken des Komponisten.

9

TROLDHAUGEN

Vom Troldhaugen – Griegs schönem Heim zehn Kilometer südlich von Bergen – überblickt man den Nordisfjord. "Hierher, wo es am allerschönsten ist – Das neue Opus, mein bisher bestes. Kein Opus hat mich bisher mehr begeistert als dieses." So äußerte sich Grieg 1884 zur Zeit der Bauarbeiten auf Troldhaugen. Hier wurde er zu einer Reihe seiner wichtigsten Werke angeregt.

249   250   251

252

■ **240-251** Art Director: JUNN PAASCHE-AASEN Designer: JUNN PAASCHE-AASEN Copywriters: FINN BENESTAD, DAG SCHJELDERUP-EBBE Client: THE ROYAL NORWEGIAN MINISTRY OF FOREIGN AFFAIRS ■ **240-251** A SERIES OF 12 POSTERS CELEBRATING THE 150TH ANNIVERSARY OF THE NORWEGIAN COMPOSER EDVARD GRIEG. BY MEANS OF PORTRAITS, LAND-SCAPES AND OBJECTS, THE POSTERS TELL THE STORY OF THE MAN AND HIS WORK. ● **240-251** EINE REIHE VON 12 PLAKATEN ANLÄSSLICH DES 150STEN GEBURTSTAGES DES NORWEGISCHEN KOMPONISTEN EDVARD GRIEG. ANHAND VON PORTRÄTS, LANDSCHAFTSBILDERN UND OBJEKTEN WIRD DIE GESCHICHTE DES MANNES UND SEINES MUSIKALISCHEN WERKES ERZÄHLT. ▲ **240-251** SÉRIE DE 12 AFFICHES PUBLIÉES POUR LA COMMÉMORATION DU 150E ANNIVERSAIRE D'EDVARD GRIEG. Y SONT ÉVOQUÉES LA JEUNESSE, LES ÉTUDES, LA MATURITÉ, LA FEMME, L'ŒUVRE ET SON INSPIRATION, LES RAPPORTS DU MUSICIEN ET DE LA NATURE ET L'HÉRITAGE MUSICAL. ELLES SONT ORNÉES DE PHOTOS DES LIEUX ET DES OBJETS DE SA VIE. (NOR)

■ **252** Art Director/Designer: GARY MALLEN Photographer: MICHAEL RUSH Agency: MALLEN AND FRIENDS ADVERTISING ARTS & DESIGN Client: KANSAS CITY BLUES & JAZZ FESTIVAL ■ **252** STREET POSTER FOR A BLUES AND JAZZ FESTIVAL. ● **252** FÜR EIN BLUES- UND JAZZFESTIVAL. ▲ **252** DESTINÉE À L'AFFICHAGE DE RUES, L'ANNONCE D'UN FESTIVAL DE BLUES ET DE JAZZ. (USA)

LET THE MUSIC TAKE YOU THERE

SONY.

SONY AUTOSOUND

253

254

■ 253 ART DIRECTOR/DESIGNER: WESLEY SHAW PHOTOGRAPHER: DON CARROLL COPYWRITER: RHONDA SMITH AGENCY: WORDS AND PICTURES CLIENT: SONY CORPORATION ■ 253 DISPLAY POSTER MAILED TO DEALERS FOR SONY AUTOSOUND. THE FINISHED PHOTOGRAPH IS COMPOSED OF FOUR DIFFERENT CHROMES: THE LANDSCAPE, THE CLOUDS, THE BEAM OF LIGHT AND A MODEL CAR. THE PHOTOS WERE SCANNED AND THEN COMPOSED ON A PAINTBOX COMPUTER. ● 253 FÜR HÄNDLER BESTIMMTES DISPLAY-PLAKAT FÜR SONY-AUTOSOUND. DAS BILD BESTEHT AUS VIER AUFNAHMEN: LANDSCHAFT, WOLKEN, LICHTSTRAHL UND MODELLAUTO. ▲ 253 AFFICHE RÉALISÉE À L'AIDE DE QUATRE PHOTOS—LE PAYSAGE, LES NUAGES, LE RAYON LUMINEUX ET UN MODELE RÉDUIT DE VOITURE—PASSÉES AU SCANNER ET TRAVAILLÉES SUR ORDINATEUR À L'AIDE D'UN PAINTBOX. (USA)

■ 254 ART DIRECTOR: STEFAN SAGMEISTER DESIGNER: ANDREW POGSON PHOTOGRAPHER: BELA BORSODI AGENCY: LEO BURNETT LTD. CLIENT: LUKAS KRAMER ■ 254 POSTER PROMOTING AN INTERNATIONAL JAZZ BAND, WITH SPACE FOR THE DATES AND LOCATIONS OF THE CONCERTS. ● 254 PLAKAT FÜR EINE INTERNATIONALE JAZZBAND. EIN LEERRAUM IST FÜR DIE ANKÜNDIGUNG EINZELER KONZERTE VORGESEHEN. ▲ 254 AFFICHE DU FESTIVAL DE JAZZ EN PLEIN AIR DE ST-GALL. (SWI)

■ 255 ART DIRECTOR/DESIGNER: JOSEPH JIBRI PHOTOGRAPHER: RAZI AGENCY: JOSEPH JIBRI GRAPHIC DESIGN CLIENT NANA DISC ■ 255 POSTER FOR A CONCERT BY AN ISRAELI ROCK BAND, EMPHASIZING THE GROUP'S NAME. ● 255 FÜR EINE ISRAELISCHE ROCKBAND, DEREN NAME IN DEN MITTELPUNKT GERÜCKT WIRD. ▲ 255 POUR UN CONCERT D'UN GROUPE ROCK ISRAÉLIEN. (ISR)

■ 256, 257 ART DIRECTOR: DANNY BOONE PHOTOGRAPHERS: DEAN HAWTHORNE 256, STOCK 257 COPYWRITER: JOE ALEXANDER AGENCY: THE MARTIN AGENCY CLIENT: THE RICHMOND SYMPHONY ■ 256, 257 POSTERS PROMOTING THE RICHMOND SYMPHONY. ● 256, 257 «FÜR EINEN ABEND IN DER STADT, EMPFEHLEN WIR FOLGENDE TAKTE» (SPIEL MIT DEM ENGLISCHEN WORT BAR); «STELLEN SIE IHREN KINDERN EINEN MUSIKER VOR, DER NIE EIN VIDEO GEMACHT HAT.» PLAKATWERBUNG FÜR EIN SINFONIEORCHESTER. ▲ 256, 257 «POUR UNE SOIRÉE EN VILLE, NOUS RECOMMANDONS LES BARS SUIVANTS»; «FAITES-CONNAITRE À VOS ENFANTS UN MUSICIEN QUI N'A JAMAIS FAIT DE VIDÉO.» PROMOTION D'UN ORCHESTRE CLASSIQUE. (USA)

255

For a night on the town, we recommend the following bars.

Live music. Exciting atmosphere. Huge crowds. And best of all: no cover charge. For reservations, call 788-1212 or 782-3900.

The Richmond Symphony

256

Introduce your kids to a musician who's never made a video.

The Richmond Symphony

257

258

259

■ 258, 259 ART DIRECTOR: GILBERT E. BAIER DESIGNER: KONRAD ERBELDING AGENCY: FORMART WERBEAGENTUR GMBH CLIENT: M.C.F. DE FREYMING MERLEBACH ■ 258, 259 "DIFFERENT FACETS OF CONTEMPORARY HUNGARIAN ART." POSTERS ANNOUNCING EXHIBITIONS OF GRAPHIC DESIGN AND PHOTOGRAPHY AND OF PAINTING AND SCULPTURE. THEY WORK EITHER TOGETHER OR AS TWO INDIVIDUAL POSTERS. ● 258, 259 «VERSCHIEDENEN FACETTEN DER ZEITGENÖSSISCHEN UNGARISCHEN KUNST.» FÜR EINE GRAPHIK- UND PHOTOGRAPHIE- SOWIE FÜR EINE BILDER- UND SKULPTURENAUSSTELLUNG. SIE KÖNNEN ZUSAMMEN ODER EINZELN GEHÄNGT WERDEN. ▲ 258, 259 DEUX AFFICHES ANNONCANT DES EXPOSITIONS D'ARTISTES HONGROIS. (GER)

■ 260-263 ART DIRECTOR: KAZUTOSHI YAGAMI DESIGNER: KAZUTOSHI YAGAMI PHOTOGRAPHER: KAZUTOSHI YAGAMI CLIENT: ORIBE TEI GALLERY ■ 260-263 FOR AN EXHIBITION OF THE WORKS OF KAZUTOSHI YAGAMI. ● 260-263 FÜR EINE AUSSTELLUNG VON KAZUTOSHI YAGAMI IN EINER GALERIE. ▲ 260-263 POUR UNE EXPOSITION DE KAZUTOSHI YAGAMI DANS UNE GALERIE. (JPN)

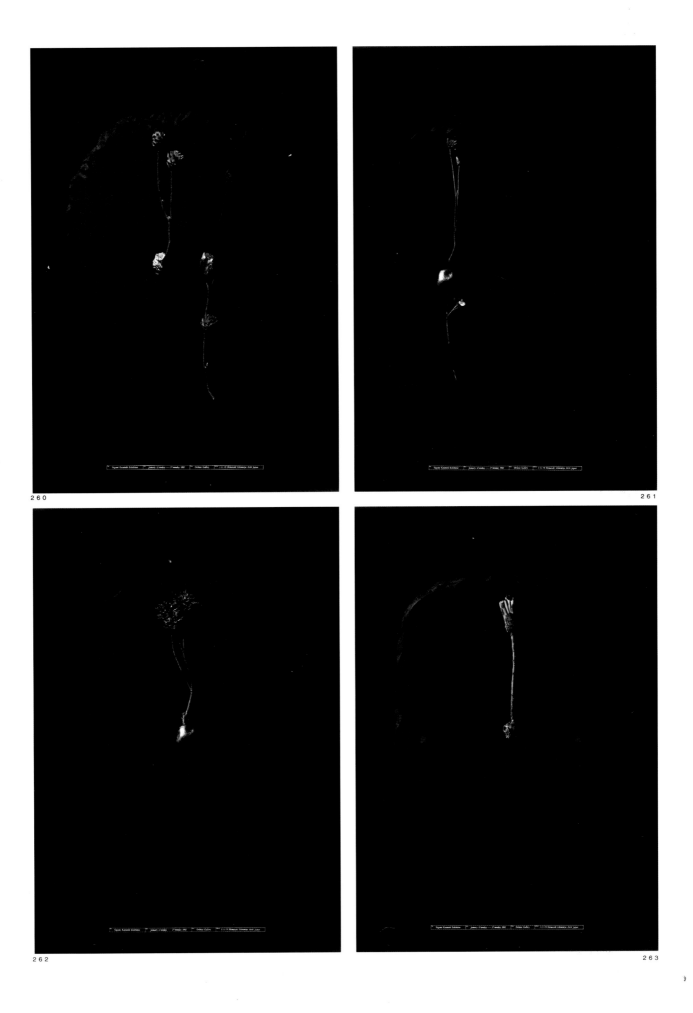

260

261

262

263

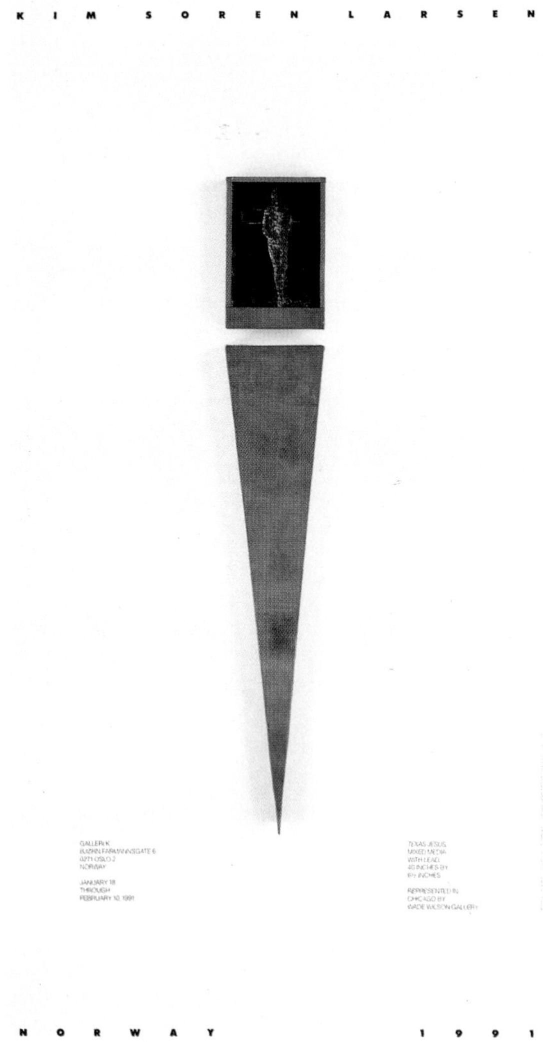
KIM SOREN LARSEN
JANUARY 18
THROUGH
FEBRUARY 10, 1991
TEXAS JESUS
MIXED MEDIA
WITH LEAD
CHICAGO BY
WADE WILSON GALLERY
NORWAY 1991

264

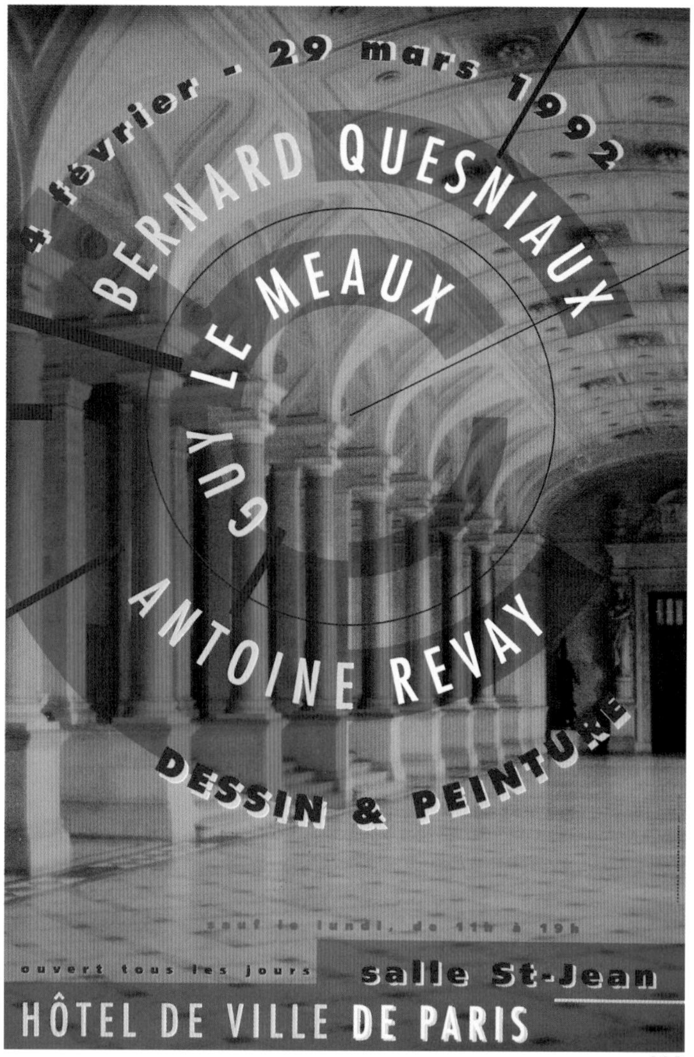
4 février - 29 mars 1992
BERNARD QUESNIAUX
GUY LE MEAUX
ANTOINE REVAY
DESSIN & PEINTURE
sauf le lundi, de 11h à 19h
ouvert tous les jours
salle St-Jean
HÔTEL DE VILLE DE PARIS

265

■ **264** ART DIRECTOR: EUGENE BELLINI DESIGNER: KIM SMITH ILLUSTRATOR/CLIENT: KIM SOREN LARSEN AGENCY: BELLINI DESIGN ■ **264** "TEXAS JESUS"—A POSTER ANNOUNCING AN EXHIBITION OF AN AMERICAN ARTIST IN NORWAY. ● **264** FÜR EINE AUSSTELLUNG EINER AMERIKANISCHEN KÜNSTLERIN IN OSLO. ▲ **264** POUR L'EXPOSITION D'UNE ARTISTE AMÉRICAINE EN NORVEGE. (NOR)

■ **265** ART DIRECTOR: BERNARD BAISSAIT DESIGNER: FREDERIC BORTOLOTTI AGENCY: COMPAGNIE BERNARD BAISSAIT CLIENT: MAIRIE DE PARIS ■ **265** POSTER ANNOUNCING A GROUP EXHIBITION IN PARIS'S CITY HALL. ● **265** ANKÜNDIGUNG EINER GRUPPENAUSSTELLUNG IM PARISER RATSHAUS. ▲ **265** POUR UNE EXPOSITION DE GROUPE À L'HOTEL DE VILLE DE PARIS. (FRA)

■ **266, 267** ART DIRECTOR: MAKOTO SAITO DESIGNER: MAKOTO SAITO ILLUSTRATOR: MAKOTO SAITO CLIENT: DAI NIPPON PRINTING CO., LTD. ■ **266, 267** POSTERS FOR AN EXHIBITION UNDER THE TITLE OF "TRANS ART 91." ● **266, 267** ZWEI PLAKATE FÜR EINE AUSSTELLUNG MIT DEM TITEL «TRANS ART 91.» ▲ **266, 267** DEUX AFFICHES POUR L'EXPOSITION «TRANS ART 91.» (JPN)

266

267

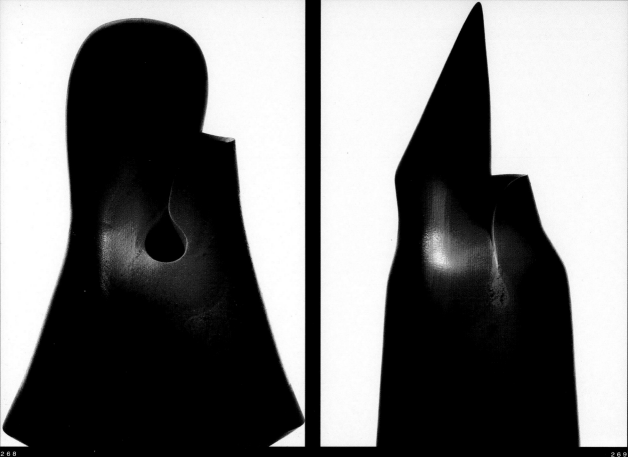

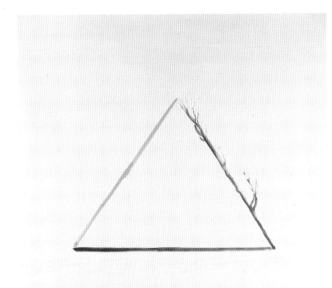

ILSE WEBER
ZEICHNUNGEN, AQUARELLE UND GEMÄLDE

KUNSTHAUS ZÜRICH 15. MÄRZ – 10. MAI 1992

ÖFFNUNGSZEITEN: DI BIS DO 10-21 UHR, FR BIS SO 10-17 UHR, OSTERN: DO 16.4. 10-15 UHR, SA 18.4. UND MO 20.4. 10-17 UHR
KARFREITAG 17.4. UND OSTERSONNTAG 19.4. GESCHLOSSEN, SECHSELÄUTEN, MO 27.4. UND 1. MAI FR 15. GESCHLOSSEN

270

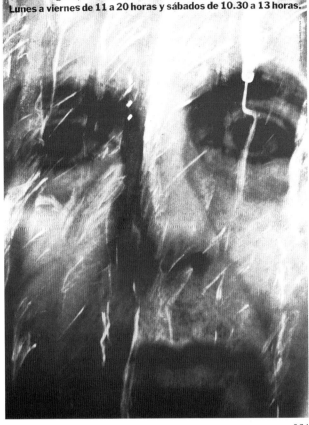

Dante Saganías, pinturas recientes. 30 de marzo al 16 de abril.
Galería Lagard, Suipacha 1216, Buenos Aires. Tel. 393 7822.
Lunes a viernes de 11 a 20 horas y sábados de 10.30 a 13 horas.

271

■ (THIS SPREAD) 268, 269 ART DIRECTOR/DESIGNER: ICHIRO MITANI PHOTOGRAPHER: GAKUJI TANAKA AGENCY: MITANI ICHIRO DESIGN CLIENT: TAKASHIMAYA ■ 268, 269 POSTERS ANNOUNCING A CERAMICS EXHIBITION OF SHIMIZU ROKUBEI IN A GALLERY OF THE TAKASHIMAYA DEPARTMENT STORE. THE INFORMATION IS BLIND-EMBOSSED ● (DIESE DOPPELSEITE) 268, 269 PLAKATE FÜR EINE AUSSTELLUNG DES JAPANISCHEN TÖPFERS SHIMIZU ROBKBEI. DIE INFORMATION AUF DEM PLAKAT IST BLIND-GEPRÄGT. ▲ (CETTE DOUBLE PAGE) 268, 269 AFFICHES POUR L'EXPOSITION D'UN POTIER DANS UN GRAND MAGASIN. (JPN)

■ (THIS SPREAD) 270 DESIGNER: PETER ZIMMERMANN ARTIST: ILSE WEBER CLIENT: KUNSTHAUS ZÜRICH ■ 270 POSTER FOR AN EXHIBITION BY A SWISS ARTIST IN ZÜRICH. ● (DIESE DOPPELSEITE) 270 PLAKAT FÜR EINE AUSSTELLLUNG DER SCHWEIZERI-SCHEN KÜNSTLERIN ILSE WEBER. ▲ (CETTE DOUBLE PAGE) 270 AFFICHE DE L'EXPOSITION D'UNE FEMME PEINTRE SUISSE. (SWI)

■ (THIS SPREAD) 271 DESIGNER/ILLUSTRATOR: GUSTAVO PEDROZA AGENCY: GUSTAVO PEDROZA CLIENT: DANTE SAGANIAS ■ 271 FOR AN EXHIBITION OF THE PAINTER DANTE SAGANIAS IN THE LAGARD ART GALLERY. ● (DIESE DOPPELSEITE) 271 FÜR EINE AUSSTELLUNG VON DANTE SAGANIAS. ▲ (CETTE DOUBLE PAGE) 271 POUR UNE EXPOSITION DU PEINTRE DANTE SAGANIAS. (ARG)

■ (FOLLOWING SPREAD) 272 ART DIRECTOR/DESIGNER: JULIE SZAMOCKI PHOTOGRAPHER: GARY MORTENSEN COPYWRITER: DAVID RYAN AGENCY: YAMAMOTO MOSS CLIENT: NÖRWEST CORPORATION ■ 272 POSTER FOR AN EXHIBITION ON LIGHTING DESIGN FROM 1900 TO 1940. ● (FOLGENDE DOPPELSEITE) 272 FÜR EINE AUSSTELLUNG VON LEUCHTEN AUS DER ZEIT ZWISCHEN 1900 UND 1940. ▲ (DOUBLE PAGE SUIVANTE) 272 ANNONCE D'UNE EXPOSITION SUR L'ÉCLAIRAGE MODERNISTE DE 1900 À 1940. (USA)

■ (FOLLOWING SPREAD) 273 ART DIRECTOR: RALPH SCHRAIVOGEL DESIGNER: RALPH SCHRAIVOGEL CLIENT: MUSEUM FÜR GESTALTUNG ■ 273 "WITH THE WIND AT YOUR BACK," AN EXHIBITION PRESENTING THE WORKS OF FEMALE ARTISTS WHO RECEIVED THE SWISS NATIONAL SCHOLARSHIP FOR APPLIED ARTS. ● (FOLGENDE DOPPELSEITE) 273 «IM RÜCKENWIND,» AUS-STELLUNG DER STIPENDIATINNEN DES EIDGENÖSSISCHEN STIPENDIUMS FÜR ANGEWANDTE KUNST. ▲ (DOUBLE PAGE SUI-VANTE) 273 POUR UNE EXPOSITION DES TRAVAUX DES LAURÉATS DE LA BOURSE FÉDÉRALE DES ARTS APPLIQUÉS EN 1990. (SWI)

274

275

276

277

278

■ **274, 276** ART DIRECTOR/DESIGNER: KAZUMASA NAGAI AGENCY: NIPPON DESIGN CENTER CLIENTS: HOKKAIDO MUSEUM OF MODERN ART 274, TOKYO DESIGNERS SPACE 276 ■ **274, 276** POSTERS FOR EXHIBITIONS ON "WORLD GLASS NOW" AND POSTERS BY KAZUMASA NAGAI. ● **274, 276** FÜR AUSSTELLUNGEN ÜBER ZEITGENÖSSISCHE GLASKUNST UND PLAKATE VON KAZUMASA NAGAI. ▲ **274, 276** POUR UNE EXPOSITION SUR LE VERRE CONTEMPORAIN ET UNE EXPOSITION PERSONNELLE DE KAZUMASA NAGAI. (JPN)

■ **275** ART DIRECTOR/DESIGNER: SHIN MATSUNAGA CLIENT: TAGAWA MUSEUM OF ART ■ **275** FOR A ONE-MAN SHOW BY SHIN MATSU-NAGA. ● **275** FÜR EINE EINZELAUSSTELLUNG SHIN MATSUNAGAS. ▲ **275** POUR UNE EXPOSITION DE SHIN MATSUNAGA. (JPN)

■ **277** ART DIRECTOR: MASAKAZU TANABE DESIGNER: MASAKAZU TANABE AGENCY: MEDIA CO., LTD. CLIENT: NIPPON DESIGNER GAKUIN ■ **277** FOR AN EXHIBITION OF THE COLLECTION OF A JAPANESE DESIGNERS' ASSOCIATION. ● **277** FÜR DIE PLAKAT-SAMMLUNG EINES JAPANISCHEN DESIGNER-VERBANDES. ▲ **277** D'UNE COLLECTION D'AFFICHES DE DESIGNERS JAPONAIS. (JPN)

■ **278** DESIGNER/ILLUSTRATOR: TAKU TASHIRO CLIENT: TOKYO ILLUSTRATORS SOCIETY ■ **278** FOR THE TOKYO ILLUSTRATORS SO-CIETY. ● **278** FÜR DEN VERBAND DER ILLUSTRATOREN IN TOKIO. ▲ **278** POUR LA SOCIÉTÉ DES ILLUSTRATEURS DE TOKYO. (JPN)

279

280

■ 279 DESIGNER: SEYMOUR CHWAST ILLUSTRATOR: SEYMOUR CHWAST AGENCY: THE PUSHPIN GROUP CLIENT: IBM GALLERY ■ 279 POSTER ANNOUNCING AN EXHIBITION COMMEMORATING 125 YEARS OF MUSICAL THEATER. ● 279 ANKÜNDIGUNG EINER AUSSTELLUNG ZUM 125JÄHRIGEN BESTEHEN DES MUSIKTHEATERS. ▲ 279 D'UNE EXPOSITION SUR 125 ANS DE COMÉDIE MUSICALE. (USA)

■ 280 DESIGNER/ILLUSTRATOR: ANDRÉS SALVAREZZA AGENCY: ATOM GRAPHICS, INC. CLIENT: LABORATORY OF METROPOLITAN ARCHITECTURE ■ 280 INVITATION TO A ROUNDTABLE, "THE LENSES IN THE CITIES," EXPLORING THE RELATIONSHIIP BETWEEN PHOTOGRAPHY AND ARCHITECTURE. ● 280 «DIE OBJEKTIVE IN DER STADT»—EINLADUNG ZU EINEM GESPRÄCH ÜBER PHOTOGRAPHIE UND ARCHITEKTUR. ▲ 280 ANNONCE D'UN COLLOQUE SUR LE RAPPORT ENTRE LA PHOTOGRAPHIE ET L'ARCHITECTURE. (SPA)

281

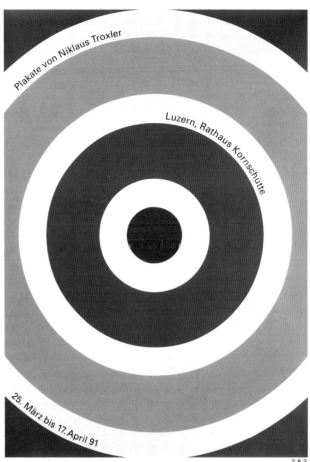

282

■ **281** DESIGNER: CLAUDE KUHN CLIENT: NATURHISTORISCHES MUSEUM DER BURGERGEMEINDE BERN ■ **281** POSTER ANNOUNC-
ING THE REOPENING OF THE GEOLOGY DEPARTMENT OF THE NATURAL HISTORY MUSEUM IN BERNE. ● **281** PLAKAT ZUR
BEKANNTGABE DER WIEDERERÖFFNUNG DER GEOLOGISCHEN ABTEILUNG DES NATURHISTORISCHEN MUSEUMS IN BERN. ▲ **281**
AFFICHE ANNONÇANT LA RÉOUVERTURE DU DÉPARTEMENT GÉOLOGIE DU MUSÉE D'HISTOIRE NATURELLE DE BERNE. (SWI)

■ **282** ART DIRECTOR/DESIGNER/ILLUSTRATOR: NIKLAUS TROXLER AGENCY: NIKLAUS TROXLER GRAFIK-STUDIO CLIENT: KULTURAMT
STADT LUZERN ■ **282** FOR AN EXHIBITION OF POSTERS BY THE SWISS ARTIST NIKLAUS TROXLER. ● **282** FÜR EINE
AUSSTELLUNG DER PLAKATE VON NIKLAUS TROXLER. ▲ **282** POUR UNE EXPOSITION D'AFFICHES DE NIKLAUS TROXLER. (SWI)

283

284

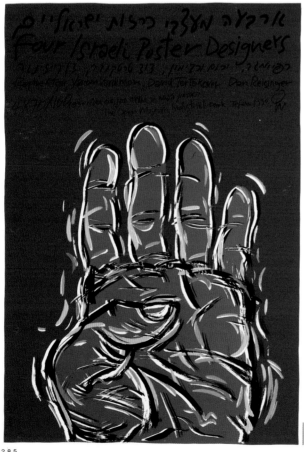

285

286

תערוכות הרצאות סרטים מוסיקה

287

■ **283** ART DIRECTOR: RITA MARSHALL DESIGNER: RITA MARSHALL ILLUSTRATOR: ETIENNE DELESSERT AGENCY: DELESSERT-MARSHALL CLIENT: MUSÉE JENISCH ■ 283 "PROPHETS AND PRETENDERS," AN EXHIBITION OF THE BLACK-AND-WHITE WORK OF ETIENNE DELESSERT. ● 283 «PROPHETEN UND SCHARLATANE,» EINE AUSSTELLUNG DER ARBEITEN VON ETIENNE DELESSERT IN SCHWARZWEISS. ▲ 283 POUR UNE EXPOSITION D'ŒUVRES PICTURALES EN NOIR ET BLANC D'ETIENNE DELESSERT. (SWI)

■ **284** ART DIRECTOR/DESIGNER: GARY KOEPKE PHOTOGRAPHER: STEVE MARSEL AGENCY: KOEPKE DESIGN GROUP CLIENTS: MATTHEW CARTER, SEYBOULD SEMINARS ■ 284 FOR AN EXPOSITION AND SEMINAR BY MATTHEW CARTER, A TYPE DESIGNER. CLASSICAL TYPE IS JUXTAPOSED WITH COMPUTER-DESIGNED TYPE. ● 284 FÜR EINE AUSSTELLUNG UND EIN SEMINAR: ES GEHT UM EINE GEGENÜBERSTELLUNG KLASSISCHER UND COMPUTERGENERIERTER TYPOGRAPHIE. ▲ 284 ANNONCE D'UNE EXPOSITION ET D'UN SÉMINAIRE: L'AFFICHE JUXTAPOSE UNE TYPOGRAPHIE CLASSIQUE ET DES CARACTERES COMPOSÉS SUR ORDINATEUR. (USA)

■ **285** DESIGNER: RAPHIE ETGAR CLIENT: THE OPEN MUSEUM ■ 285 POSTER FOR AN EXHIBITION OF FOUR ISRAELI GRAPHIC DESIGNERS, SYMBOLIZED BY THE FOUR FINGERS OF THE HAND. ● 285 FÜR EINE AUSSTELLUNG VON VIER ISRAELISCHEN GRA-PHIK-DESIGNERN. ▲ 285 POUR UNE EXPOSITION DE QUATRE ARTISTES, SYMBOLISÉS PAR LES QUATRE DOIGTS DE LA MAIN. (ISR)

■ **286** ART DIRECTOR/DESIGNER: K.G. OLSSON ARTIST: EDUARDO CHILLIDA AGENCY: K.G. OLSSON CLIENT: KONSTMUSEET, ARKIV FÖR DEKORATIV KONST ■ 286 POSTER FOR AN EXHIBITION OF "PUBLIC ART IN LUND 1990," SHOWING A WORK BY EDUARDO CHILLIDA. ● 286 ANKÜNDIGUNG DER AUSSTELLUNG «ÖFFENTLICHER KUNST IN LUND 1990» MIT EINEM KUNSTWERK VON EDUARDO CHILLIDA. ▲ 286 AFFICHE DE L'EXPOSITION: «L'ART PUBLIC À LUND EN 1990,» ILLUSTRÉ D'UNE ŒUVRE D'EDUARDO CILLIDA. (SWE)

■ **287** ART DIRECTOR/DESIGNER: JOSEPH JIBRI PHOTOGRAPHERS: JOSEPH JIBRI, REBECCA STERNBERG AGENCY: JOSEPH JIBRI GRAPHIC DESIGN CLIENT: BUGRASHOV GALLERY ■ 287 POSTER DESIGNED AS PART OF A MONTHLY PROGRAM OF CULTURAL ACTIVITIES AND EVENTS AT A GALLERY. IT WAS CREATED DURING THE 1991 GULF WAR AND PRINTED AFTER THE WAR. ● 287 «KEIN LEBENSRETTER IM DIENST.» PLAKAT IM RAHMEN DER KULTURELLEN VERANSTALTUNGEN EINER GALERIE. ES ENTSTAND WÄHREND DES GOLFKRIEGES UND DRÜCKT DIE STIMMUNG IN TEL-AVIV AUS. ▲ 287 «PAS DE GARDES DU CORPS EN SERVICE.» CETTE AFFICHE A ÉTÉ CRÉÉE DURANT LA GUERRE DU GOLFE ET EXPOSÉE UNE FOIS LE CONFLIT TERMINÉ À TEL AVIV. (ISR)

91 OBJECTS BY 91 DESIGNERS   GALLERY 91, N.Y.   DESIGN BY SHIN MATSUNAGA '91

288

Sponsored by
**Bell of
Pennsylvania**
in support
of the
Philadelphia
Zoo's new
carnivore exhibit.
Poster sales
will also
be used to
support this
endeavor.

■ (PREVIOUS SPREAD) **288** ART DIRECTOR/DESIGNER: SHIN MATSUNAGA CLIENT: GALLERY 91 ■ **288** POSTER FOR AN EXHIBITION AT GALLERY 91 IN NEW YORK. ● **288** (VORANGEHENDE DOPPELSEITE) FÜR EINE AUSSTELLUNG IN EINER NEW YORKER GALERIE. ▲ **288** (DOUBLE PAGE PRÉCÉDENTE) POUR L'EXPOSITION «91 OBJETS DE 91 DESIGNERS» À LA GALERIE 91 DE NEW YORK. (USA)

■ (PREVIOUS SPREAD) **289** DESIGNER/ILLUSTRATOR: MILTON GLASER CLIENT: PHILADELPHIA ZOO ■ **289** FOR AN EXHIBITION AT THE PHILADELPHIA ZOO. ● (VORANGEHENDE DOPPELSEITE) **289** «DAS REICH DER FLEISCHFRESSER,» PLAKAT FÜR EINE AUSSTELLUNG IM ZOO VON PHILADELPHIA. ▲ (DOUBLE PAGE PRÉCÉDENTE) **289** POUR L'EXPOSITION «LE ROYAUME DES CARNIVORES.» (USA)

■ (THIS SPREAD) **290** DESIGNER: KLAUS E. GÖLTZ PHOTOGRAPHER: HANS FINSLER CLIENT: SCHWEIZERISCHE STIFTUNG FÜR DIE PHOTOGRAPHIE ■ **290** "NEW ROADS IN PHOTOGRAPHY," A POSTER ANNOUNCING AN EXHIBITION OF THE WORK OF HANS FINSLER (1891-1972). THE PHOTOGRAPH SHOWN IS ENTITLED "TWO EGGS, POSITIVE" (C. 1930). ● (DIESE DOPPELSEITE) **290** «ZWEI EIER, POSITIV" (UM 1930)—ANKÜNDIGUNG EINER AUSSTELLUNG DES PHOTOGRAPHISCHEN WERKES VON HANS FINSLER (1891-1972). ▲ (CETTE DOUBLE PAGE) **290** AFFICHE ANNONÇANT UNE EXPOSITION DE L'ŒUVRE DU PHOTOGRAPHE HANS FINSLER (1891-1972). LA PHOTOGRAPHIE REPRÉSENTÉE, DATANT D'ENVIRON 1930, S'INTITULE «DEUX ŒUFS, POSITIF.» (SWI)

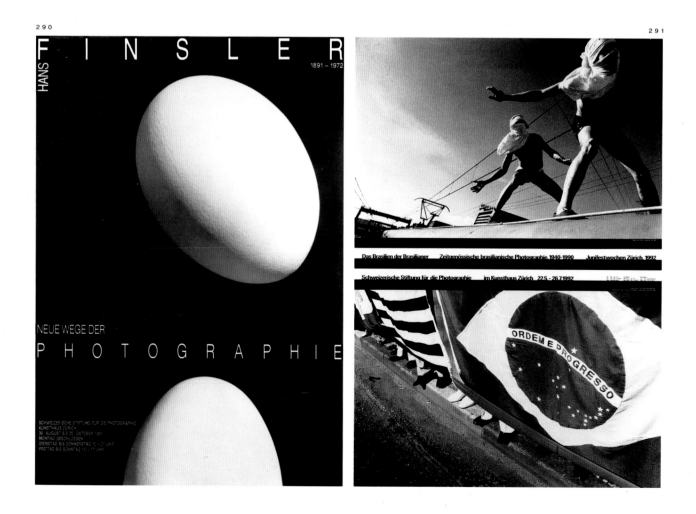

CHRISTINA HOPE
1ST COAST ESPRIT DE CORPS

CHRISTINA HOPE
MARIO VILLA GALLERY · NEW ORLEANS

292

293

■ (THIS SPREAD) **291** DESIGNER: WERNER JEKER PHOTOGRAPHERS: ROGERIO REIS, WALTER FIRMO CLIENT: KUNSTHAUS ZÜRICH ■ **291** "THE BRAZIL OF THE BRAZILIANS," AN EXHIBITION OF CONTEMPORARY BRAZILIAN PHOTOGRAPHY IN ZÜRICH'S MUSEUM OF ART. THE PHOTO ON TOP IS "TRAIN SURFERS," RIO 1991. AT THE BOTTOM IS "FUNERAL SERVICE FOR PRESIDENT TANCREDO NEVES," SAO PAULO 1985. ● (DIESE DOPPELSEITE) **291** AUSSTELLUNGSPLAKAT. DER TITEL DES PHOTOS OBEN: »ZUG-SURFER,« RIO 1991, UNTEN: «TRAUERFEIER FÜR PRÄSIDENT TANCREDO NEVES,» SAO PAULO 1985. ▲ (CETTE DOUBLE PAGE) **291** «LE BRÉSIL DES BRÉSILIENS,» ANNONCE D'UNE EXPOSITION DE PHOTOGRAPHIE BRÉSILIENNE CONTEMPORAINE. LA PHOTO DU HAUT S'INTITULE: «SURFERS DE TRAINS,» RIO, 1991; CELLE DU BAS: «FUNÉRAILLES DU PRÉSIDENT TANCREDO NEVES,» SAO PAULO, 1985. (SWI)

■ (THIS SPREAD) **292, 293** PHOTOGRAPHER: CHRISTINA HOPE ■ **292, 293** POSTERS FEATURING UNDERWATER PHOTOGRAPHS BY CHRISTINA HOPE. THEY ARE USED FOR SELF-PROMOTION AND AS ANNOUNCEMENTS OF EXHIBITIONS. ● (DIESE DOPPELSEITE) **292, 293** UNTERWASSERAUFNAHMEN DER PHOTOGRAPHIN CHRISTINA HOPE. SIE WERDEN ALS EIGENWERBUNG UND ZUR ANKÜNDIGUNG VON AUSSTELLUNGEN VERWENDET. ▲ (CETTE DOUBLE PAGE) **292, 293** AFFICHES MONTRANT DES PHOTOS SOUS-MARINES DE CHRISTINA HOPE. ELLES SONT UTILISÉES COMME AUTOPROMOTION ET POUR L'ANNONCE D'EXPOSITIONS. (GER)

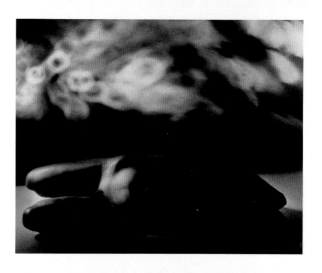

CONFUSED GRAVITATION

YURIKO TAKAGI

294

295

■ **294** ART DIRECTOR: JOEL FULLER DESIGNER/ILLUSTRATOR: CLAUDIA DE CASTRO COPYWRITERS: FRANK CUNNINGHAM, JOEL FULLER, MARK CANTORE, CLAUDIA DE CASTRO AGENCY: PINKHAUS DESIGN CORP. CLIENT: AIGA MIAMI ■ **294** POSTER ANNOUNCING A VISIT TO MIAMI BY THE TRAVELING NATIONAL AIGA SHOW. THIS ANNOUNCEMENT WAS ACTUALLY PRINTED OVER THE ORIGINAL AIGA POSTER, SO THAT THE DESIGN WOULD BE SEEN AS A TEXTURE BENEATH THE NEW MESSAGE. ● **294** PLAKAT FÜR EINE WANDERAUSSTELLUNG DER AIGA MIAMI. DIE ANKÜNDIGUNG WURDE ÜBER DAS URSPRÜNGLICHE AIGA-PLAKAT GEDRUCKT, DAS DIE HINTERGRUNDSTRUKTUR LIEFERT. ▲ **294** AFFICHE POUR L'EXPOSITION ITINÉRANTE DU CONCOURS DE L'AIGA À MIAMI. L'ANNONCE A ÉTÉ IMPRIMÉE SUR L'AFFICHE ORIGINALE DE L'AIGA, CELLE-CI FOURNISSANT AINSI LA STRUCTURE DU FOND. (USA)

■ **295** ART DIRECTOR: KENICHI SAMURA DESIGNER: KENICHI SAMURA PHOTOGRAPHER: YURIKO TAKAGI AGENCY: NUMBER ONE DESIGN OFFICE INC. CLIENT: ZEIT-FOTO SALON ■ **295** ANNOUNCEMENT OF A PHOTO EXHIBITION IN TOKYO. ● **295** ANKÜNDIGUNG EINER AUSSTELLUNG MIT PHOTOGRAPHIEN VON YURIKO TAKAGI. ▲ **295** AFFICHE ANNONÇANT UNE EXPOSITION DE PHOTOS À TOKYO. (JPN)

■ **296** ART DIRECTOR/DESIGNER: ROBERT SCHALLENBERG COPYWRITER: EBERHARD HÜTTER AGENCY: HÜTTER UND SCHALLENBERG CLIENT: PESCH WOHNEN ■ **296** "JAPANESE DESIGN IN HARMONY WITH EUROPEAN LIVING CULTURE." POSTER ANNOUNCING A SPECIAL EXHIBITION IN A FURNITURE STORE. ● **296** GROSSFLÄCHENPLAKAT FÜR EINE SONDERAUSSTELLUNG IM EINRICHTUNGS-HAUS PESCH. ▲ **296** AFFICHE GÉANTE POUR UNE EXPOSITION SPÉCIALE INTITULÉE «ACCENTS EXTREME-ORIENTAUX.» (GER)

■ **297** ART DIRECTOR/DESIGNER: FERNANDO MEDINA ILLUSTRATOR: FERNANDO MEDINA COPYWRITER: FERNANDO MEDINA AGENCY: TRIOM DESIGN CLIENT: TRAMA VISUAL ■ **297** POSTER ANNOUNCING EXHIBITIONS AND LECTURES BY THE GRAPHIC DESIGNER FERNANDO MEDINA IN VARIOUS MEXICAN CITIES. ● **297** DIESES PLAKAT INFORMIERT ÜBER DIE AUSSTELLUNGEN UND VORTRÄGE DES GRAPHIK-DESIGNERS FERNANDO MEDINA IN MEXIKANISCHEN STÄDTEN. ▲ **297** CETTE AFFICHE INFORME DES EXPOSITIONS ET DES CONFÉRENCES DU DESIGNER GRAPHIQUE FERNANDO MEDINA DANS DES VILLES MEXICAINES. (MEX)

日本のセンスと欧風リビング

Japanisches Design in harmonischer Verbindung

〝東洋のタッチ〟一大セール

mit europäischer Wohnkultur.

特別展 1988年3月迄

Große Sonderausstellung „Fernöstliche Akzente" bis März '88.

斬新なインテリアハウスペッシュ

Einmalig im Einrichtungshaus Pesch/Köln.

pesch
wohnen

Kaiser-Wilhelm-Ring 12–34 · 5000 Köln 1 · Tel. 02 21/16 13-0
Pesch-Parkanlage · Einfahrt Von-Werth-Straße

H&S Köln

296

FERNANDO MEDINA
EN MÉXICO

CARTEL CONMEMORATIVO DEL CURSO "DISEÑO DE CARTEL" IMPARTIDO POR FERNANDO MEDINA · C.C. OLLIN YOLIZTLI · SOCICULTUR · DDF · 12-17 MARZO 1990 · PRIMERA BIENAL INTERNACIONAL DEL CARTEL EN MÉXICO

297

298

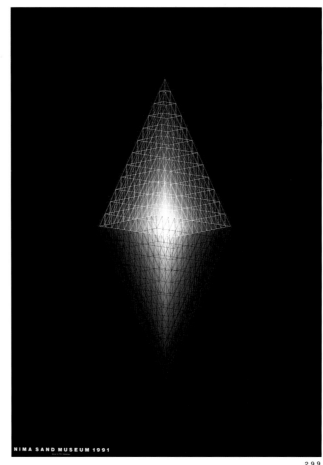

299

300

301

302

■ 298, 299 ART DIRECTOR: SHIN MATSUNAGA DESIGNER: SHIN MATSUNAGA AGENCY: I&S CORPORATION 298 CLIENTS: SEZON
MUSEUM OF ART 298 NIMA SAND MUSEUM 299 ■ 298, 299 POSTERS FOR AN EXHIBITION OF CONTEMPORARY JAPANESE ART AT
THE SEZON MUSEUM AND FOR THE NIMA SAND MUSEUM. ● 298, 299 PLAKATE FÜR EINE AUSSTELLUNG ZEITGENÖSSISCHER
JAPANISCHER KUNST IM SEZOM MUSEUM IN TOKIO UND ALS WERBUNG FÜR DAS NIMA SAND MUSEUM IN SHIMANE. ▲ 298, 299
AFFICHES POUR UNE EXPOSITION D'ART JAPONAIS CONTEMPORAIN AU SEZOM MUSEUM ET POUR LE NIMA SAND MUSEUM. (JPN)

■ 300 DESIGNER: CLAUDE KUHN CLIENT: NATURHISTORISCHES MUSEUM DER BURGERGEMEINDE BERN ■ 300 POSTER PROMOTION
FOR THE MUSEUM OF NATURAL HISTORY IN BERNE, SWITZERLAND. ● 300 PLAKATWERBUNG FÜR DAS NATURHISTORISCHE MU-
SEUM DER BURGERGEMEINDE BERN. ▲ 300 AFFICHE PUBLICITAIRE POUR LE MUSÉE D'HISTOIRE NATURELLE DE BERNE. (SWI)

■ 301, 302 ART DIRECTOR: SUSAN FASICK-JONES DESIGNER: SUSAN FASICK-JONES ILLUSTRATOR: TIM EASTLAND AGENCY: PETER
GOOD GRAPHIC DESIGN CLIENT: MYSTIC SEAPORT MUSEUM ■ 301, 302 FROM A SERIES OF POSTERS SPOTLIGHTING THE
COLLECTION OF THE MYSTIC SEAPORT MUSEUM. SHOWN ARE A COURTHOUSE FIGURE AND A SHIP'S CHANDLERY FIGURE. ●
301, 302 AUS EINER REIHE VON PLAKATEN, AUF DENEN EINIGE DER ZAHLREICHEN ARTEFAKTE DES MYSTIC-SEAPORT-MUSEUMS
VORGESTELLT WERDEN: DIE FIGUREN STAMMEN AUS EINEM GERICHTSGEBÄUDE UND AUS DEN BESTÄNDEN EINES SCHIFFSAUS-
RÜSTERS. ▲ 301, 302 D'UNE SÉRIE D'AFFICHES SUR LESQUELLES SONT PRÉSENTÉS QUELQUES-UNS DES NOMBREUX OBJETS
DU MYSTIC SEAPORT MUSEUM: LES FIGURES PROVIENNENT D'UN PALAIS DE JUSTICE ET DES STOCKS D'UN ARMATEUR. (USA)

303

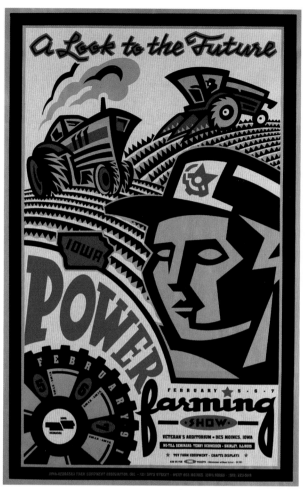

304

■ 303 ART DIRECTOR: BERNARD BAISSAIT DESIGNER: FREDERIC BORTOLOTTI AGENCY: COMPAGNIE BERNARD BAISSAIT CLIENT:
FONDATION ÉLECTRICITÉ DE FRANCE ■ 303 POSTER FOR AN EXHIBITION ON THE EVOLUTION OF ARCHITECTURE LINKED TO
ELECTRICITY. ● 303 AUSSTELLUNG ÜBER DIE ENTWICKLUNG DER ARCHITEKTUR IM ZUSAMMENHANG MIT DER ELEKTRIZITÄT. ▲
303 SÉRIGRAPHIE POUR UNE EXPOSITION QUI PRÉSENTAIT L'ÉVOLUTION DE L'ARCHITECTURE LIÉE À L'ÉLECTRICITÉ. (FRA)

■ 304 ART DIRECTOR/DESIGNER/ILLUSTRATOR: JOHN SAYLES AGENCY: SAYLES GRAPHIC DESIGN CLIENT: IOWA-NEBRASKA FARM
EQUIPMENT ASSOC. ■ 304 THIS POSTER FOR AN ANNUAL FARM-EQUIPMENT EXHIBITION WAS SILK-SCREENED ON RECYCLED PA-
PER TO ACHIEVE A RUSTIC LOOK. ● 304 PLAKAT FÜR EINE LANDWIRTSCHAFTSMASCHINEN-AUSSTELLUNG. SIEBDRUCK AUF
PACKPAPIER. ▲ 304 AFFICHE POUR UNE EXPOSITION DE MACHINES AGRICOLES EN SÉRIGRAPHIE SUR PAPIER KRAFT. (USA)

CELEBRATION FOR

THE NATIVE AMERICAN
AUGUST 23-25, 1991
ASPEN, COLORADO
BENEFITING THE
SMITHSONIAN NATIONAL
MUSEUM OF THE
AMERICAN INDIAN

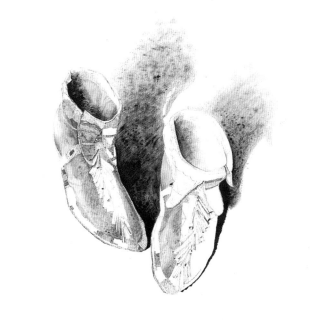

WALK WITH ME

305

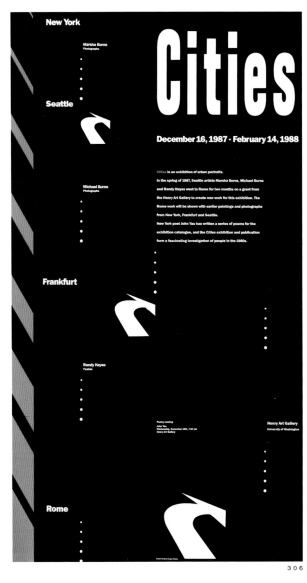

306

■ 305 Art Director: JACK SUMMERFORD Designer: JACK SUMMERFORD Illustrator: JACK UNRUH Client: SMITHSONIAN INSTITUTION ■ 305 THIS POSTER WAS DESIGNED TO PROMOTE AND RAISE MONEY FOR THE NEW SMITHSONIAN NATIONAL MUSEUM OF THE AMERICAN INDIAN. ● 305 FUND-RAISING-PLAKAT FÜR DAS NEUE SMITHSONIAN NATIONAL MUSEUM OF THE AMERICAN INDIAN. ▲ 305 AFFICHE POUR LE NOUVEAU SMITHSONIAN NATIONAL MUSEUM OF THE AMERICAN INDIAN. (USA)

■ 306 Art Director: DOUGLAS WADDEN Designer: DOUGLAS WADDEN Client: HENRY ART GALLERY ■ 306 THE DESIGNER OF THIS POSTER WAS INSTRUCTED TO SHOW NO IMAGES. IT ANNOUNCES AN EXHIBITION OF STRAIGHTFORWARD URBAN PHOTO-GRAPHS AND PASTELS FROM DIFFERENT CITIES. ● 306 BEI DIESEM PLAKAT MUSSTE DER GESTALTER OHNE BILDER AUSKOM-MEN. ANGEKÜNDIGT WIRD EINE AUSSTELLUNG VON PHOTOGRAPHIEN UND PASTELLZEICHNUNGEN, DIE IN VERSCHIEDENEN STÄD-TEN ENTSTANDEN SIND. ▲ 306 LE DESIGNER AVAIT POUR MANDAT DE CRÉER UNE AFFICHE SANS AVOIR RECOURS À DES IMAGES. IL S'AGISSAIT D'ANNONCER UNE EXPOSITION DE PHOTOS ET DE PASTELS RÉALISÉS DANS DES VILLES DIFFÉRENTES. (USA)

307

308

309

310

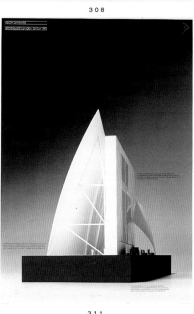

311

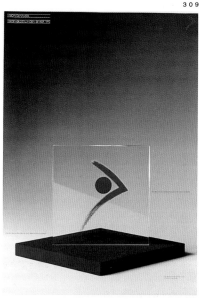

312

■ 307-312 ART DIRECTOR/DESIGNER: PER ARNOLDI PHOTOGRAPHER: FINN ROSTED COPYWRITER: PER ARNOLDI AGENCY: PER ARNOLDI
CLIENT: DANISH MINISTRY OF INDUSTRY ■ 307-312 POSTERS FROM AN IMAGE CAMPAIGN FOR DENMARK'S CONTRIBUTION TO
EXPO 92 IN SEVILLE, SPAIN. ● 307-312 PLAKATE AUS EINER IMAGEKAMPAGNE FÜR DEN DÄNISCHEN PAVILLON AN DER EXPO 92
IN SEVILLA. ▲ 307-312 AFFICHES D'UNE CAMPAGNE DE PRESTIGE POUR LE PAVILLON DANOIS DE L'EXPO 92 DE SÉVILLE. (SPA)

■ 313 ART DIRECTOR/DESIGNER/ILLUSTRATOR/COPYWRITER/STYLIST: ANDREAS KARL AGENCY: KIENOW + PARTNER CLIENT: MINISTERIUM
FÜR BILDUNG + KULTUR RHEINLAND-PFALZ ■ 313 OFFICIAL POSTER FOR THE "CULTURAL SUMMER IN RHEINLAND-PFALZ,"
REFERRING TO THE CULTURAL VARIETY IN THIS PART OF GERMANY. ● 313 OFFIZIELLES VERANSTALTUNGSPLAKAT FÜR DEN
«KULTURSOMMER RHEINLAND-PFALZ 1992,» MIT DEM AUF DIE KULTURELLE VIELFALT IN DIESEM BUNDESLAND AUFMERKSAM
GEMACHT WIRD. ▲ 313 AFFICHE OFFICIELLE DE MANIFESTATIONS CULTURELLES ORGANISÉES EN ÉTÉ DANS LE LAND DU
RHEINLAND-PFALZ: L'ACCENT EST MIS SUR LA DIVERSITÉ DE LA CULTURE QU'OFFRE CETTE RÉGION D'ALLEMAGNE. (GER)

KULTURSOMMER '92

SOMMERTHEATER
KLOSTERRUINE LIMBURG
Bad Dürkheim

INTERNATIONALES
JAZZFESTIVAL
Kammgarn Kaiserslautern

ZAUBERFLÖTE PUR
Chawwerusch-Theater unterwegs

BALLETT DER WELT
Theater im Pfalzbau. Ludwigshafen

SCHLOSSTAGE
PANTOMIME-FESTIVAL
Idar-Oberstein

MOSELFESTWOCHEN

'OPEN WALD'
Natur und Kultur

TAL-TOTAL
Der Erlebnistag
im Tal der Loreley

VILLA MUSICA
in Burgen und Schlössern

THEATERTAGE
in der Landskrone Oppenheim

DOROTHY PARKER
Szenen und Chansons.
Kammerspiele Mainz

KULTURBEUTEL

LANDESJUGEND-
BLASORCHESTER

INTERNATIONALES
THEATERFESTIVAL HAMBACH

AHNUNG DER STILLE
Tanztheater Regenbogen unterwegs

STAATSTHEATER MAINZ
„CONTACT '92"
Tage des polnischen Theaters

FEMME CULTURELLE
Mainz

'BURGENZAUBER'
Theater für Kinder aus Europa

EURO-T(R)ANS '92
Trans-Europe Halles- und
Internationales Tanztheaterfestival.
Kulturfabrik Koblenz

'VER-RÜCKTE GRENZEN'
Rocktheater-Revue in und um Trier

RHEINISCHE PHILHARMONIE

FIDELIO OPEN-AIR
EHRENBREITSTEIN
Theater der Stadt Koblenz

KINDER- UND
JUGENDTHEATERFESTIVAL
Speyer

INTERNATIONALES
AMATEUR BIG BAND-FESTIVAL
Koblenz

LANDESJUGENDCHOR

KUZ-SOMMER
Mainz

LAHNECK LIVE
Lahnstein

INTERNATIONALE
ORGELFESTWOCHEN

KULTUR FÜR KURZE
Montabaur

JUGENDNACHWUCHSFESTIVAL
Rock & Pop am Deutschen Eck.
Koblenz

OPEN OHR FESTIVAL
Mainz

GAUKLERFESTIVAL
Koblenz

JAZZ UND KUNST
IN WEINGÜTERN

STAATSPHILHARMONIE
RHEINLAND-PFALZ

JACQUES OFFENBACH-
FESTIVAL Bad Ems

MUSIK MIT
PFEFFERMINZGESCHMACK
Schloßtreff Deidesheim

DEUTSCHES MOZARTFEST
ZWEIBRÜCKEN
Oper im Zirkus

FEST DER NATIONEN
Trier

JAZZ-ORCHESTER
RHEINLAND-PFALZ

FESTIVAL DER FANTASIE
Jockgrim

BURGFESTSPIELE MAYEN

Eine Initiative des Landes Rheinland-Pfalz

Sie erhalten:
Infos und Kultursommer-Programmheft
bei allen Veranstaltern, beim Büro Kultursommer
im Ministerium für Bildung und Kultur.
Postfach 3220, 6500 Mainz und unter 01 30/82 55 82
Aktuelle Programmhinweise: Im Südwesttext auf Videotext-Tafel 505

RHEINLAND-PFALZ

313

314

315

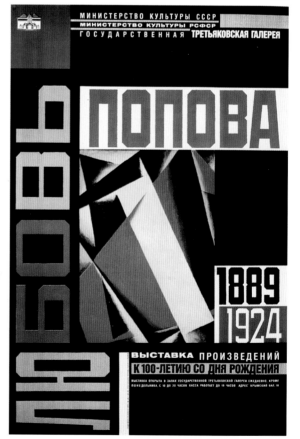

316

317

318

■ **314** ART DIRECTOR/DESIGNER: ENRICO SEMPI PHOTOGRAPHER: MARIO FINOTTI AGENCY: TANGRAM STRATEGIC DESIGN CLIENT: COMUNE DI NOVARA ■ **314** POSTER ANNOUNCING AN EXHIBITION OF CZECH AND SLOVAKIAN ART. ● **314** FÜR EINE AUSSTELLUNG TSCHECHISCHER UND SLOVAKISCHER KUNST IN ITALIEN. ▲ **314** POUR UNE EXPOSITION D'ART TCHEQUE ET SLOVAQUE. (ITA)

■ **315** DESIGNER: RAPHIE ETGAR CLIENT: ARTS & CRAFTS FAIR ■ **315** LARGE-FORMAT POSTER FOR A JERUSALEM STREET FESTIVAL. ● **315** PLAKAT FÜR EIN FESTIVAL IN JERUSALEM. ▲ **315** AFFICHE POUR UN FESTIVAL DE RUES À JÉRUSALEM. (ISR)

■ **316** ART DIRECTOR: LISA NAFTOLIN DESIGNERS: LISA NAFTOLIN, HARRIS BHANDARI PHOTOGRAPHER: CARLO CATENAZZI AGENCY/CLIENT: ART GALLERY OF ONTARIO ■ **316** INSTEAD OF REFERRING TO THE NATIONALITIES OF THE ANNOUNCED ARTISTS, THIS POSTER STRESSES WHERE THEY WERE GOING. ● **316** STATT DIE NATIONALITÄT DER ANGEKÜNDIGTEN KÜNSTLER HERAUSZUSTELLEN, WIRD BEI DIESEM PLAKAT DER AUSSTELLUNGSORT IN DEN MITTELPUNKT GERÜCKT. ▲ **316** AU LIEU DE METTRE L'ACCENT SUR LA NATIONALITÉ DES ARTISTES PRÉSENTÉS, L'AFFICHE ÉVOQUE LE LIEU DE L'EXPOSITION. (CAN)

■ **317** ART DIRECTOR/DESIGNER: PETER KRASICHKOV ILLUSTRATOR: LUBOV POPOVA COPYWRITER: NATALY KURENKOVA AGENCY: DROMGRAPHICA CLIENT: TRETYAKOV GALLERY ■ **317** POSTER FOR AN EXHIBITION IN MOSCOW OF LUBOV POPOVA, A RUSSIAN AVANT-GARDE ARTIST. ● **317** PLAKATANKÜNDIGUNG EINER AUSSTELLUNG DES RUSSISCHEN AVANTGARDE-KÜNSTLERS LUBOV POPOVA IN MOSKAU. ▲ **317** AFFICHE ANNONÇANT UNE EXPOSITION DE L'ARTISTE D'AVANT-GARDE RUSSE LUBOV POPOVA. (RUS)

■ **318** ART DIRECTORS: SAVAS CEKIC, SAHIN AYMERGEN DESIGNERS: SAVAS CEKIC, SAHIN AYMERGEN AGENCY: VALÖR DESIGN PROMOTION AGENCY CLIENT: TÖBANK ART GALLERY ■ **318** FOR AN ART EXHIBITION IN A TURKISH GALLERY. ● **318** FÜR EINE KUNSTAUSSTELLUNG IN EINER TÜRKISCHEN GALERIE. ▲ **318** POUR UNE EXPOSITION D'ART DANS UNE GALERIE TURQUE. (TUR)

BYRON TEMPLE

319

320

GIL STENGEL

■ **319, 320** ART DIRECTOR/DESIGNER: JULIUS FRIEDMAN PHOTOGRAPHER: GEOFFREY CARR AGENCY: IMAGES CLIENTS: BYRON TEMPLE
319 GIL STENGEL 320 ■ **319, 320** POSTERS ANNOUNCING EXHIBITIONS OF BYRON TEMPLE AND GIL STENGEL, FOCUSING ON THE
CERAMIC WORK OF THE TWO ARTISTS. ● **319, 320** PLAKATE FÜR AUSSTELLUNGEN VON BYRON TEMPLE UND GIL STENGEL. DAS
HAUPTGEWICHT LIEGT AUF DER PRÄSENTATION IHRER KERAMISCHEN ARBEITEN. ▲ **319, 320** AFFICHES POUR DES EXPOSITIONS
DE BYRON TEMPLE ET GIL STENGEL. L'ACCENT EST MIS SUR LA PRÉSENTATION DE LEURS CRÉATIONS EN CÉRAMIQUE. (USA)

SOCIAL

GESELLSCHAFT

SOCIAL

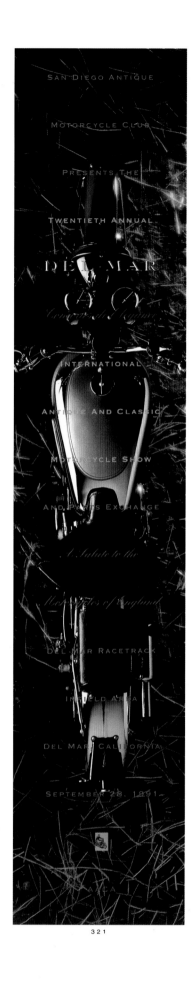

321

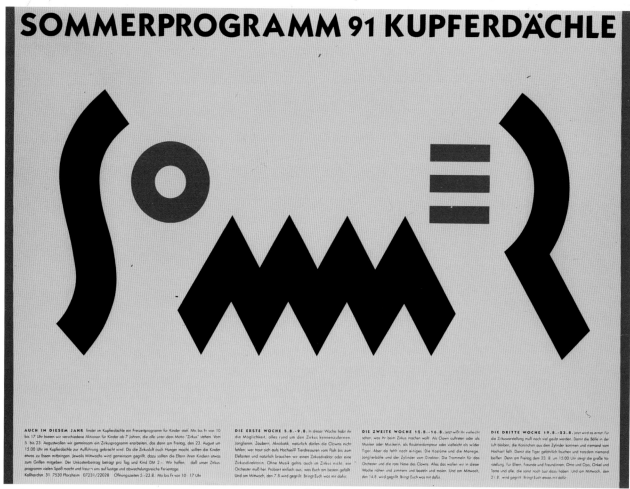

SOMMERPROGRAMM 91 KUPFERDÄCHLE

AUCH IN DIESEM JAHR findet im Kupferdächle ein Freizeitprogramm für Kinder statt. Mo bis Fr von 10 bis 17 Uhr bieten wir verschiedene Aktionen für Kinder ab 7 Jahren, die alle unter dem Motto "Zirkus" stehen. Vom 5. bis 23. Augustwollen wir gemeinsam ein Zirkusprogramm erarbeiten, das dann am Freitag, dem 23. August um 15.00 Uhr im Kupferdächle zur Aufführung gebracht wird. Da die Zirkusluft auch Hunger macht, sollten die Kinder etwas zu Essen mitbringen. Jeweils Mittwochs wird gemeinsam gegrillt, dazu sollten die Eltern ihren Kindern etwas zum Grillen mitgeben. Der Unkostenbeitrag beträgt pro Tag und Kind DM 2.– Wir hoffen, daß unser Zirkusprogramm vielen Spaß macht und Insur'n uns auf lustige und abwechslungsreiche Ferientage. Kollhardtstr. 31. 7530 Pforzheim 07231/22028 Öffnungszeiten 5.–23.8. Mo bis Fr von 10.–17 Uhr

DIE ERSTE WOCHE 5.8.–9.8. In dieser Woche habt ihr die Möglichkeit, alles rund um den Zirkus kennenzulernen. Jonglieren, Zaubern, Akrobatik, natürlich dürfen die Clowns nicht fehlen; wer traut sich aufs Hochseil? Tierdressuren vom Floh bis zum Elefanten und natürlich brauchen wir einen Zirkusdirektor oder eine Zirkusdirektorin. Ohne Musik gehts auch im Zirkus nicht; ein Orchester muß her. Probiert einfach aus, was Euch am besten gefällt. Und am Mittwoch, den 7.8. wird gegrillt. Bringt Euch was mit dafür.

DIE ZWEITE WOCHE 12.8.–16.8. Jetzt wißt ihr vielleicht schon, was ihr beim Zirkus machen wollt. Als Clown auftreten oder als Musiker oder Musikerin, als Raubtierdompteur oder vielleicht als wilder Tiger. Aber da fehlt noch einiges. Die Kostüme und die Manege. Jonglierbälle und der Zylinder vom Direktor. Die Trommeln für das Orchester und die rote Nase des Clowns. Alles das wollen wir in dieser Woche nähen und zimmern und basteln und malen. Und am Mittwoch, den 14.8. wird gegrillt. Bringt Euch was mit dafür.

DIE DRITTE WOCHE 19.8.–23.8. Jetzt wird es ernst. Für die Zirkusvorstellung muß noch viel geübt werden. Damit die Bälle in der Luft bleiben, die Kaninchen aus dem Zylinder kommen und niemand vom Hochseil fällt. Damit die Tiger gefährlich fauchen und trotzdem niemand beißen. Denn am Freitag dem 23.8. um 15.00 Uhr steigt die große Vorstellung. Für Eltern, Freunde und Freundinnen, Oma und Opa, Onkel und Tante und alle, die sonst noch Lust dazu haben. Und am Mittwoch, den 21.8. wird gegrillt. Bringt Euch etwas mit dafür.

323

■ (PREVIOUS SPREAD) 321 ART DIRECTOR: JOSE SERRANO DESIGNERS: JOSE SERRANO, SCOTT MIRES PHOTOGRAPHER: CHRIS WIMPEY AGENCY: MIRES DESIGN, INC. CLIENT: SAN DIEGO ANTIQUE MOTORCYCLE CLUB ■ 321 POSTER FOR A CLASSIC MOTOR-CYCLE CONCOURSE HELD AT A FAMOUS HORSE-RACING TRACK IN DEL MAR, CALIFORNIA. ● (VORANGEHENDE DOPPELSEITE) 321 PLAKAT FÜR DIE ANKÜNDIGUNG EINES KLASSISCHEN MOTORRADRENNENS AUF EINER BERÜHMTEN PFERDERENNBAHN. ▲ (DOUBLE PAGE PRÉCÉDENTE) 321 AFFICHE POUR UNE COURSE DE MOTOS SE DÉROULANT SUR UN CÉLÈBRE HIPPODROME. (USA)

■ (PREVIOUS SPREAD) 322 ART DIRECTOR: OSCAR MARINE BRANDI DESIGNER: OSCAR MARINE BRANDI AGENCY: OMB DISEÑO GRAFICO CLIENT: SWATCH ■ 322 POSTER ANNOUNCING AN INTERNATIONAL SNOWBOARD CHAMPIONSHIP IN SOUTHERN SPAIN. THE SPONSOR, THE SWATCH COMPANY, WANTED AN UNMISTAKABLE SPANISH STYLE. ● (VORANGEHENDE DOPPELSEITE) 322 ANKÜNDIGUNG EINES SCHNEEBRETT-WETTBEWERBS IN SÜDSPANIEN. DIE SONNENBRILLE DES TOREROS IST EIN HINWEIS AUF DAS PRODUKT, DAS DER SPONSOR SWATCH AUF DEM SPANISCHEN MARKT EINFÜHREN WILL. ▲ (DOUBLE PAGE PRÉCÉDENTE) 322 ANNONCE D'UN CHAMPIONNAT INTERNATIONAL DE SNOWBOARD AU SUD DE L'ESPAGNE. LE TORERO PORTE DES LUNETTES DE SOLEIL QUE LE SPONSOR DE CETTE MANIFESTATION, LA SWATCH, SOUHAITE LANCER SUR LE MARCHÉ ESPAGNOL. (SPA)

■ (THIS SPREAD) 323 ART DIRECTOR/DESIGNER: SASCHA LOBE AGENCY: ATELIER PETER KRAUS CLIENT: JUGENDKULTURTREFF KUP-FERDÄCHLE ■ 323 POSTER FOR A SUMMER VACATION PROGRAM FOR YOUNG PEOPLE. ● (DIESE DOPPELSEITE) 323 PLAKAT FÜR EIN SOMMERFERIENPROGRAMM. ▲ (CETTE DOUBLE PAGE) 323 AFFICHE ANNONÇANT UN PROGRAMME DES VACANCES D'ÉTÉ. (GER)

■ (THIS SPREAD) 324, 325 ART DIRECTOR/DESIGNER: JAHNS + WALLAU CLIENT: STADT DÜSSELDORF ■ 324, 325 "FINALLY MAD AGAIN." POSTERS WITH AND WITHOUT IMPRINT, PROMOTING THE THREE DAYS OF THE CARNIVAL IN DÜSSELDORF. ● (DIESE DOPPELSEITE) 324, 325 KARNEVALSPLAKAT OHNE UND MIT EINDRUCK. ▲ (CETTE DOUBLE PAGE) 324, 325 AFFICHE DU CARNAVAL 1992 AVEC ET SANS LE TEXTE IMPRIMÉ ET L'ACCROCHE «ON VA ENFIN POUVOIR ENCORE FAIRE LES FOUS.» (GER)

Endlich widder jeck

29.2. - 2.3.1992
Die 3 tollen Tage · The 3 mad days · Les 3 jours fofâtres · De 3 dollen dagen · Los 3 días locos · I 3 giorni matti · 狂喜の 3 日間 仮装行列

2.3.1992 · Rosenmontagszug · Carnival Parade · La Cavalcade du Lundi Gras · Carnevalsoptocht · El desfile del Carneval · La parata del Carnevale · バラの月曜日

Düsseldorfer Carneval

Design: Mario Jahns • Rüdi Wißler

326

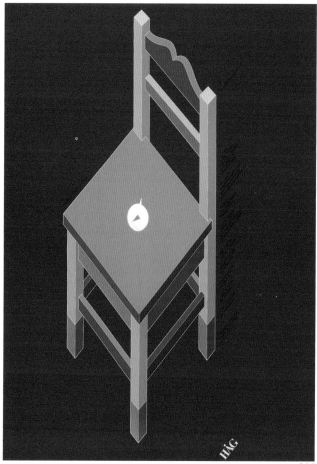

327

■ **326** ART DIRECTOR/DESIGNER/ILLUSTRATOR: MIKE WHEATON PHOTOGRAPHER: DICK BAKER COPYWRITER: TOM JORDAN AGENCY: HOFFMAN YORK & COMPTON CLIENT: INDIAN SUMMER FESTIVALS ■ **326** THIS POSTER HAD TO COMMUNICATE THE FACT THAT THE EVENT WAS AN INDIAN CULTURE FESTIVAL THAT TAKES PLACE IN THE FALL. ● **326** FÜR EIN AUSSCHLIESSLICH INDIANISCHES KULTURFESTIVAL, DAS IM HERBST STATTFINDET. ▲ **326** AFFICHE POUR UN FESTIVAL DÉDIÉ À LA CULTURE INDIENNE. (GER)

■ **327** ART DIRECTOR/DESIGNER: BRUNO OLDANI PHOTOGRAPHER: BRUNO OLDANI CLIENT: HAG A/S ■ **327** DIRECT-MAIL POSTER SERVING AS AN ANNOUNCEMENT OF AND INVITATION TO A VERNISSAGE ORGANIZED BY HAG FURNITURE. ● **327** EINLADUNG ZU EINER VERNISSAGE DES MÖBELHERSTELLERS HAG. ▲ **327** INVITATION À UN VERNISSAGE DU FABRICANT DE MEUBLES HAG. (NOR)

■ **328** ART DIRECTOR/DESIGNER/ILLUSTRATOR/COPYWRITER: JOHN SAYLES AGENCY: SAYLES GRAPHIC DESIGN CLIENT: ADC OF CINCINNATI ■ **328** THIS POSTER ANNOUNCES A SPEAKING ENGAGEMENT BY THE DESIGNER JOHN SAYLES AT THE ART DIRECTORS CLUB OF CINCINNATI. ● **328** ANKÜNDIGUNG EINES VORTRAGES DES GRAPHIK-DESIGNERS JOHN SAYLES IM ADC VON CINCINNATI. ▲ **328** POUR UNE CONFÉRENCE DU DESIGNER GRAPHIQUE JOHN SAYLES AU ART DIRECTORS CLUB DE CINCINNATI. (USA)

■ **329** ART DIRECTOR: JACK ANDERSON DESIGNERS: JACK ANDERSON, DAVID BATES AGENCY: HORNALL ANDERSON DESIGN WORKS ■ **329** AN ANNOUNCEMENT FOR THE WESTERN WASHINGTON ALL-BRITISH FIELD MEET, AN EXHIBITION OF BRITISH CARS. ● **329** FÜR EIN VETERANENTREFFEN. ▲ **329** ANNONCE D'UNE RENCONTRE DE VÉTÉRANS AMATEURS DE VIEILLES VOITURES. (USA)

328

329

330

331

■ **330** ART DIRECTORS: SCOTT MEDNICK, LOID DER DESIGNER/ILLUSTRATOR: LOID DER AGENCY: THE MEDNICK GROUP CLIENT: EDUCATION FIRST ■ **330** THIS POSTER IS MEANT TO PERSUADE STUDENTS TO ATTEND CLASSES. THE DESIGN AND COPY HAD TO APPEAL TO YOUNG PEOPLE. ● **330** MIT DIESEM PLAKAT WERDEN STUDENTEN AUFGEFORDERT, DIE VORLESUNGEN ZU BESUCHEN. GESTALTUNG UND TEXT SIND AUF JUNGE MENSCHEN AUSGERICHTET. ▲ **330** CETTE AFFICHE DOIT INCITER LES ÉTUDIANTS À FRÉQUENTER LES COURS. LE DESIGN ET LE TEXTE DEVAIENT SPÉCIALEMENT S'ADRESSER AUX JEUNES. (USA)

■ **331** ART DIRECTOR: STEVE LISKA DESIGNERS: KIM NYBERG, STEVE LISKA AGENCY: LISKA AND ASSOCIATES CLIENT: AIGA NEW YORK ■ **331** POSTER ANNOUNCING THE AIGA NATIONAL CONFERENCE IN CHICAGO. SHOWN IS A PORTRAIT OF CHICAGO'S FORMER MAYOR, RICHARD J. DALEY. ● **331** ANKÜNDIGUNG DER NATIONALEN KONFERENZ DER AIGA IN CHICAGO MIT EINEM PORTRÄT DES VERSTORBENEN BÜRGERMEISTERS VON CHICAGO, RICHARD J. DALEY. ▲ **331** ANNONCE DE LA CONFÉRENCE NATIONALE DE L'AIGA, ORNÉE DU PORTRAIT DU DERNIER MAIRE DE CHICAGO, AUJOURD'HUI DÉCÉDÉ, RICHARD J. DALEY. (USA)

■ **332** ART DIRECTOR: JENNIFER MORLA DESIGNER: JENNIFER MORLA ILLUSTRATOR: JENNIFER MORLA AGENCY: MORLA DESIGN CLIENT: STANFORD ALUMNI ASSOCIATION ■ **332** POSTER FOR THE STANFORD CONFERENCE ON DESIGN. THE THEME IS THE BRINGING TOGETHER OF MEN AND WOMEN FROM THE ARCHITECTURAL AND DESIGN PROFESSIONS. ● **332** ANKÜNDIGUNG EINER ARCHITEKTUR- UND DESIGN-KONFERENZ IN STANFORD, KALIFORNIEN. DIE VISUELLE BOTSCHAFT BETRIFFT DAS ZUSAMMENKOMMEN VON MÄNNERN UND FRAUEN AUS DIESEN FACHBEREICHEN. ▲ **332** AFFICHE D'UNE CONFÉRENCE SUR LE DESIGN ET L'ARCHITECTURE À STANFORD EN CALIFORNIE QUI RÉUNIT DES HOMMES ET DES FEMMES DE LA PROFESSION. (USA)

■ (FOLLOWING SPREAD) **333** ILLUSTRATOR: DAVID LANCE GOINES CLIENT: CHEZ PANISSE ■ **333** (FOLLOWING SPREAD) POSTER ANNOUNCING A SPECIAL MARKET OF THE SUPPLIERS OF A RESTAURANT. ● (NÄCHSTE DOPPELSEITE) **333** AUF DEM HIER ANGE-KÜNDIGTEN MARKT PRÄSENTIEREN DIE LIEFERANTEN EINES RESTAURANTS IHRE WAREN. ▲ (DOUBLE PAGE SUIVANTE) **333** POUR UNE FOIRE À L'OCCASION DE LAQUELLE LES FOURNISSEURS D'UN RESTAURANT PRÉSENTERONT LEURS PRODUITS. (USA)

■ (FOLLOWING SPREAD) **334** ART DIRECTOR/DESIGNER/ILLUSTRATOR/AGENCY: VANDERBYL DESIGN CLIENT: *EXHIBITOR* MAGAZINE ■ **334** POSTER COMMEMORATING AN EXHIBITION VENDOR SHOW. ● (NÄCHSTE DOPPELSEITE) **334** PLAKAT FÜR EINE AUSSTELLUNG. ▲ (DOUBLE PAGE SUIVANTE) **334** AFFICHE POUR UNE EXPOSITION DE CONSTRUCTEURS DE STANDS D'EXPOSITION. (USA)

333

338

339

■ **338** ART DIRECTOR/DESIGNER/ILLUSTRATOR/COPYWRITER: REX PETEET AGENCY: SIBLEY/PETEET CLIENT: WHITE ROCK MARATHON ■ **338** A POSTER ANNOUNCING A FAMOUS MARATHON COURSE. MERCURY'S CONTEMPLATIVE POSE SUGGESTS THE CONCENTRATION AND DEDICATION REQUIRED TO TRAIN FOR AND RUN A MARATHON. ● **338** FÜR EINE BERÜHMTEN MARATHON. DIE POSE MERKURS ERINNERT AN DIE ERFORDERTE KONZENTRATION UND HINGABE. ▲ **338** ANNONCE D'UN CÉLEBRE MARATHON. LA POSE DE MERCURE SUGGERE LA CONCENTRATION ET L'APPLICATION QUE REQUIERENT L'ENTRAINEMENT ET LA COURSE. (USA)

■ **339** ART DIRECTORS: ROBIN RICKABAUGH, HEIDI RICKABAUGH DESIGNERS: JON OLSEN, ROBIN RICKABAUGH ILLUSTRATOR: JON OLSEN AGENCY: PRINCIPIA GRAPHICA CLIENT: CASCADE RUNOFF ■ **339** THE T-SHIRT, THE MOST IMPORTANT PART OF THE CAMPAIGN FOR THIS RUNNING EVENT, IS FEATURED ON A POSTER. THE IMAGERY IS A COMPOSITE OF DIFFERENT RUNNERS. ● **339** DAS T-SHIRT ALS WICHTIGSTER BESTANDTEIL DER KAMPAGNE FÜR DIESEN LAUFWETTKAMPF LIEFERTE DAS THEMA FÜR DAS PLAKAT. DER AUFDRUCK IST EINE KOMPOSITION DER VERSCHIEDENEN TEILNEHMER. ▲ **339** LE T-SHIRT, L'ÉLÉMENT LE PLUS IMPORTANT DE LA CAMPAGNE DE PUBLICITÉ DE CETTE COURSE À PIED, A FOURNI LE SUJET DE CETTE AFFICHE. (USA)

■ **340** ART DIRECTOR/DESIGNER: JOSEPH PARSLEY AGENCY: NIKE DESIGN ■ **340** POSTER CELEBRATING THE 20TH ANNIVERSARY OF THE PORTLAND MARATHON. ● **340** JUBILÄUMSPLAKAT. ▲ **340** POUR LE 20E ANNIVERSAIRE DU MARATHON DE PORTLAND. (USA)

340

Seventh Annual International Rowing & Paddling Regatta · Mission Bay to San Diego Bay · Peninsula Family YMCA · San Diego, California · April 21, 1991

341

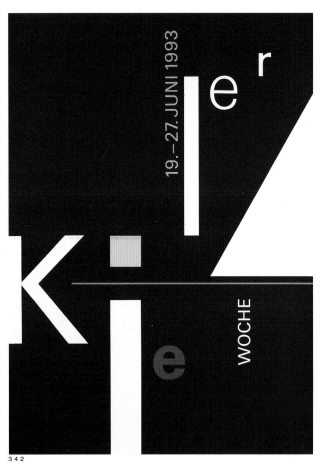

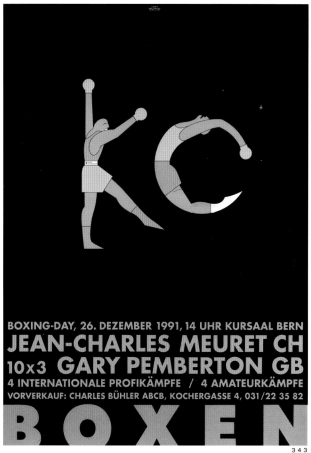

342

343

■ 341 ART DIRECTOR: JOSE SERRANO DESIGNERS: JOSE SERRANO, GERRY BUSTAMANTE ILLUSTRATOR: GERRY BUSTAMANTE AGENCY: MIRES DESIGN CLIENT: PENINSULA FAMILY YMCA ■ 341 POSTER FOR AN ANNUAL ROWING AND PADDLING REGATTA. ● 341 FÜR EINE JÄHRLICHE RUDER- UND PADDEL-REGATTA. ▲ 341 POUR UNE RÉGATE ANNUELLE D'AVIRON ET DE CANOE-KAYAK. (USA)

◣ 342 ART DIRECTION/AGENCY: BAUMANN & BAUMANN DESIGNERS: BARBARA BAUMANN, GERD BAUMANN CLIENT: STADT KIEL ■ 342 A POSTER FOR THE "KIELER WOCHE," AN INTERNATIONAL SAILING EVENT. ● 342 PLAKAT UND IDENTITÄT FÜR DIE KIELER WOCHE 1993. ▲ 342 POUR LA «KIELER WOCHE 1993,» UNE COURSE DE BATEAUX À VOILE ORGANISÉE SUR LA MER BALTIQUE. (GER)

■ 343 DESIGNER: CLAUDE KUHN CLIENT: CHARLY BÜHLER BOXSCHULE ■ 343 A SILK-SCREEN POSTER ANNOUNCING A BOXING DAY. ● 343 SIEBDRUCKPLAKAT FÜR EINE BOXVERANSTALTUNG. ▲ 343 SÉRIGRAPHIE POUR L'ANNONCE D'UN MATCH DE BOXE. (SWI)

344

345

346

347

348

349

350

351

352

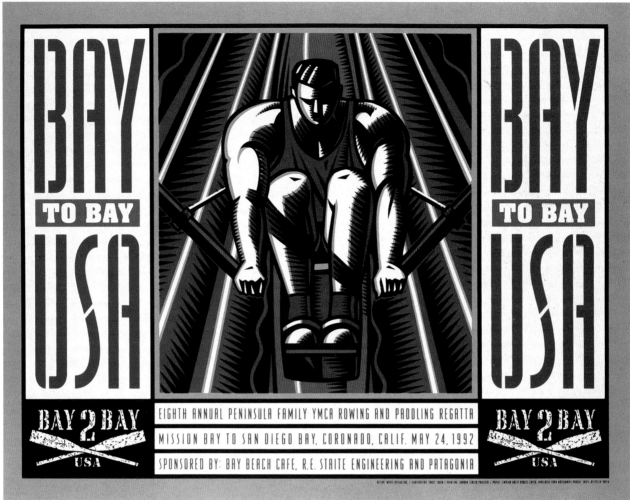

353

■ (THIS SPREAD) 344-352 CREATIVE DIRECTOR: BRENT OPPENHEIMER ART DIRECTOR: MADELEINE BENNETT DESIGNERS: MADELEINE BENNETT, BRENT OPPENHEIMER PHOTOGRAPHERS: ALLSPORT/NASA 344, 345, 347, 349-352 NBA/NASA 346 KISHIMOTO/NASA 348 PHOTO MONTAGE: JONES BLOOM AGENCY: ADDISON CLIENT: COOB'92 S.A. ■ 344-352 EXAMPLES FROM THE OFFICIAL SPORTS POSTER COLLECTION CELEBRATING AND PROMOTING THE RANGE OF SPORTS AT THE 1992 OLYMPIC GAMES IN BARCELONA. ● (DIESE DOPPELSEITE) 344-352 BEISPIELE DER OFFIZIELLEN PLAKATREIHE DER OLYMPIADE IN BARCELONA 1992. ▲ (CETTE DOUBLE PAGE) 344-352 EXEMPLES DE LA SÉRIE D'AFFICHES OFFICIELLES DES JEUX OLYMPIQUES DE BARCELONE 1992. (SPA)

■ (THIS SPREAD) 353 ART DIRECTOR/DESIGNER: JOSE SERRANO ILLUSTRATOR: TRACY SABIN AGENCY: MIRES DESIGN CLIENT: PENINSULA FAMILY YMCA ■ 353 POSTER PRINTED ON KRAFT STOCK, PROMOTING A FAMILY WATER-SPORTS EVENT. ● (DIESE DOPPELSEITE) 353 AUF PACKPAPIER GEDRUCKTES PLAKAT FÜR EINEN WASSERSPORT-ANLASSES FÜR FAMILIEN. ▲ (CETTE DOUBLE PAGE) 353 AFFICHE IMPRIMÉE SUR PAPIER KRAFT POUR L'ANNONCE D'UNE MANIFESTATION DE SPORT NAUTIQUE. (USA)

■ (FOLLOWING SPREAD) 354 ART DIRECTOR/DESIGNER/ILLUSTRATOR/COPYWRITER/STYLIST: BORIS LJUBICIC AGENCY: STUDIO INTER-NATIONAL ■ 354 A COMMENT ON THE WAR IN CROATIA. ● (NÄCHSTE DOPPELSEITE) 354 «DIE KRAWATTE IST AUS KROATIEN.» KOMMENTAR ZUM KRIEG IN KROATIEN. ▲ (DOUBLE PAGE SUIVANTE) 354 UN COMMENTAIRE SUR LA GUERRE EN CROATIE. (CRO)

■ (FOLLOWING SPREAD) 355 ART DIRECTOR: SHIN MATSUNAGA DESIGNER: SHIN MATSUNAGA CLIENT: JAPAN GRAPHIC DESIGNERS ASSOCIATION, INC. ■ 355 "WHAT'S DONE CANNOT BE UNDONE," A PEACE POSTER PUBLISHED BY THE JAPAN GRAPHIC DESIGNERS ASSOCIATION. ● (NÄCHSTE DOPPELSEITE) 355 «WAS GESCHEHEN IST, LÄSST SICH NICHT UNGESCHEHEN MACHEN,» EIN FRIEDENSPLAKAT DER JAPAN GRAPHIC DESIGNERS ASSOCIATION. ▲ (DOUBLE PAGE SUIVANTE) 355 «CE QUI S'EST PASSÉ NE SE LAISSE PAS RÉPARER,» UNE AFFICHE POUR LA PAIX DE L'ASSOCIATION DES DESIGNERS GRAPHIQUES JAPONAIS. (JPN)

THE TIE IS CROATIAN

354

PEACE
What's done cannot be undone.

1991

Designed by Shin Matsunaga
Printed in Japan by Kyodo Printing Co. Ltd

355

ALL THOSE IN FAVOR OF THE
DEATH PENALTY, RAISE YOUR HAND.

As we see it, the United States is in with some pretty unseemly company. Isn't it time we took a firm stand against the death penalty? To find out what you can do, call us. **AMNESTY INTERNATIONAL USA.1-800-55AMNESTY**

356

IN VIRGINIA, CHILD ABUSE IS
ILLEGAL UNLESS YOU USE THIS.

Killing children is still a legal form of punishment in Virginia and has so far claimed a total of 29 young lives. How many more must die before we put a stop to it? Call Amnesty International USA if you want to help. **AMNESTY INTERNATIONAL USA.1-800-55AMNESTY**

357

MAYBE THE DEATH PENALTY SHOULD
HAVE BEEN ELIMINATED A LONG TIME AGO.

Every time the state kills it affects each one of us. Let's stop it. Call Amnesty International USA if you'd like to know how to help. **AMNESTY INTERNATIONAL USA.1-800-55AMNESTY**

358

MOST STATES WOULD HAVE
PUT THESE KIDS IN REFORM SCHOOL.
VIRGINIA PUT THEM TO DEATH.

Clem Oxie and Bill James are just two of the 29 children who have been executed in Virginia. Let's change the laws that allow this to happen. Call Amnesty International USA if you'd like to know how to help. **AMNESTY INTERNATIONAL USA.1-800-55AMNESTY**

359

360

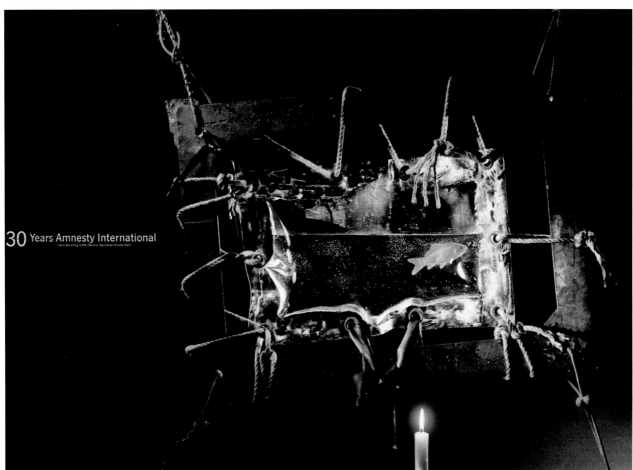

30 Years Amnesty International
Hans Bockting (UNA) Reinier Gerritsen Amsterdam

361

■ **356-359** Aʀᴛ Dɪʀᴇᴄᴛᴏʀ: JERRY TORCHIA Pʜᴏᴛᴏɢʀᴀᴘʜᴇʀ: STOCK 356, 357, 359 Aʀᴛɪsᴛ: ALBRECHT DÜRER 358 Cᴏᴘʏᴡʀɪᴛᴇʀ: TRIPP WESTBROOK Aɢᴇɴᴄʏ: THE MARTIN AGENCY Cʟɪᴇɴᴛ: AMNESTY INTERNATIONAL ■ **356-359** A SERIES OF POSTERS PUBLISHED BY AMNESTY INTERNATIONAL OF VIRGINIA. ● **356-359** PLAKATREIHE HERAUSGEGEBEN VON AMNESTY INTERNATIONAL VIRGINIA: «WER FÜR DIE TODESSTRAFE IST, ERHEBE DIE HAND»; «IN VIRGINIA IST KINDESMISSHANDLUNG ILLEGAL, ES SEI DENN, MAN BENUTZT DIESEN HIER»; «VIELLEICHT HÄTTE DIE TODESSTRAFE SCHON VOR LANGER ZEIT ABGESCHAFFT WERDEN SOLLEN»; «IN DEN MEISTEN STAATEN WÄREN DIESE KINDER IN EINER BESSERUNGSANSTALT GELANDET, IN VIRGINIA LANDETEN SIE IN DER TODESZELLE.» ▲ **356-359** AFFICHES PUBLIÉES PAR AMNESTY INTERNATIONAL EN VIRGINIE: «QUE CEUX QUI SONT POUR LA PEINE DE MORT LEVENT LA MAIN»; «EN VIRGINIE, LA VIOLENCE CONTRE LES ENFANTS EST INTERDITE, SAUF POUR CEUX QUI UTILISENT CELLE-LÀ»; «PEUT-ETRE QUE LA PEINE DE MORT AURAIT DU ETRE ABOLIE VOICI LONGTEMPS»; «DANS LA PLUPART DES ETATS, ON AURAIT MIS CES ENFANTS DANS UNE MAISON DE CORRECTION, EN VIRGINIE, ON LES A CONDAMNÉ À MORT.» (USA)

■ **360** Dᴇsɪɢɴᴇʀ: SIMON SERNEC Cʟɪᴇɴᴛ: ULUPUH ■ **360** AN APPEAL TO STOP THE WAR IN CROATIA. ● **360** «KEIN KRIEG MEHR IN KROATIEN.» EIN APPELL GEGEN DEN KRIEG IN KROATIEN. ▲ **360** UN APPEL À FAIRE CESSER LA GUERRE EN CROATIE. (CRO)

■ **361** Aʀᴛ Dɪʀᴇᴄᴛᴏʀ/Dᴇsɪɢɴᴇʀ: HANS BOCKTING Pʜᴏᴛᴏɢʀᴀᴘʜᴇʀ: REINIER GERRITSEN Aɢᴇɴᴄʏ: UNA Cʟɪᴇɴᴛ: AMNESTY INTERNA-TIONAL ■ **361** ONE OF A SERIES OF POSTERS BY 50 DESIGNERS, COMMEMORATING 30 YEARS OF AMNESTY INTERNATIONAL. ● **361** AUS EINER SERIE VON PLAKATEN VON 50 DESIGNERN ZUM 30JÄHRIGEN BESTEHEN VON AMNESTY INTERNATIONAL. ▲ **361** L'UNE DES AFFICHES D'UNE SÉRIE DE 50 DESIGNERS POUR COMMÉMORER LES 30 ANS D'AMNESTY INTERNATIONAL. (NLD)

362

363

■ **362** ART DIRECTOR/DESIGNER/COPYWRITER: YAROM VARDIMON CLIENT: ICU PUBLICATIONS ■ **362** THE MESSAGE OF THIS SILK-SCREEN POSTER ON RECYCLED PAPER IS THAT EXTREMISM PRODUCES MILITARY CONFRONTATIONS, WHICH INEVITABLY PRODUCE EXPLOSIONS. ● **362** SIEBDRUCKPLAKAT AUF RECYCLING-PAPIER: EXTREME FÜHREN ZU MILITANTEN POSITIONEN, DIE UNWEIGERLICH ZU EXPLOSIONEN FÜHREN. ▲ **362** AFFICHE SÉRIGRAPHIÉE SUR PAPIER RECYCLÉ: LES EXTRÉMISMES ABOUTISSENT SOUVENT À DES POSITIONS QUI, MILITAIREMENT, CONDUISENT INEXORABLEMENT À DES EXPLOSIONS. (ISR)

■ **363** ART DIRECTOR/DESIGNER: JOAO MACHADO ILLUSTRATOR: JOAO MACHADO CLIENT: ETATS UNIS D'EUROPE ■ **363** A VIEW OF A UNITED EUROPE. ● **363** EIN AUSBLICK AUF EIN VEREINIGTES EUROPA. ▲ **363** UNE PERSPECTIVE SUR L'EUROPE UNIE. (POR)

■ **364, 365** ART DIRECTOR/DESIGNER/ILLUSTRATOR: VOJKO TOMINC COPYWRITER: BORIS MAZALIN AGENCY: VOJKO TOMINC ART DESIGN STUDIO CLIENT: OBALNA SINDIKALNA ORGANIZACIJA ■ **364, 365** POSTER URGING A GENERAL STRIKE IN SLOVENIA AND STATING THE REQUESTS OF THE UNIONS. SHOWN ARE VERSIONS IN TWO LANGUAGES. ● **364, 365** AUFRUF ZUM GENERALSTREIK IN SLOWENIEN. DAS PLAKAT INFORMIERT ÜBER DIE FORDERUNGEN DER GEWERKSCHAFTEN. ▲ **364, 365** UN APPEL À LA GREVE GÉNÉRALE EN SLOVÉNIE. L'AFFICHE EXPOSE EN DEUX LANGUES DIFFÉRENTES LES REVENDICATIONS DES SYNDICATS. (SLO)

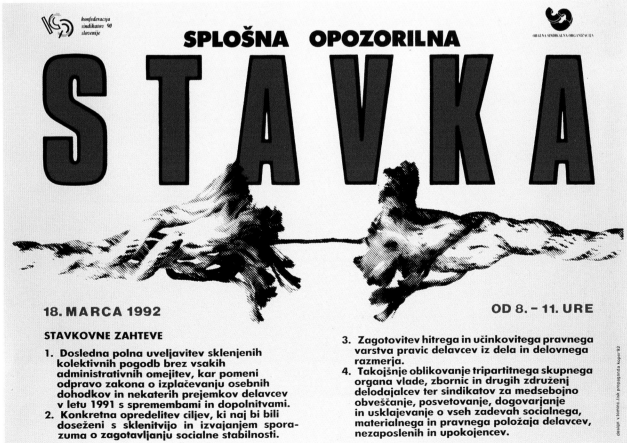

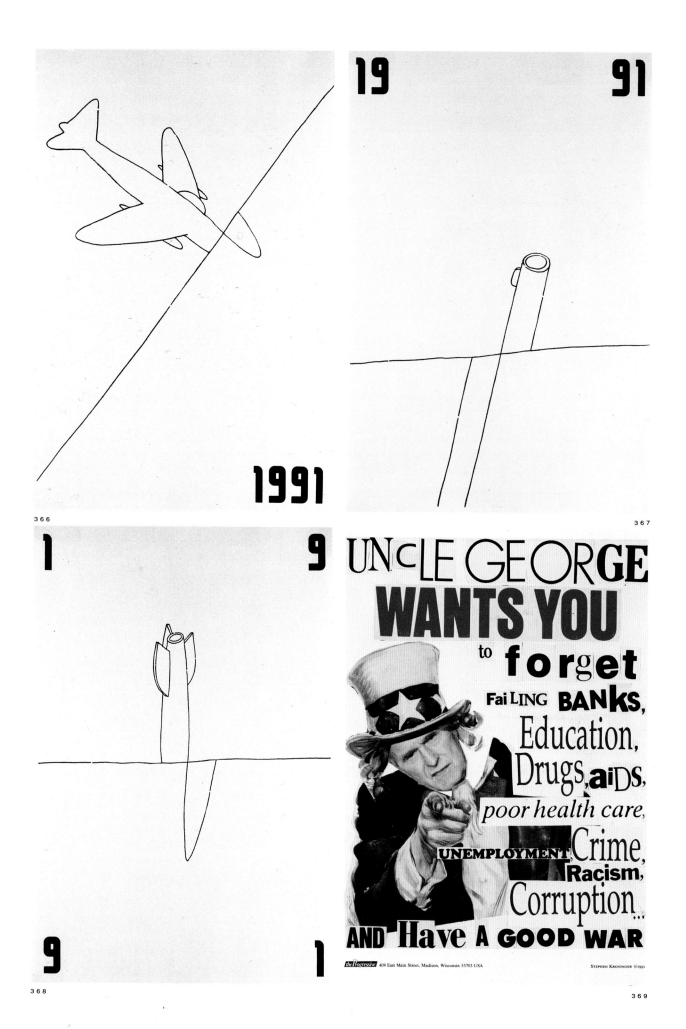

AMERICA TODAY 500 YEARS LATER

370

371

■ **366-368** ᴀʀᴛ Dɪʀᴇᴄᴛᴏʀ/Dᴇsɪɢɴᴇʀ/Iʟʟᴜsᴛʀᴀᴛᴏʀ: LANNY SOMMESE Cʟɪᴇɴᴛ: SOMMESE DESIGN ■ **366-368** THE BREAKUP OF THE SOVIET BLOC AND THE END OF THE ARMS RACE ARE THE THEMES OF THIS POSTER SERIES. ● **366-368** THEMA DIESER PLAKATREIHE IST DER ZERFALL DES OSTBLOCKS UND DAS ENDE DES RÜSTUNGSWETTLAUFS. ▲ **366-368** LA DÉSINTÉGRATION DU BLOC SOVIÉTIQUE ET LA FIN DE LA COURSE AUX ARMEMENTS SONT LES SUJETS DE CETTE SÉRIE D'AFFICHES. (USA)

■ **369** ᴀʀᴛ Dɪʀᴇᴄᴛᴏʀ/Dᴇsɪɢɴᴇʀ: PATRICK JB FLYNN Iʟʟᴜsᴛʀᴀᴛᴏʀ: STEPHEN KRONINGER Cʟɪᴇɴᴛ: *THE PROGRESSIVE* ■ **369** POSTER DEPICTING GEORGE BUSH AS UNCLE SAM. ● **369** GEORGE BUSH SCHLÄGT DEN LEUTEN VOR, DIE SOZIALEN MISSSTÄNDE ZU VERGESSEN UND WÜNSCHT IHNEN STATT DESSEN EINEN «SCHÖNEN» KRIEG. ▲ **369** AFFICHE REPRÉSENTANT GEORGE BUSH EN ONCLE SAM QUI DEMANDE AUX AMÉRICAINS D'OUBLIER LES PROBLEMES SOCIAUX ET LEUR SOUHAITE «UNE BONNE GUERRE.» (USA)

■ **370** ᴀʀᴛ Dɪʀᴇᴄᴛᴏʀ: PER ARNOLDI Dᴇsɪɢɴᴇʀ: PER ARNOLDI Cʟɪᴇɴᴛ: TRAMA VISUAL ■ **370** "AMERICA, 500 YEARS LATER," A BITING COMMENTARY ON AMERICAN HISTORY. ● **370** «AMERIKA, 500 JAHRE SPÄTER,» EIN BISSIGER KOMMENTAR ZUR AMERIKANISCHEN GESCHICHTE. ▲ **370** «AMÉRIQUE, 500 ANS APRES,» UN COMMENTAIRE CINGLANT SUR L'HISTOIRE DE L'AMÉRIQUE. (DEN)

■ **371** ᴀʀᴛ Dɪʀᴇᴄᴛᴏʀ/Dᴇsɪɢɴᴇʀ: PETER FELDER Tᴇxᴛ: PABLO NERUDA Aɢᴇɴᴄʏ: PETER FELDER GDA, GRAFIK-DESIGN Cʟɪᴇɴᴛ: BILDUNGSHAUS BATSCHUNS ■ **371** "500 YEARS OF CONQUEST IN AMERICA." FOUR-COLOR SILK-SCREENSCREEN POSTER PRINTED IN AN EDITION OF 100 PIECES. THE BENEFITS FROM ITS SALES GO TO INDIANS IN BRAZIL. ● **371** DER ERLÖS AUS DEM VERKAUF DIESES IN 100ER AUFLAGE HERGESTELLTEN SIEBDRUCKPLAKATES KOMMT INDIANERN IN BRASILIEN ZUGUTE. ▲ **371** «500 ANS DE CONQUETE DE L'AMÉRIQUE.» AFFICHE SÉRIGRAPHIQUE EN QUADRICHROMIE PUBLIÉE EN UN TIRAGE DE 100 EXEMPLAIRES; LES BÉNÉFICES DE LA VENTE ÉTAIENT DESTINÉS AUX INDIENS DU BRÉSIL. ELLE COMPORTE UNE CITATION DE PABLO NERUDA. (AUT)

■ **372-377** ART DIRECTOR/DESIGNER/ILLUSTRATOR/COPYWRITER: CORNELIA SCHÜTTE ■ **372-377** POSTERS AGAINST CHILD ABUSE: "IT JUST WOULDN'T SLEEP," "150,000 VICTIMS OF SEXUAL ABUSE PER YEAR," "I HARDLY HAD A MINUTE FOR MYSELF," "IT WAS ALL TOO MUCH FOR ME," "I COULDN'T STAND THE CRYING ANYMORE," "THE NOISE LENA MADE WAS UNBEARABLE." ● **372-377** PLA-KATE GEGEN KINDESMISSHANDLUNG. ▲ **372-377** «IL NE VOULAIT PAS DORMIR»; «150 000 VICTIMES D'ABUS SEXUELS CHAQUE ANNÉE» (EN ALLEMAGNE); «JE N'AVAIS MEME PAS UNE MINUTE DE LIBRE POUR MOI»; «C'EN ÉTAIT TROP POUR MOI»; «JE NE POU-VAIS PLUS SUPPORTER CES CRIS»; «LENA FAISAIT UN BRUIT INSUPPORTABLE.» CONTRE LA VIOLENCE SUR LES ENFANTS. (GER)

■ **378-381** ART DIRECTOR: JOHN HORNALL DESIGNERS: JULIA LAPINE, DAVID BATES, HEIDI HATLESTAD, BRIAN O'NEILL ILLUSTRATOR: HORNALL ANDERSON DESIGN WORKS COPYWRITERS: PAMELA MASON-DAVEY, NEIL STARKMAN AGENCY: HORNALL ANDERSON DESIGN WORKS CLIENT: ROBERTS, FITZMAHAN & ASSOCIATES/COMPREHENSIVE HEALTH EDUCATION FOUNDATION ■ **378-381** POSTERS CONVEYING ANTI-DRUG MESSAGES IN A POSITIVE, SOPHISTICATED MANNER. ● **378-381** PLAKATE GEGEN DROGEN. DER TON IST POSITIV UND ANSPRUCHSVOLL. ▲ **378-381** AFFICHES CONTRE LA DROGUE. LE TON EST POSITIF ET RESPONSABLE. (USA)

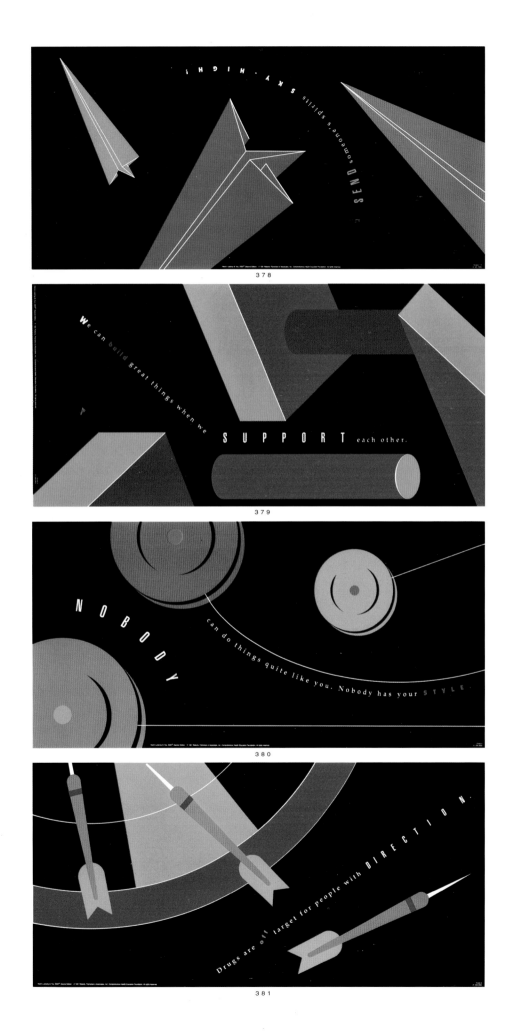

378

379

380

381

Javnosti
Umetnik
Arhitekta
Planer
Zanatlija
İnzenjer
Sociolog
İstoriçar
Pisac
Politiçar

Halk
Sanatçı
Mimar
Planlamacı
El Sanatçısı
Mühendis
Sosyolog
Tarihçi
Yazar
Politikacı

A Közönség
A Müvész
Az Épitész
A Tervezö
A Kézmüves
A Mérnök
A Tàrsadalomtudós
A Történész
Az Iró
A Politikus

To Koινό
ο Καλλιτέχνης
ο Αρχιτέκτονας
ο Πολεοδόμος
ο Τεχνίτης
ο Μηχανικός
ο Κοινωνικός Επιστήμονας
ο Ιστορικός
ο Συγγραφέας
ο Πολιτικός

das Publikum
der Künstler
der Architekt
der Stadtplaner
der Handwerker
der Ingenieur
der Sozialwissenschaftler
der Historiker
der Schriftsteller
der Politiker

The Public
The Artist
The Architect
The Planner
The Craftsman
The Engineer
The Social Scientist
The Historian
The Writer
The Politician

Občané
Umělci
Architekti
Projektanti
Řemeslníci
Inženýři
Sociologové
Historici
Spisovatelé
Politici

İletişim kurmayı yeniden öğrenmek.

Μαθαίνοντας να επικοινωνούν ξανά.

Uçimo da opštimo ponovo.

Ujra Kommunikálni tanulunk.

Učme se opět dorozumět.

Von neuem lernen zu kommunizieren.

Learning to communicate again.

Şehirlerimizin çağdaş mimari çevresinin iyileştirilmesine katkıda bulunacak birleşik bir Sanat ve Mimarlık dili yaratmak. Αναπτύσσοντας μια κοινή καλλιτεχνική και αρχιτεκτονική γλώσσα που συμβάλλει στη βελτίωση του σύγχρονου αρχιτεκτονικού περιβάλλοντος των πόλεων μας. R a z v o j jedinstvenog Umetničkog i Arhitektonskog jezika koji doprinosi unapredzivanju savremene arhitekture okoline u našim gradovima. Egységes képzó-és Épitómüvészeti nyelvet alakitunk ki, amely segiti mai épitészeti környezetünk javitásat varosainkban. Rozvíjejme spolecné Uměni a Architekturu projevu, který přispěje ke zdokonalení současné architektury prostředí uvnitř našich měst. Entwicklung einer Kunst und Architektur verbindenden Sprache, die zu einer Verbesserung des gegenwärtigen gebauten Umfelds in unseren Städten beitragen soll. Developing a unified Art and Architectural language which contributes to an improvement of the contemporary architectural environment within our cities.

Whaur Extremes Meet

İstanbul
12-19 Mayıs 1990, "Cankurtaran Parkı"

Αθήνα
21 - 25 Μαΐου 1990, "Ζαππειον"

Beograd
27-31 Maj 1990, "Manjez Park"

Budapest
1-5 Junis 1990, "Flórián Tér"

Praha
6-11 Června 1990, "Maj, Metro-Narodni"

Berlin
12-17 Junis 1990, "Mariannenplatz"

Glasgow
1st-31st July 1990, "Glasgow Green"

GLASGOW 1990
EUROPEAN CULTURAL FOUNDATION
Subsidised by the Scottish Arts Council
ARUP Consulting Engineers
The British Council
EMINÖNÜ BELEDİYESİ
EMLAK BANKASI
British Rail International

386

387

■ 382-385 ART DIRECTOR/DESIGNER: BÜLENT ERKMEN COPYWRITER: GAVIN RENWICK AGENCY: REKLAMEVI/YOUNG & RUBICAM CLIENT: SCOTTISH ART COUNCIL ■ 382-385 FOUR-PART POSTER FOR A SERIES OF CONFERENCES ON ART AND ARCHITECTURE. ● 382-385 VIERTEILIGES PLAKAT FÜR VORTRÄGE ÜBER KUNST UND ARCHITEKTUR. «WO EXTREME AUFEINANDERTREFFEN.» ▲ 382-385 AF-FICHE QUADRIPARTITE POUR DES CONFÉRENCES SUR L'ART ET L'ARCHITECTURE: «LÀ OU LES EXTREMES SE REJOIGNENT.» (GBR)

■ 386, 387 ART DIRECTOR: MCRAY MAGLEBY DESIGNER: MCRAY MAGLEBY ILLUSTRATOR: MCRAY MAGLEBY SILK-SCREENER: RORY ROBINSON COPYWRITER: NORM DARAIS AGENCY: BYU GRAPHICS CLIENT: BRIGHAM YOUNG UNIVERSITY ■ 386, 387 POSTERS INFORMING STUDENTS OF REGISTRATION DEADLINES. ● 386, 387 MIT DIESEN PLAKATEN WERDEN DIE STUDENTEN AN DIE EIN-SCHREIBETERMINE ERINNERT. ▲ 386, 387 CES AFFICHES INFORMENT LES ÉTUDIANTS DES DATES LIMTES D'INSCRIPTION. (USA)

388

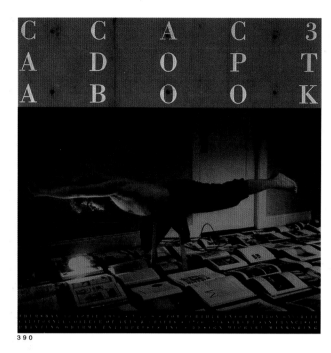

390

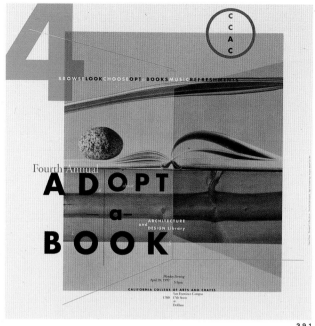

391

■ (PREVIOUS SPREAD) **388** Aʀᴛ Dɪʀᴇᴄᴛᴏʀ/Dᴇsɪɢɴᴇʀ: ZEMPAKU SUZUKI Pʜᴏᴛᴏɢʀᴀᴘʜᴇʀ: HIROSHI YODA Sᴛʏʟɪsᴛ: ASAKO FUKUNAGA Aɢᴇɴᴄʏ: B-BI STUDIO INCORPORATED Cʟɪᴇɴᴛ: HIKO MIZUNO COLLEGE OF JEWELRY ■ **388** POSTER FOR THE HIKO MIZUNO COLLEGE OF JEWELRY IN TOKYO. ● (VORANGEHENDE DOPPELSEITE) **388** FÜR DAS HIKO MIZONO COLLEGE FÜR SCHMUCK-DESIGNER. ▲ (DOUBLE PAGE PRÉCÉDENTE) **388** POUR LE HIKO MIZONO COLLEGE, UNE ÉCOLE DE DESIGN DE BIJOUX. (JPN)

■ (PREVIOUS SPREAD) **389** Aʀᴛ Dɪʀᴇᴄᴛᴏʀ: SILAS H. RHODES Dᴇsɪɢɴᴇʀ: PAULA SCHER Aʀᴛɪsᴛ: PAULA SCHER Aɢᴇɴᴄʏ: PENTAGRAM DESIGN, NEW YORK Cʟɪᴇɴᴛ: SCHOOL OF VISUAL ARTS NEW YORK ■ **389** POSTER AIMED AT POTENTIAL STUDENTS. ● (VORANGEHENDE DOPPELSEITE) **389** PLAKAT ALS WERBUNG FÜR DIE SCHOOL OF VISUAL ARTS IN NEW YORK. ▲ (DOUBLE PAGE PRÉCÉDENTE) **389** AFFICHE DE L'ÉCOLE D'ARTS VISUELS À NEW YORK POUR LE RECRUTEMENT D'ÉTUDIANTS. (USA)

■ (THIS SPREAD) **390, 391** Aʀᴛ Dɪʀᴇᴄᴛᴏʀs/Dᴇsɪɢɴᴇʀs: MICHAEL MANWARING 390, LUCILLE TENAZAS 391 Pʜᴏᴛᴏɢʀᴀᴘʜᴇʀ: MICHAEL MANWARING 390, PETER DE LORY 391 Aɢᴇɴᴄʏ: THE OFFICE OF MICHAEL MANWARING Cʟɪᴇɴᴛ: CALIFORNIA COLLEGE OF ARTS & CRAFTS ■ **390, 391** THE PUBLIC IS INVITED TO PARTICIPATE IN EXPANDING THE LIBRARY OF THIS ART SCHOOL BY "ADOPTING" A BOOK. ● (DIESE DOPPELSEITE) **390, 391** «ADOPTIEREN SIE EIN BUCH.» AUFFORDERUNG ZUM AUFBAU DER BIBLIOTHEK DES CALIFORNIA COLLEGE OF ARTS AND CRAFTS. ▲ (CETTE DOUBLE PAGE) **390, 391** «ADOPTEZ UN LIVRE.» CETTE AFFICHE INVITE LE PUBLIC À PARTICIPER À L'AGRANDISSEMENT DE LA BIBLIOTHEQUE DU CALIFORNIA COLLEGE OF ARTS AND CRAFTS. (USA)

■ (THIS SPREAD) **392** Aʀᴛ Dɪʀᴇᴄᴛᴏʀ: JOHN MULLER Dᴇsɪɢɴᴇʀs: JOHN MULLER, SCOTT CHAPMAN Iʟʟᴜsᴛʀᴀᴛᴏʀ: MARTY ROPER Cᴏᴘʏᴡʀɪᴛᴇʀ: DOUG EDWARDS Aɢᴇɴᴄʏ: MULLER + CO. Cʟɪᴇɴᴛ: KANSAS CITY MUSEUM ■ **392** POSTER ANNOUNCING A NEW EXHIBIT OPENING AT THE KANSAS CITY MUSEUM. ● (DIESE DOPPELSEITE) **392** FÜR EINE AUSSTELLUNG IM MUSEUM VON KANSAS CITY. ▲ (CETTE DOUBLE PAGE) **392** ANNONCE D'UNE EXPOSITION INTITULÉE «SCIENCE CITY» AU MUSÉE DE KANSAS CITY. (USA)

AMUSEMENT ENTERTAINMENT FUN EDUCATION EXCITEMENT EXPERIENCE

KANSAS CITY MUSEUM

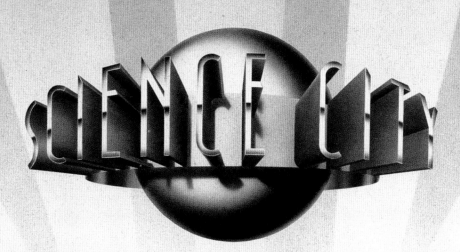

KANSAS CITY MUSEUM'S SCIENCE CITY OFFERS AN

EDUCATIONAL ADVENTURE FOR THE MINDS OF OUR

CHILDREN AND GRANDCHILDREN. BUILT BY A PUBLIC-

PRIVATE PARTNERSHIP AT THE CULTURAL CENTER OF

OUR CITY, SCIENCE CITY WILL BE AN INNOVATIVE NATIONAL

ATTRACTION FOR OUR SCHOOLS, FAMILIES AND TOURISTS.

ITS HANDS-ON EXHIBITS LET YOU TOUCH TOMORROW.

392

393

■ 393 DESIGNER: MICHAEL BIERUT PHOTOGRAPHER: REVEN T.C. WURMAN AGENCY: PENTAGRAM DESIGN CLIENT: RINGLING SCHOOL OF ART AND DESIGN ■ 393 THIS POSTER WAS USED IN HIGH SCHOOLS AS A RECRUITMENT TOOL FOR AN ART SCHOOL. ● 393 DAS PLAKAT MACHT STUDENTEN AUF EINE KUNSTSCHULE AUFMERKSAM. ▲ 393 CETTE AFFICHE D'UNE ÉCOLE D'ART CHERCHE À RECRUTER DES ÉTUDIANTS EN SIGNALANT QUE L'INSTITUTION SE TROUVE DANS UNE RÉGION FORTEMENT ENSOLEILLÉE. (USA)

■ 394, 395 ART DIRECTOR/DESIGNER: MICHAEL CRONAN AGENCY: CRONAN DESIGN, INC. CLIENT: CALIFORNIA COLLEGE OF ARTS & CRAFTS ■ 394, 395 FROM A SERIES OF POSTERS FOR THE CCAC. ● 394, 395 AUS EINER PLAKATREIHE FÜR EINE AM MEER GELEGENE KUNSTSCHULE. ▲ 394, 395 UNE SÉRIE D'AFFICHES POUR UNE ÉCOLE D'ART SITUÉE AU BORD DE LA MER. (USA)

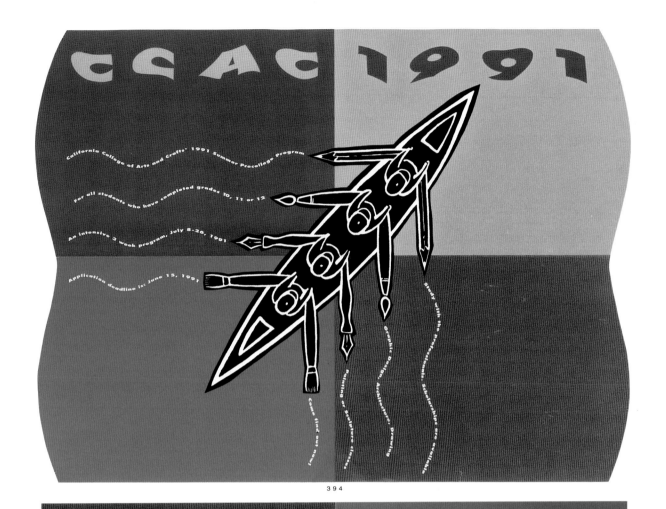

394

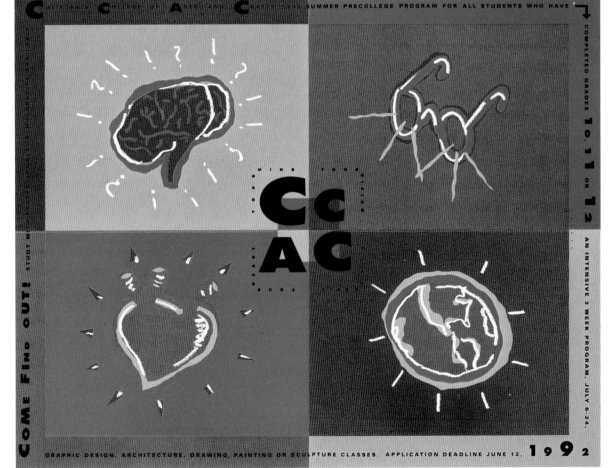

395

396

■ 396 ART DIRECTOR/DESIGNER: JASON KEDGLEY PHOTOGRAPHERS: JASON KEDGLEY, CAROL MOSS COPYWRITERS: JASON KEDGLEY, CRAIL MELLOWS, ANNMARIE KIDDLE CLIENT: LONDON COLLEGE OF PRINTING ■ 396 POSTER FOR THE MEDIA PRODUCTION DESIGN COURSE OF THE LONDON COLLEGE OF PRINTING. A 1960S OLYMPIC TYPEWRITER SERVED AS A MODEL. ● 396 PLAKAT FÜR DEN MEDIA-PRODUKTIONSKURSUS AM LONDON COLLEGE OF PRINTING. DAS KONZEPT BASIERT AUF DEM THEMA SCHREIB-MASCHINE. EINE OLYMPIC AUS DEN SECHZIGER JAHREN DIENTE ALS AUSGANGSPUNKT. ▲ 396 AFFICHE POUR LE COURS DE PRO-DUCTION DE MÉDIAS DU LONDON COLLEGE OF PRINTING. LE CONCEPT EST BASÉ SUR LE THEME DE LA MACHINE À ÉCRIRE. (GBR)

■ 397 DESIGNER/ILLUSTRATOR: SCOTT RAMSEY AGENCY: SCOTT RAMSEY DESIGN CLIENT: JOSTENS LEARNING CORPORATION ■ 397 A POSTER FOR PRISONS AND CORRECTIONAL FACILITIES, COMMUNICATING THE VALUE OF EDUCATION, WITH THE AIM OF EQUIPPING INMATES FOR THEIR EVENTUAL RELEASE. ● 397 DIESES PLAKAT IST AN DIE INSASSEN VON STRAFANSTALTEN GE-RICHTET. ES INFORMIERT ÜBER DEN WERT EINER AUSBILDUNG BEI DER WIEDEREINGLIEDERUNG. ▲ 397 AFFICHE ADRESSÉE AUX PRISONNIERS DE MAISONS D'ARRET: ELLE LES INFORME DE L'IMPORTANCE DE LA FORMATION POUR UNE RÉINSERTION. (USA)

397

398

399

400

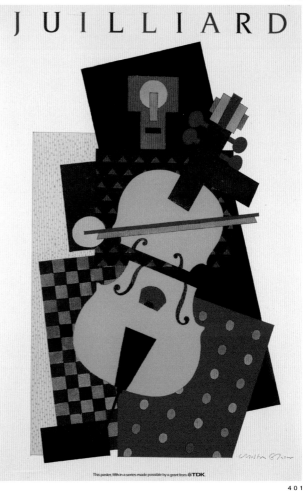

401

402

403

■ 398 ART DIRECTOR: RICHARD DANNE DESIGNER: GARY SKEGGS ILLUSTRATOR: MIN JAE HONG COPYWRITER: LORETTA LAWRENCE KEANE AGENCY: RICHARD DANNE & ASSOCIATES CLIENT: FASHION INSTITUTE OF TECHNOLOGY ■ 398 RECRUITMENT POSTER PROMOTING THE FASHION INSTITUTE OF TECHNOLOGY IN NEW YORK. ● 398 «ALLE STRASSEN FÜHREN ZUM F.I.T.» PLAKAT FÜR DAS FASHION INSTITUTE OF TECHNOLOGY IN NEW YORK. ▲ 398 «TOUS LES CHEMINS CONDUISENT AU F.I.T.» (FASHION INSTITUTE OF TECHNOLOGY). AFFICHE S'ADRESSANT AUSSI BIEN AUX LYCÉENS QU'AUX CONSEILLERS PROFESSIONNELS. (USA)

■ 399 ART DIRECTOR/DESIGNER/ILLUSTRATOR: LAURIE ROSENWALD COPYWRITER: DAVID HALES CLIENT: UNIVERSITY OF SOUTHERN CALIFORNIA ■ 399 POSTER FOR AN EVENT ON THE USC CAMPUS. ● 399 PLAKAT DER UNIVERSITY OF CALIFORNIA. ▲ 399 AFFICHE POUR UNE MANIFESTATION SE DÉROULANT DANS LE CADRE DU CAMPUS DE L'UNIVERSITÉ DE CALIFORNIE. (USA)

■ 400 ART DIRECTOR: JANET LEVY DESIGNER: LAURIE ROSENWALD ILLUSTRATORS: PARSONS STUDENTS COPYWRITERS: LAURIE ROSENWALD, JANET LEVY AGENCY: PARSONS SCHOOL OF DESIGN CLIENT: PARSONS SCHOOL OF DESIGN ■ 400 POSTER FOR THE PARSONS SCHOOL OF DESIGN, FEATURING STUDENTS' WORKS. ● 400 PLAKAT FÜR DIE PARSONS SCHOOL OF DESIGN MIT STUDENTENARBEITEN. ▲ 400 AFFICHE POUR LA PARSONS SCHOOL OF DESIGN REPRÉSENTANT DES TRAVAUX DES ÉTUDIANTS. (USA)

■ 401 DESIGNER/ILLUSTRATOR: MILTON GLASER AGENCY: MILTON GLASER INC. CLIENT: THE JUILLIARD SCHOOL ■ 401 POSTER FOR THE JUILLIARD SCHOOL. ● 401 PLAKAT FÜR DIE JUILLIARD-MUSIKSCHULE. ▲ 401 AFFICHE D'UNE ACADÉMIE DE MUSIQUE. (USA)

■ 402 DESIGNERS: SUSANNE SÖFFKER, FRANCES UCKERMANN CLIENT: UNIVERSITÄT KASSEL ■ 402 POSTER ANNOUNCING A SPECIAL PROGRAM ON FEMINIST ISSUES AT THE UNIVERSITY OF KASSEL. ● 402 ANKÜNDIGUNG EINER VERANSTALTUNG DER UNIVERSITÄT KASSEL. ▲ 402 ANNONCE D'UN COLLOQUE CONSACRÉ AUX QUESTIONS FÉMINISTES À L'UNIVERSITÉ DE KASSEL. (GER)

■ 403 ART DIRECTOR/DESIGNER: OLE FLYV CHRISTENSEN ILLUSTRATOR: OLE FLYV CHRISTENSEN AGENCY: OLE FLYV CHRISTENSEN CLIENT: AALBORG UNIVERSITETSCENTER ■ 403 AIRBRUSH AND GOUACHE POSTER FOR THE AALBORG UNIVERSITY, AIMED AT RECRUITING NEW STUDENTS. ● 403 PLAKAT (AIRBRUSH UND GOUACHE) ALS WERBUNG DER UNIVERSITÄT VON AALBORG. ▲ 403 AFFICHE (AÉROGRAPHE ET GOUACHE) DE L'UNIVERSITÉ DE AALBORG POUR LE RECRUTEMENT DE NOUVEAUX ÉTUDIANTS. (DEN)

404

405

■ **404** ART DIRECTOR: STEVE PATTEE DESIGNERS: STEVE PATTEE, KELLY STILES, TIM SCHUMANN AGENCY: PATTEE DESIGN CLIENT: IABC ■ **404** POSTER FOR ANNUAL FALL SEMINARS ON MORE EFFECTIVE COMMUNICATION. ● **404** FÜR EIN SEMINAR ÜBER WIRKUNGSVOLLE KOMMUNIKATION. ▲ **404** ANNONCE D'UN SÉMINAIRE SUR LE THEME D'UNE COMMUNICATION EFFICACE. (USA)

■ **405** ART DIRECTORS: CHARLES S. ANDERSON, DANIEL OLSON DESIGNERS: CHARLES S. ANDERSON, DANIEL OLSON, TODD HAUSWIRTH AGENCY: C.S. ANDERSON DESIGN COMPANY CLIENT: DALLAS SOCIETY OF VISUAL COMMUNICATIONS ■ **405** POSTER ANNOUNCING A SPEAKING ENGAGEMENT. ● **405** ANKÜNDIGUNG EINES VORTRAGS BEI DER DALLAS SOCIETY OF VISUAL COMMUNICATIONS. ▲ **405** AFFICHE ANNONÇANT UNE CONFÉRENCE DE LA DALLAS SOCIETY OF VISUAL COMMUNICATIONS. (USA)

■ **406-408** DESIGNER: CHOR-MAN FAN CLIENT: VIRGINIA POLYTECHNIC INSTITUTE & STATE UNIVERSITY ■ **406-408** POSTERS PROMOTING DIFFERENT EVENTS OF A THREE-DAY SYMPOSIUM ON THE ARCHITECT LOUIS I. KAHN. ● **406-408** PLAKATE FÜR VER-SCHIEDENE VERANSTALTUNGEN EINES DREITÄGIGEN SYMPOSIUMS ÜBER DEN ARCHITEKTEN LOUIS I. KAHN. ▲ **406-408** AFFICHES POUR DIVERSES MANIFESTATIONS DANS LE CADRE D'UN SYMPOSIUM DE TROIS JOURS SUR L'ARCHITECTE LOUIS I. KAHN. (USA)

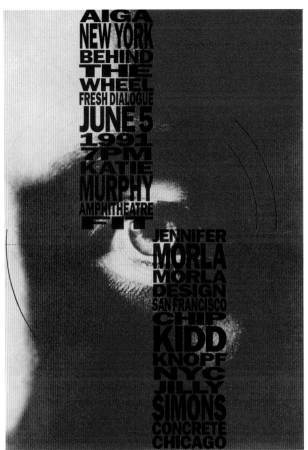

410

411

■ 409 ART DIRECTOR/DESIGNER: ANITA MEYER TYPOGRAPHERS: ANITA MEYER, NICOLE JUEN, MATTHEW MONK COPYWRITER: ALCAN ALUMINIUM LTD. AGENCY: PLUS DESIGN INC. CLIENT: ALCAN ALUMINIUM LTD. ■ 409 POSTER ANNOUNCING ALCAN'S 1992 LECTURE SERIES, ON THE SUBJECT OF RECYCLING PROCESSES. THE POSTER IS PRINTED ON CARDBOARD WITH TYPOGRAPHY GENERATED BY STENCILS AND AN ANTIQUE TYPEWRITER. ● 409 PLAKAT FÜR EINE VON DEM ALUMINIUMKONZERN ALCAN VERANSTALTETEN VORTRAGSREIHE ZUM THEMA ARCHITEKTUR UND RECYCLING-PROZESSE. ES IST AUF KARTON GEDRUCKT. DIE SCHRIFT WURDE MIT SCHABLONEN UND EINER ALTEN SCHREIBMASCHINE ERSTELLT. ▲ 409 AFFICHE ANNONÇANT UNE SÉRIE DE CONFÉRENCES SUR LE THEME DE L'ARCHITECTURE ET DES TECHNIQUES DE RECYCLAGE, ORGANISÉE PAR LA SOCIÉTÉ ALCAN, LE GÉANT DE L'ALUMINIUM. LE TEXTE A ÉTÉ RÉALISÉ AU MOYEN DE PONCIFS ET D'UNE VIEILLE MACHINE À ÉCRIRE. (USA)

■ 410 ART DIRECTOR: JENNIFER MORLA DESIGNERS: JENNIFER MORLA, SHARRIE BROOKS PHOTOGRAPHER: BYBEE STUDIOS AGENCY: MORLA DESIGN CLIENT: AIGA ■ 410 BUS-SHELTER POSTER FOR A LECTURE SERIES ON RADICAL DESIGN. ● 410 FÜR EINE VOR-TRAGSREIHE ÜBER BAHNBRECHENDES DESIGN. ▲ 410 ANNONCE D'UNE SÉRIE DE CONFÉRENCES SUR LE DESIGN «RADICAL.» (USA)

■ 411 ART DIRECTOR: RICHARD POULIN DESIGNER: RICHARD POULIN PHOTOGRAPHER: DEBORAH KUSHMA AGENCY: RICHARD POULIN DESIGN GROUP, INC. CLIENT: AIGA NEW YORK ■ 411 POSTER ANNOUNCING LECTURES BY WELL-KNOWN DESIGNERS. ● 411 MIT DIESEM PLAKAT KÜNDIGT DAS AIGA NEW YORK EINE VORTRAGSREIHE BEKANNTER GRAPHIK-DESIGNER AN. ▲ 411 L'AIGA DE NEW YORK ANNONCE SUR CETTE AFFICHE UNE SÉRIE DE CONFÉRENCES DE DESIGNERS GRAPHIQUES BIEN CONNUS. (USA)

FRED HAS A BETTER IDEA... *(or at least knows where to find one). Well, maybe, maybe not. You can be the judge on January 16th when Fred Woodward, the former art director of TEXAS MONTHLY talks about five years on the assembly line at ROLLING STONE, where quality is still Job One. Motor in for drinks at 6:00 p.m. at the Ellipse Ballroom in the Stouffer Hotel (2222 on the beautiful North Stemmons Freeway in Dallas) and hear wild tales of all-night closings, the secret type laboratory, and blood on the drawing boards after eleventh-hour cover switcheroos. Stick around for the program, which begins at 7:00, and learn how to handle imperial photographers, space-hog editors, money-mad suits and other New York Types who don't know what he goes through to spin this rag out EVERY TWO WEEKS! Ahem. It costs DSVC members nothing, students $3.00 and interested civilians $10.00. Cheap.*

412

■ **412** ART DIRECTOR: FRED WOODWARD DESIGNER: FRED WOODWARD CLIENT: DSVC ■ **412** "FRED HAS A BETTER IDEA... (OR AT LEAST KNOWS WHERE TO FIND ONE)." POSTER ANNOUNCING A LECTURE BY FRED WOODWARD ON HIS FIVE YEARS AS AN ART DIRECTOR WITH *ROLLING STONE*. ● **412** «FRED HAT EINE BESSERE IDEE... (ODER WEISS WENIGSTENS, WIE ER DAZU KOMMT).» ANKÜNDIGUNG EINES VORTRAGS VON FRED WOODWARD ÜBER SEINE FÜNFJÄHRIGE ERFAHRUNG ALS ART DIRECTOR DER ZEIT-SCHRIFT *ROLLING STONE*. ▲ **412** «FRED A UNE MEILLEURE IDÉE... (IL SAIT DU MOINS OU EN TROUVER UNE).» AFFICHE ANNONÇANT UNE CONFÉRENCE DE FRED WOODWARD SUR SES CINQ ANNÉES DE DIRECTION ARTISTIQUE AUPRES DE *ROLLING STONE*. (USA)

■ **414** ART DIRECTOR/DESIGNER: JOHN CLARK COPYWRITER: VIRGINIA PEPPER AGENCY: LOOKING CLIENT: ART CENTER COLLEGE OF DESIGN (EUROPE) ■ **414** POSTER ANNOUNCING THE EVENTS OF A TRIMESTER AT THE ART CENTER COLLEGE OF DESIGN (EUROPE). ● **414** ANKÜNDIGUNG DER VERANSTALTUNGEN AM ART CENTER COLLEGE OF DESIGN (EUROPE). ▲ **414** ANNONCE DES DIVERSES MANIFESTATIONS PROPOSÉES AU COURS D'UN TRIMESTRE PAR LE ART CENTER COLLEGE OF DESIGN (EUROPE). (SWI)

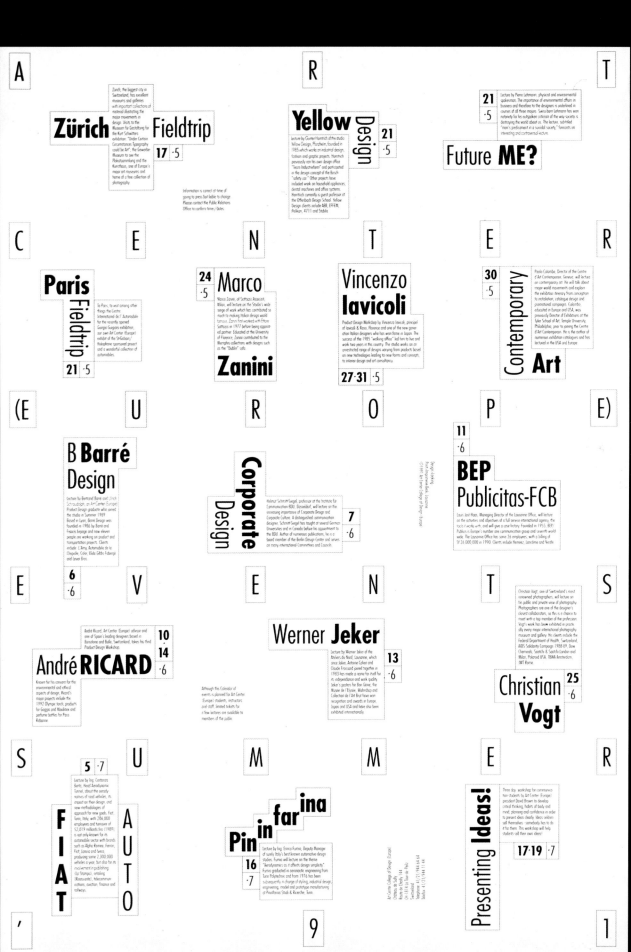

A

Zürich Fieldtrip 17 ·5

Zürich, the biggest city in Switzerland, has excellent museums and galleries with important collections of material illustrating the major movements in design. Visits to the Museum für Gestaltung to the Kurt Schwitters exhibition "Unter Gewissen Circumstances Typography could be Art", the Schweizer Museum to see the Plakatsammlung and the Kunsthaus, one of Europe's major art museums, and home of a fine collection of photography.

Information is correct at time of going to press but liable to change. Please contact the Public Relations Office to confirm times/dates.

R

Yellow Design 21 ·5

Lecture by Günter Horntrich of the studio Yellow Design, Pforzheim, founded in 1985 which works on industrial design, fashion and graphic projects. Horntrich previously ran his own design office "Team Industiedesign" and participated in the design concept of the Bosch "safety car." Other projects have included work on household appliances, dental machines and office systems. Horntrich currently is guest professor at the Offenbach Design School. Yellow Design clients include ABB, EFFEM, Pelikan, 4711 and Stabilo.

T

21 ·5 Lecture by Pierre Lehmann, physicist and environmental spokesman. The importance of environmental affairs in business and therefore to the designer is underlined in courses of all three majors. Swiss-born Lehmann has won notoriety for his outspoken criticism of the way society is destroying the world about us. His lecture, subtitled "man's predicament in a suicidal society," forecasts an interesting and controversial vectum.

Future ME?

C

Paris Fieldtrip 21 ·5

So Paris, to visit among other things the Centre International de l'Automobile for the recently opened Giorgio Guigaro exhibition, our own Art Center (Europe) exhibit at the 'Art-Station/ Aérophone sponsored project and a wonderful collection of automobiles.

E

N

24 ·5

Marco Zanini

Marco Zanini, of Sottsass Associati, Milan, will lecture on the Studio's wide range of work which has contributed so much to making Italian design world famous. Zanini first worked with Ettore Sottsass in 1977 before being appointed partner. Educated at the University of Florence, Zanini contributed to the Memphis collections with designs such as the "Dublin" sofa.

T

Vincenzo Iavicoli 27·31 ·5

Product Design Workshop by Vincenzo Iavicoli, principal of Iavicoli & Rossi, Florence and one of the new generation Italian designers who has won fame in Japan. The success of the 1985 "walking office" led him to live and work two years in the country. The studio works on an unrestricted range of designs varying from products based on new technologies leading to new forms and concepts, to interior design and art consultancy.

E

R

30 ·5

Contemporary Art

Paolo Colombo, Director of the Centre d'Art Contemporain, Geneva, will lecture on contemporary art. He will talk about major world movements and explore the exhibition itinerary from conception to installation, catalogue design and promotional campaign. Colombo, educated in Europe and USA, was previously Director of Exhibitions at the Tyler School of Art, Temple University, Philadelphia, prior to joining the Centre d'Art Contemporain. He is the author of numerous exhibition catalogues and has lectured in the USA and Europe.

(E

B Barré Design 6 ·6

Lecture by Bertrand Barré and Ulrich Schraudolph, an Art Center (Europe) Product Design graduate who owned the studio in Summer 1989. Based in Lyon, Barré Design was founded in 1986 by Barré and Frères. Laspage and now eleven people are working on product and transportation projects. Clients include: L'Amy, Automobiles de la Chapelle, Color, Elida Gibbs Fabergé and Lever Bros.

U

N

Corporate Design 7 ·6

Helmut Schmitt-Siegel, professor at the Institute für Communication BDU, Düsseldorf, will lecture on the increasing importance of Corporate Design and Corporate Culture. A distinguished communication designer, Schmitt-Siegel has taught at several German Universities and in Canada before his appointment to the BDU. Author of numerous publications, he is a board member of the Berlin Design Center and serves on many international Committees and Councils.

Design Lecturing
Printed in Switzerland
© 1991 Art Center College of Design (Europe)

P

11 ·6

BEP Publicitas-FCB

Louis Jost Haan, Managing Director of the Lausanne Office, will lecture on the activities and objectives of a full service international agency, the topics it works with, and will give a case history. Founded in 1955, BEP/ Publicitas is Europe's number one communication group and seventh world wide. The Lausanne Office has some 26 employees, with a billing of Sf 26,000,000 in 1990. Clients include Hennicz, Lancôme and Nestlé.

E)

E

6 ·6

André RICARD 10·14 ·6

André Ricard, Art Center (Europe) advisor and one of Spain's leading designers based in Barcelona and Italia, Switzerland, takes his third Product Design Workshop.

Known for his concern for the environmental and ethical aspects of design, Ricard's major projects include the 1992 Olympic torch, products for Gaggia and Moulinex and perfume bottles for Paco Rabanne.

Although this Calendar of events is planned for Art Center (Europe) students, instructors and staff, limited tickets for a few lectures are available to members of the public.

V

Werner Jeker 13 ·6

Lecture by Werner Jeker of the Ateliers du Nord, Lausanne, which saw Jeker, Antoine Cohen and Claude Frossard joined together in 1983 has made a name for itself for its independence and work quality. Jeker's posters for Ben Geneva, the Musée de l'Elysée, Waterdsap and Collection de l'Art Brut have won recognition and awards in Europe, Japan and USA and have also been exhibited internationally.

N

Christian Vogt 25 ·6

Christian Vogt, one of Switzerland's most renowned photographers, will lecture on his public and private view of photography. Photographers are one of the designer's closest collaborators, so this is a chance to meet with a top member of the profession. Vogt's work has been exhibited in practically every major international photography museum and gallery. His clients include the Federal Department of Health, Switzerland, AIDS Solidarity Campaign 1988-89, Dow Chemicals, Saatchi & Saatchi London and Milan, Polaroid USA, IBMA Amsterdam, IWT Rome.

T

S

S

5 ·7

FIAT AUTO

Lecture by Ing. Costanzo Bertz, Head Aerodynamics Tunnel, about the aerody namics of road vehicles, its impact on their design, and new methodologies of approach for new goods. Fiat, Turin, Italy, with 286,000 employees and turnover of 52,019 milliards lire (1989) is not only known for its automobile sector with brands such as Alpha Romeo, Ferrari, Fiat, Lancia and Iveco, producing some 2,300,000 vehicles a year, but also for its involvement in publishing (La Stampa), retailing (Rinascente), telecommunications, aviation, finance and railways.

U

M

Pininfarina 16 ·7

Lecture by Ing. Enrico Fumia, Deputy Manager of surely Italy's best known automotive design studios. Fumia will lecture on the theme "Aerodynamics or it affects design simplicity." Fumia graduated in aeronautic engineering from Turin Polytechnic and from 1976 has been subsequently in charge of styling, industrial design, engineering, model and prototype manufacturing at Pininfarina Studi & Ricerche, Turin.

Art Center College of Design (Europe)
Château de Sully
Route de Chailly 144
CH-1814 La Tour-de-Peilz
Switzerland
Telephone 41/21/944 44 44
Telefax 41/21/944 11 44

M

E

Presenting Ideas! 17·19 ·7

Three day workshop for communication majors by Art Center (Europe) president David Brown to develop critical thinking, habits of body and mind, planning and confidence in order to present ideas clearly. Ideas seldom sell themselves — somebody has to do it for them. This workshop will help students sell their own ideas!

R

'

9

1

BIERUTAH

Michael Bierut
gets together
with Salt Lake City,
Utah!

Eighteen years ago,
Michael Bierut
decided he wanted to
be a graphic designer.

Twelve years ago,
he joined
Vignelli Associates,
New York
where he began
by doing mechanicals
and ended up
as Vice President,
Graphic Design.

Eighteen months ago
he became
a partner in the
New York office of the
international
design firm Pentagram.

Next week he's
coming to Utah to
present his work.

How did he get
from there to here?

Come to AIHLC
and find out.

Art Directors
Salt Lake City
Wednesday
March 11, 1992
6:30pm
Refreshments
7:00pm
Presentation

Free to
AIHLC members
$10 for guests

The Salt Lake
Art Center
Crane Auditorium

The
American
Institute of
Graphic Arts,
Los Angeles
presents
•
Paula Scher:
East Meets West

AIGA/LA
Annual Patron
Sponsor Night

Wednesday,
March 4,
1992
6:30 pm
Reception/
Patron Exhibition
7:30 pm
Speaker
Presentation

416

■ **415** Designer: MICHAEL BIERUT Agency: PENTAGRAM DESIGN Client: ART DIRECTORS SALT LAKE CITY ■ **415** ANNOUNCEMENT FOR A LECTURE BY MICHAEL BIERUT IN UTAH. THE LOCATION AND THE LECTURER'S NAME MADE FOR AN INCONGRUOUS JUXTAPOSITION. ● **415** ANKÜNDIGUNG EINES VORTRAGS DES AMERIKANISCHEN DESIGNERS MICHAEL BIERUT IM STAATE UTAH. DER NAME DES VORTRAGENDEN LIESS SICH IDEAL MIT DEM ORT KOMBINIEREN. ▲ **415** AFFICHE ANNONÇANT UNE CONFÉRENCE DU DESIGNER AMÉRICAIN MICHAEL BIERUT DANS L'UTAH. LE NOM DE CE DERNIER A ÉTÉ JUXTAPOSÉ AU NOM DU LIEU. (USA)

■ **416** Designer: PAULA SCHER Agency: PENTAGRAM DESIGN Client: AIGA LOS ANGELES ■ **416** POSTER FOR A SPEAKING ENGAGEMENT BY PAULA SCHER IN LOS ANGELES. THE LAST TWO LETTERS OF HER NAME ARE SEPARATED TO PLAY OFF THE NAME OF THE CITY. ● **416** ANKÜNDIGUNG EINES VORTRAGS DER DESIGNERIN PAULA SCHER IN LOS ANGELES. DIE LETZTEN BEIDEN BUCHSTABEN IHRES VORNAMENS WURDEN DURCH DIE INFORMATION AUSEINANDERGEZOGEN UND LIEFERN GLEICHZEITIG DEN HINWEIS AUF VERANSTALTUNGSORT LOS ANGELES. ▲ **416** ANNONCE D'UNE CONFÉRENCE DE PAULA SCHER À LOS ANGELES. LES DEUX DERNIERES LETTRES DE SON PRÉNOM ONT ÉTÉ DISPOSÉES DE MANIERE À ÉVOQUER L.A. (USA)

417

418

1992ing

419

The JAGDA Peace and Environment Poster Exhibition '14 here.
Designed in Tokyo/Tokyo.

■ **417, 418** ART DIRECTOR/DESIGNER: TAKAHARU MATSUMOTO AGENCY: TAKAHARU MATSUMOTO ■ **417, 418** THE POLLUTION OF THE ENVIRONMENT WAS THE SUBJECT OF A POSTER SERIES UNDER THE TITLE OF "MOTHER EARTH." THE SEASHELL, REPRESENTING THE OLDEST CREATURE ON EARTH, STANDS FOR ALL CREATURES OF THE OCEAN ENDANGERED BY THE POLLUTION. THE "D" STANDS FOR DEATH. THE CIGARETTE IS A SYMBOL OF POLLUTION CAUSED BY HUMANS, WHO ARE ALSO HARMING THEMSELVES. ● **417, 418** DIE BEDROHUNG DER UMWELT IST DAS THEMA EINER PLAKATSERIE UNTER DEM TITEL «MUTTER ERDE.» DIE MUSCHEL ALS ÄLTESTES LEBEWESEN WURDE STELLVERTRETEND FÜR ALLE KREATUREN GEWÄHLT, DIE DURCH DIE GEWÄS- SERVERSCHMUTZUNG VOM AUSSTERBEN BEDROHT SIND. DAS «D» STEHT FÜR «DEATH» (TOD). DIE ZIGARETTE IST EIN SYMBOL FÜR DIE DURCH DEN MENSCHEN VERURSACHTE ZERSTÖRUNG, DER SELBST VOR DEM EIGENEN KÖRPER NICHT HALT MACHT. ▲ **417, 418** LES MENACES QUI PESENT SUR L'ENVIRONNEMENT SONT LE SUJET DE CETTE SÉRIE D'AFFICHES INTITULÉES «LA TERRE MERE.» LE COQUILLAGE, LA PLUS ANCIENNE TRACE DE VIE SUR LA TERRE, SYMBOLISE TOUTES LES CRÉATURES MENACÉES D'EXTINCTION À CAUSE DE LA POLLUTION DES EAUX. LE «D» EST L'INITIALE DU MOT «DEATH» (LA MORT). LA CIGA- RETTE EST UN SYMBOLE DES DESTRUCTIONS CAUSÉES PAR L'HOMME, INCAPABLE DE PRÉSERVER SON PROPRE CORPS. (JPN)

■ **419** ART DIRECTOR/DESIGNER: TADANORI ITAKURA AGENCY: ITAKURA DESIGN INSTITUTE INC. CLIENT: JAPAN GRAPHIC DESIGNERS ASSOCIATION ■ **419** POSTER FOR THE EXHIBITION "PEACE AND ENVIRONMENT" BY THE JAPAN GRAPHIC DESIGNERS ASSOCIATION. IT IS A COMBINATION OF A SILK-SCREEN AND AN OFFSET PRINT. ● **419** PLAKAT FÜR EINE AUSSTELLUNG DER JAPAN GRAPHIC DESIGNERS ASSOCIATION UNTER DEM TITEL «FRIEDE UND UMWELT.» ES HANDELT SICH UM EINE KOMBINATION VON OFFSET- UND SIEBDRUCK. ▲ **419** AFFICHE POUR UNE EXPOSITION DE L'ASSOCIATION DES DESIGNERS GRAPHIQUES DU JA- PON, INTITULÉE «PAIX ET ENVIRONNEMENT.» IL S'AGIT D'UNE COMBINAISON D'IMPRESSION OFFSET ET DE SÉRIGRAPHIE. (JPN)

つかった紙をゴミと呼ぶのは,そろそろやめにしませんか

420

リサイクルは、生活の知恵ではありません。生存の知恵

421

地球の環境？
どんどんよくなってる
じゃないか。へへ

THE ENVIRONMENT? FOR
SOME OF US IT'S GETTING
BETTER EVERY DAY.
The average person living in Japan throws
away 1 kilogram of garbage every day. Adding
industrial waste, that's enough each year to bury
the city of Osaka more than 5 meters deep.
日本人の家庭から出るゴミは、平均すると、1人1日約1kg。
日本全体でうまれるゴミ（産業廃棄物も含む）は、
大阪市を毎年5mずつ埋めつくす計算になります。

422

YOUR RECYCLING MONEY COULD SUPPORT A LARGE FAMILY.

PROTECT WILDLIFE. DONATE YOUR RECYCLING MONEY TO EARTH SHARE.

423

享年四十六億歳

424

■ **420, 421** ART DIRECTOR: DAISUKE NAKATSUKA DESIGNER: YASUHIKO MATSUMOTO PHOTOGRAPHER: TORU KOGURE COPYWRITER: HIDEO OKANO AGENCY: NAKATSUKA DAISUKE INC. CLIENT: RENGO CO., LTD. ■ **420, 421** "MAYBE IT'S TIME TO STOP CALLING USED PAPER 'TRASH'"; "RECYCLING IS THE KEY NOT TO LIVING BUT TO SURVIVAL." EXAMPLES FROM A SERIES OF ENVIRONMENTAL POSTERS. ● **420, 421** «VIELLEICHT IST ES ZEIT, ALTPAPIER NICHT MEHR 'ABFALL' ZU NENNEN»; «RECYCLING IST NICHT DER SCHLÜSSEL ZUM LEBEN, SONDERN ZUM ÜBERLEBEN.» AUS EINER PLAKATREIHE ZUM THEMA UMWELT. ▲ **420, 421** «PEUT-ETRE EST-IL TEMPS D'ARRETER DE CONSIDÉRER LE VIEUX PAPIER COMME UN DÉCHET.» «LE RECYCLAGE N'EST PAS LA CLÉ DE LA VIE, MAIS DE LA SURVIE.» D'UNE SÉRIE D'AFFICHES SUR LE THEME DE LA PROTECTION DE L'ENVIRONNEMENT. (JPN)

■ **422** ART DIRECTOR/DESIGNER: JUTARO ITOH ILLUSTRATOR: KOICHI SHIMODA COPYWRITERS: KOHEI MURAKAMI, JOHN L. MCREERY AGENCY: ITOH DESIGN INC. CLIENT: JAPAN GRAPHIC DESIGNERS ASSOCIATION ■ **422** A STATEMENT ON THE PROBLEM OF WASTE DISPOSAL. ● **422** «DIE UMWELT? FÜR EINIGE VON UNS WIRD SIE TÄGLICH BESSER.» ▲ **422** «L'ENVIRONNEMENT? POUR QUEL-QUES-UNS D'ENTRE NOUS, IL EST TOUS LES JOURS MEILLEUR.» AVEC LES DÉCHETS PRODUITS CHAQUE ANNÉE PAR LA POPU-LATION ET L'INDUSTRIE JAPONAISES, ON POURRAIT ENTERRER LA VILLE D'OSAKA SOUS CINQ METRES DE DÉTRITUS. (JPN)

■ **423** ART DIRECTOR: CLIFF SORAH ILLUSTRATOR: KEN GOLDAMMER COPYWRITER: TRIPP WESTBROOK AGENCY: THE MARTIN AGENCY CLIENT: REYNOLDS RECYCLING ■ **423** AN APPEAL TO RETURN ALUMINUM PRODUCTS AND DONATE THE REFUNDS TO AN ENVIRONMENTAL CAUSE. ● **423** «MIT IHREM PFANDGELD KÖNNTEN SIE EINE GROSSE FAMILIE ERNÄHREN.» HIER GEHT ES UM DIE WIEDERVERWERTUNG VON ALUMINIUM UND DEN EINSATZ DES PRO KILO BEZAHLTEN GELDES FÜR UMWELTSCHUTZPROJEKTE. ▲ **423** «L'ARGENT CONSACRÉ AU RECYCLAGE POURRAIT NOURRIR UNE GRANDE FAMILLE.» IL EST QUESTION ICI DU RECYCLAGE DE L'ALUMINIUM, L'ARGENT GAGNÉ SUR CHAQUE KILO ÉTANT INVESTI DANS DES PROJETS EN FAVEUR DE L'ENVIRONNEMENT. (USA)

■ **424** ART DIRECTOR: TOSHIO IWATA DESIGNER: TOSHIO IWATA PHOTOGRAPHER: TETSUYA ABE COPYWRITER: TOSHIO IWATA CLIENT: JAPAN GRAPHIC DESIGNERS ASSOCIATION ■ **424** "DEAD AT THE AGE OF 46 HUNDRED MILLION YEARS." THIS POSTER, AN APPEAL TO PROTECT THE EARTH, SHOWS A JAPANESE-STYLE FUNERAL OF THE PERSONIFIED EARTH. ● **424** «GESTORBEN IM ALTER VON 46 HUNDERT MILLIONEN JAHREN.» DIESES PLAKAT, EIN APPELL ZUM SCHUTZ DER ERDE, ZEIGT EINE BEERDIGUNG DER PERSONIFIZIERTEN ERDE IM JAPANISCHEN STIL. ▲ **424** «MORTE À L'AGE DE 46 CENTAINES DE MILLIONS D'ANNÉES.» LES FUNÉRAILLES DE LA TERRE PERSONNIFIÉE SUR UNE AFFICHE JAPONAISE, UN APPEL A LA SAUVEGARDE DE LA PLANETE. (JPN)

425

426

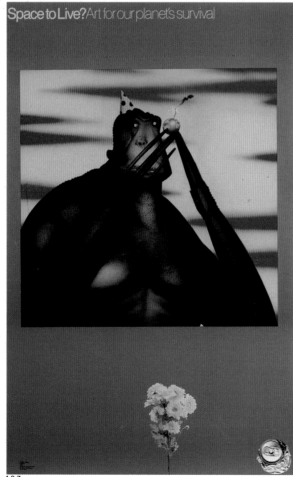

427

428

429

430

■ **425** ART DIRECTOR: JENNIFER MORLA DESIGNERS: JENNIFER MORLA, JEANETTE ARAMBURU AGENCY: MORLA DESIGN CLIENT: AIGA SAN FRANCISCO ■ **425** AN APPEAL TO THE PUBLIC TO TAKE ACTION ON ENVIRONMENTAL ISSUES. ● **425** «WISSEN, DAS NICHT IN DIE TAT UMGESETZT WIRD, ZERSTÖRT.» APPELL AN DIE ÖFFENTLICHKEIT ZUM SCHUTZ DER UMWELT. ▲ **425** «SAVOIR MAIS NE PAS AGIR DÉTRUIT.» UN APPEL AU PUBLIC À S'ENGAGER ACTIVEMENT DANS LA PROTECTION DE L'ENVIRONNEMENT. (USA)

■ **426** ART DIRECTOR: JOHN BIELENBERG DESIGNER: BIELENBERG DESIGN PHOTOGRAPHER: ALLEN ASHTON AGENCY: BIELENBERG DE-SIGN CLIENT: AIGA SAN FRANCISCO ■ **426** "THE DIMINISHING OZONE LAYER IS INVISIBLE BUT WE ARE INSANE TO IGNORE THE PROBLEM." ● **426** «DIE ZERSTÖRUNG DER OZONSCHICHT IST UNSICHTBAR, ABER ES IST WAHNSINN, DAS PROBLEM ZU IGNORIEREN.» ▲ **426** «LA DESTRUCTION DE LA COUCHE D'OZONE NE SE VOIT PAS, MAIS C'EST DE LA FOLIE D'IGNORER CE PROBLEME.» (USA)

■ **427** ART DIRECTOR/DESIGNER/ILLUSTRATOR: BILL MAYER AGENCY: BILL MAYER, INC. CLIENT: UNITED NATIONS ■ **427** POSTER FOR A UNITED NATIONS SHOW TO CREATE ENVIRONMENTAL AWARENESS. ● **427** «LEBENSRAUM? KUNST FÜR DIE UMWELT»—FÜR EINE UN-AUSSTELLUNG. ▲ **427** «ESPACE VITAL? L'ART AU SERVICE DE L'ENVIRONNEMENT»—POUR UNE EXPOSITION DE L'ONU. (USA)

■ **428** DESIGNER/ILLUSTRATOR: SEYMOUR CHWAST AGENCY: THE PUSHPIN GROUP CLIENT: MERYL PENNER/THE EARTH DAY COMMITTEE ■ **428** AN APPEAL TO TAKE ACTION FOR THE SAKE OF THE ENVIRONMENT. VEGETABLE-BASED INKS ON RECYCLED PAPER. ● **428** «JETZT HANDELN»—DRUCKFARBEN AUF PFLANZENBASIS, RECYCLING-PAPIER. ▲ **428** «MAINTENANT, AGISSONS»—AFFICHE EN FAVEUR DE L'ENVIRONNEMENT. ENCRES D'IMPRIMERIE FAITES À BASE DE PLANTES, SUR PAPIER RECYCLÉ. (USA)

■ **429** ART DIRECTOR: MICHAEL MANWARING DESIGNER: MICHAEL MANWARING PHOTOGRAPHER: MICHAEL MANWARING AGENCY: THE OFFICE OF MICHAEL MANWARING CLIENT: AIGA SAN FRANCISCO ■ **429** POSTER INTENDED TO RAISE AWARENESS OF ECO-LOGICAL ISSUES. ● **429** «LIMITIERTES ANGEBOT. HANDLE JETZT.» ▲ **429** «OFFRE LIMITÉE. A SAISIR TOUT DE SUITE.» (USA)

■ **430** DESIGNER/ILLUSTRATOR: MICHAEL SCHWAB CLIENT: BELLA BLUE ■ **430** POSTER PRINTED WITH WATER-BASED SILK-SCREEN INK ON RECYCLED PAPER. ● **430** UMWELTPLAKAT, MIT WASSERLÖSLICHER SIEBDRUCKFARBE AUF RECYCLING-PAPIER GE-DRUCKT. ▲ **430** AFFICHE EN FAVEUR DE L'ENVIRONNEMENT IMPRIMÉE AVEC UNE ENCRE SÉRIGRAPHIQUE SOLUBLE À L'EAU. (USA)

■ **431** CREATIVE DIRECTOR/ART DIRECTOR/DESIGNER: KAN TAI-KEUNG PHOTOGRAPHER: C.K. WONG AGENCY: KAN TAI-KEUNG DESIGN & ASSOC. LTD. CLIENT: QUALITY PAPER SPECIALIST ■ **431** THE CONSERVATION OF NATURE AND THE USE OF RECYCLED PAPER ARE THE THEMES OF THIS POSTER. ● **431** ERHALTUNG DER NATUR UND VERWENDUNG VON RECYCLING-PAPIER SIND DAS THEMA DES PLAKATES. ▲ **431** L'AFFICHE A POUR THEME LA CONSERVATION DE LA NATURE ET L'UTILISATION DE PAPIER RECYCLÉ. (HKG)

431

■ **432-435** ART DIRECTOR/DESIGNER: KAZUMASA NAGAI AGENCY: NIPPON DESIGN CENTER CLIENT: JAPAN GRAPHIC DESIGNERS ASSOCIATION ■ **432-435** A SERIES OF SILK-SCREEN POSTERS URGING THE CONSERVATION OF SPECIES AND THE ENVIRONMENT. ● **432-435** SIEBDRUCKPLAKATE FÜR DIE ERHALTUNG DER ARTENVIELFALT UND DER UMWELT. ▲ **432-435** UNE SÉRIE D'AFFICHES SÉRIGRAPHIQUES POUR LA PROTECTION DES ESPECES MENACÉES ET DE L'ENVIRONNEMENT. (JPN)

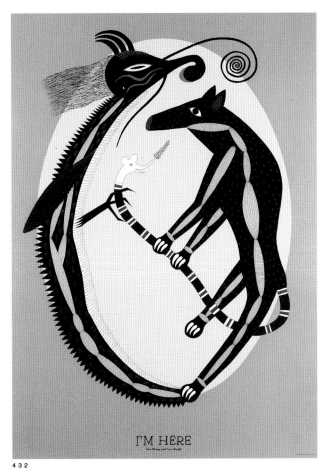

I'M HERE

432

I'M HERE

433

I'M HERE

434

I'M HERE

435

■ 436 Art Director/Designer: KENICHI SAMURA Photographer: MITSUO SHIBATA Copywriter: KENICHI SAMURA Agency: NUMBER ONE DESIGN OFFICE INC. Client: JAPAN GRAPHIC DESIGNERS ASSOCIATION ■ 436 "A CAPSULE NAMED DESIRE." A POSTER WITH AN ANTI-NUCLEAR MESSAGE. THE COPY TELLS THE STORY OF THIS PHOTOGRAPH WITH INFORMATION ON TIME AND PLACE: MITSUO SHIBATA DISCOVERED A BURNED-OUT NUCLEAR-WARHEAD CAPSULE NEAR AN AIR FORCE BASE IN ARIZONA. ● 436 «EINE KAPSEL NAMENS SEHNSUCHT.» EIN PLAKAT GEGEN ATOMWAFFEN. DER TEXT INFORMIERT ÜBER DIE AUFNAHME, UND ZWAR MIT GENAUEN ANGABEN ÜBER ORT UND ZEIT: DER JAPANISCHE PHOTOGRAPH MITSUO SHIBATA ENTDECKTE DIESE AUS-GEBRANNTE ATOMSPRENGKOPF-KAPSEL BEI EINEM LUFTWAFFENSTÜTZPUNKT IN ARIZONA. ▲ 436 «UNE OGIVE NOMMÉE DÉSIR.» LE TEXTE DE CETTE AFFICHE ANTINUCLÉAIRE DONNE DES INFORMATIONS PRÉCISES SUR LA PHOTO: LE PHOTOGRAPHE MITSUO SHIBATA A DÉCOUVERT CETTE OGIVE NUCLÉAIRE CALCINÉE À PROXIMITÉ DE LA BASE DE L'AIR FORCE EN ARIZONA. (JPN)

436

437

438

439

■ **437** ART DIRECTOR/DESIGNER/ILLUSTRATOR: JOAO MACHADO CLIENT: ECO '92 ■ **437** POSTER ANNOUNCING AN EXHIBITION OF POSTERS ON THE SUBJECT OF THE ENVIRONMENT AND DEVELOPMENT. ● **437** FÜR EINE AUSSTELLUNG VON UMWELT- UND ENTWICK-LUNGSPLAKATEN. ▲ **437** POUR UNE EXPOSITION D'AFFICHES SUR LE THÈME DE L'ENVIRONNEMENT ET DU DÉVELOPPEMENT. (POR)

■ **438, 439** ART DIRECTORS/DESIGNERS/PHOTOGRAPHERS: KRISTIN ZWIMPFER, RINALDO BARABINO COPYWRITER: CHRISTIAN LANG STYLIST: KROKODIL + CO. AGENCY: ALLCOMM CLIENT: CIBA-GEIGY ■ **438, 439** THESE POSTERS ARE AN APPEAL TO THE STAFF OF CIBA-GEIGY TO USE IMAGINATION TO HELP SAVE ENERGY. ● **438, 439** AN DIE MITARBEITER VON CIBA-GEIGY GERICHTETER ENERGIESPARAUFRUF. ▲ **438, 439** UN APPEL AUX ÉCONOMIES D'ÉNERGIE ADRESSÉ AUX COLLABORATEURS DE CIBA-GEIGY. (SWI)

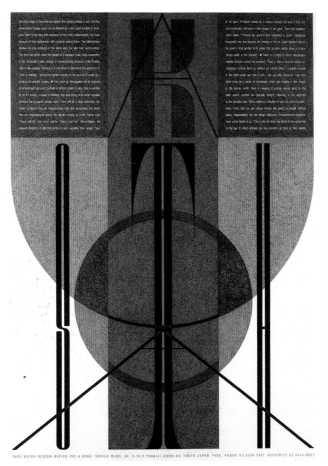

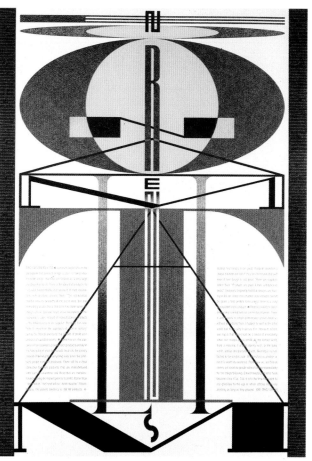

440

441

442

443

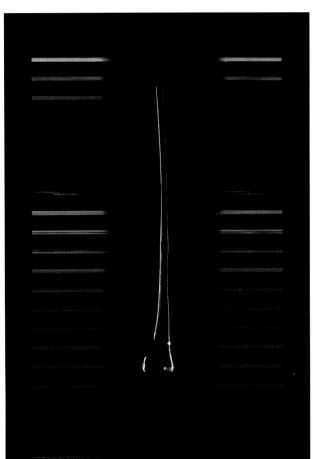

444

■ **440, 441** ART DIRECTOR: TAKU SATOH DESIGNER: TAKU SATOH COPYWRITER: TAKU SATOH AGENCY: TAKU SATOH DESIGN OFFICE INC. CLIENT: TAKU SATOH DESIGN OFFICE INC. ■ **440, 441** WITH THESE POSTERS, TAKU SATOH DESIGN OFFICE MAKES A STATEMENT ON THE RESPONSIBILITY OF PRODUCT DESIGNERS AND MANUFACTURERS TO DESIGN AND PRODUCE PRODUCTS THAT ARE ACTUALLY NEEDED. ● **440, 441** MIT DIESEN PLAKATEN ÄUSSERT DER DESIGNER TAKU SATOH SEINE MEINUNG ÜBER DIE VERANWORTUNG DER DESIGNER UND HERSTELLER, NUR WIRKLICH NOTWENDIGE PRODUKTE ZU ENTWERFEN UND HERZU-STELLEN. ▲ **440, 441** AVEC CES AFFICHES, LE DESIGNER TAKU SATOH EXPRIME SON OPINION SUR LA RESPONSABILITÉ DES DESIGNERS ET DES FABRICANTS, QUI NE DEVRAIENT CRÉER ET PRODUIRE QUE CE QUI EST ABSOLUMENT NÉCESSAIRE. (JPN)

■ **442** DESIGNER: MARIA TOMECZEK ■ **442** POSTER FOR AN INTERNATIONAL STUDENT COMPETITION ON THE SUBJECT OF RECYCLING. ● **442** DIESES PLAKAT ENTSTAND IM RAHMEN EINES STUDENTENWETTBEWERBS ZUM THEMA RECYCLING. ▲ **442** CETTE AFFICHE A ÉTÉ RÉALISÉE DANS LE CADRE D'UN CONCOURS POUR ÉTUDIANTS SUR LE THEME DU RECYCLAGE. (GER)

■ **443** ART DIRECTOR/DESIGNER: TAKAHARU MATSUMOTO AGENCY: TAKAHARU MATSUMOTO ■ **443** APPEAL TO SAVE THE ENVIRON-MENT. SILKSCREEN POSTER. ● **443** EIN HILFESCHREI DER NATUR. ▲ **443** UN APPEL À SAUVER LA NATURE. SÉRIGRAPHIE. (JPN)

■ **444** ART DIRECTOR/DESIGNER: MOTOMITSU TAKAGI PHOTOGRAPHERS: TOSHIYASU ADACHI, KYOUICHI KAMEI CLIENT: FREE LANCE DESIGNERS CLUB ■ **444** VIBRATIONS OF NATURE—A POSTER ON THE SUBJECT OF ECOLOGICAL PROBLEMS. ● **444** VIBRATIONEN DER NATUR—UMWELTPLAKAT. ▲ **444** LES VIBRATIONS DE LA NATURE—UNE AFFICHE SUR LE THEME DE L'ÉCOLOGIE. (JPN)

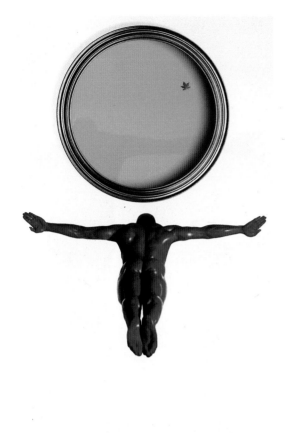

445

446

■ **445** ART DIRECTOR: JERRY GOEN DESIGNER: JERRY GOEN PHOTOGRAPHER: PETER DARLEY MILLER AGENCY: INTRALINK FILM GRAPHIC DESIGN CLIENT: GANS INKS ■ **445** POSTER PRINTED WITH SOY-BASED INKS, ADDRESSED TO PROFESSIONALS IN THE GRAPHIC-ART COMMUNITY TO PROMOTE THE USE OF ENVIRONMENTALLY FRIENDLY INKS. ● **445** PLAKAT FÜR UMWELT-FREUNDLICHE DRUCKFARBEN AUF SOJA-BASIS. ▲ **445** AFFICHE IMPRIMÉE AU MOYEN D'ENCRES À BASE DE SOJA DESTINÉE AUX PROFESSIONNELS DE L'INDUSTRIE GRAPHIQUE, AFIN DE LES INCITER À UTILISER CES PRODUITS NON-POLLUANTS. (USA)

■ **446** ART DIRECTOR: JOHN CLARK DESIGNERS: JOHN CLARK, PAUL LANGLAND PHOTOGRAPHER: OE/UEDA STUDIOS COPYWRITER: AILEEN FARNAN ANTONIER CLIENT: AIGA LOS ANGELES ■ **446** POSTER USING RECYCLED PAPER AND SOY-BASED INKS. IT ANSWERS QUESTIONS ABOUT THE USE OF THESE MATERIALS AND PRINTING IN AN ENVIRONMENTALLY RESPONSIBLE MANNER. ● **446** DIESES PLAKAT WURDE MIT FARBEN AUF SOJABASIS AUF RECYCLING-PAPIER GEDRUCKT. ES INFORMIERT ÜBER UMWELT-BEWUSSTES DRUCKEN. ▲ **446** CETTE AFFICHE A ÉTÉ IMPRIMÉE SUR PAPIER RECYCLÉ À L'AIDE D'ENCRES À BASE DE SOJA. ELLE DONNE DES INFORMATIONS SUR LES MATÉRIAUX ET LES TECHNIQUES D'IMPRESSION QUI MÉNAENT L'ENVIRONNEMENT. (USA)

■ **447** ART DIRECTOR: DOUG AKAGI DESIGNERS: DOUG AKAGI, KIMBERLY LENTZ-POWELL ILLUSTRATOR: HIROSHI AKAGI AGENCY: AKAGI DESIGN CLIENT: AIGA SAN FRANCISCO ■ **447** THIS POSTER IS MEANT TO ALERT PEOPLE TO THE DECLINE OF THE WATER QUALITY IN SAN FRANCISCO BAY. ● **447** DIESES PLAKAT SOLL DIE BEVÖLKERUNG AUF DIE EXTREME VERSCHLECHTERUNG DER WASSERQUALITÄT IN DER SAN FRANCISCO BAY AUFMERKSAM MACHEN. ▲ **447** CETTE AFFICHE A POUR BUT D'ATTIRER L'ATTEN-TION DE LA POPULATION SUR LA DÉGRADATION DRAMATIQUE DE LA QUALITÉ DES EAUX DANS LA BAIE DE SAN FRANCISCO. (USA)

■ **448** ART DIRECTOR: KENICHI SAMURA DESIGNER: KENICHI SAMURA PHOTOGRAPHERS: YURIKO TAKAGI, ATSUSHI KITAGAWARA COPYWRITER: YURIKO TAKAGI AGENCY: NUMBER ONE DESIGN OFFICE INC. CLIENT: JAPAN GRAPHIC DESIGNERS ASSOCIATION ■ **448** POSTER FOR THE JAGDA PEACE AND ENVIRONMENTAL EXHIBITION. ● **448** «ICH BIN DER ERBE DES UNIVERSUMS.» PLAKAT FÜR DIE FRIEDENS- UND UMWELTAUSSTELLUNG DER JAGDA: «I AM HERE.» ▲ **448** «JE SUIS L'HÉRITIER DE L'UNIVERS.» AF-FICHE POUR UNE EXPOSITION SUR LA PAIX ET L'ENVIRONNEMENT, INTITULÉE «JE SUIS LÀ,» ORGANISÉE PAR LA JAGDA. (JPN)

447

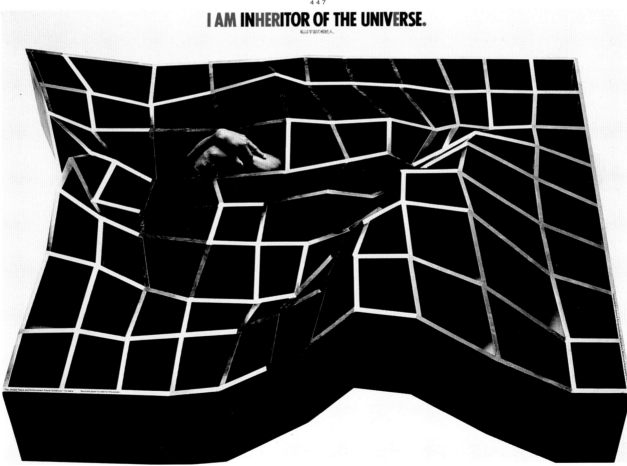

448

449

■ **449** ART DIRECTOR/DESIGNER: MERVYN KURLANSKY PHOTOGRAPHER: NICK TURNER AGENCY: PENTAGRAM DESIGN LTD. CLIENT: POLISH GOVERNMENT ■ **449** DESIGN FOR AN EARTH FLAG FOR THE POLISH PAVILION AT EXPO '92 IN SEVILLE, PROMOTING GLOBAL SOLIDARITY. ● **449** EIN APPELL ZUR ERHALTUNG DER ERDE UND ZU GEMEINSAMEN ANSTRENGUNGEN. PLAKAT FÜR DEN POLNISCHEN PAVILLON AN DER EXPO '92 IN SEVILLA. ▲ **449** UN APPEL À LA SAUVEGARDE DE LA PLANETE ET DE LA SOLIDARITÉ EN FAVEUR DE L'ENVIRONNEMENT. AFFICHE DU PAVILLON POLONAIS DE L'EXPO '92 DE SÉVILLE.(SPA)

INDEXES

VERZEICHNISSE

INDEXES

CALL FOR ENTRIES

EINLADUNG

APPEL D'ENVOIS

BOOK & MAGAZINE ORDER FORMS

BESTELLSCHEINE

BONS DE COMMANDE

C A L L   F O R   E N T R I E S

GRAPHIS DESIGN 95

ENTRY DEADLINE: NOVEMBER 30, 1993

ADVERTISING: Newspaper and magazine. **DESIGN**: Promotion brochures, catalogs, invitations, record covers, announcements, logos, corporate campaigns, calendars, books, book covers, packaging (single or series, labels or complete packages). **EDITORIAL**: Company magazines, newspapers, consumer magazines, house organs, annual reports. **ILLUSTRATION**: All categories, black-and-white or color. **ELIGIBILITY**: All work produced between December 1, 1992 and November 30, 1993, including unpublished work by professionals or students.

GRAPHIS PHOTO 94

ENTRY DEADLINE: AUGUST 31, 1993

ADVERTISING PHOTOGRAPHY: Ads, catalogs, invitations, announcements, record covers and calendars on any subject. **EDITORIAL PHOTOGRAPHY**: Photos for journals, books and corporate publications. **FINE ART PHOTOGRAPHY**: Personal studies on any subject. **UNPUBLISHED PHOTOGRAPHS**: Experimental or student work on any subject. **ELIGIBILITY**: All work produced between Sept. 1, 1992 and Aug. 31, 1993.

GRAPHIS POSTER 94

ENTRY DEADLINE: APRIL 30, 1993

CULTURAL POSTERS: Exhibitions, film, music and theater. **ADVERTISING POSTERS**: Consumer goods and self-promotion. **SOCIAL POSTERS**: Education, conferences, political issues. **ELIGIBILITY**: All work produced between May 1, 1992 and April 30, 1993.

GRAPHIS ANNUAL REPORTS 4

ENTRY DEADLINE: APRIL 30, 1993

All annual reports, brochures, and other corporate collateral material. **ELIGIBILITY**: Work published between May 1, 1991 and April 30, 1993.

RULES

By submitting work, the sender grants permission for it to be published in any Graphis book, any article in *Graphis* magazine, or any advertisement, brochure or other printed matter produced specifically for the purpose of promoting the sale of these publications.

■ **ELIGIBILITY**: All work produced in the 12-month period previous to the submission deadline, including unpublished work by professionals or students, is eligible.

■ **WHAT TO SEND**: Please send the printed pieces or duplicate transparencies (please mark the dupes with your name) accompanied by a completed entry label. ALL 35MM SLIDES MUST BE CARDBOARD-MOUNTED, NO GLASS! *We regret that entries cannot be returned.*

■ **HOW AND WHERE TO SEND**: Please tape (do not glue) the completed entry form (or a copy) to the back of each piece. Entries can be sent by air mail, air parcel post or surface mail. Please do not send anything by air freight. Write "No Commercial Value" on the package, and label it "Art for Contest." The number of photographs and transparencies enclosed should also be marked on the parcel. (If sending by air courier—Federal Express or DHL, for instance—label the package "Documents, Commercial Value $00.00.") For entries from countries with exchange controls, please contact us.

■ **SINGLE ENTRIES**: North America, U.S. $15; Germany, DM 15; all other countries, SFr 15.

■ **FOR AN ENTRY OF THREE OR MORE PIECES IN A SINGLE CONTEST**: North America, U.S. $35; Germany, DM 40; all other countries, SFr 40.

■ **STUDENTS' ENTRIES**: Free with copy of student identification.

Please make checks payable to GRAPHIS PRESS CORP., ZÜRICH, and include in parcel. A confirmation of receipt will be sent to each entrant, and all entrants will be notified of whether their work has been accepted for publication. By submitting work, you qualify for a 25 percent discount on the purchase of the published book. Please send entries to:

GRAPHIS PRESS CORP., 107 DUFOURSTRASSE CH-8008 ZÜRICH, SWITZERLAND

E I N L A D U N G

GRAPHIS DESIGN 95

EINSENDESCHLUSS: 30. NOVEMBER 1993

WERBUNG: In Zeitungen und Zeitschriften. **DESIGN**: Werbeprospekte, Kataloge, Einladungen, Schallplattenhüllen, Anzeigen, Signete, Image-Kampagnen, Kalender, Bücher, Buchumschläge, Packungen. **REDAKTIONELLES DESIGN**: Firmenpublikationen, Zeitungen, Zeitschriften, Jahresberichte. **ILLUSTRATIONEN**: Alle Kategorien, schwarzweiss oder farbig. **IN FRAGE KOMMEN**: Alle Arbeiten von Fachleuten und Studenten – auch nicht publizierte Arbeiten –, die zwischen Dezember 1992 und November 1993 entstanden sind.

GRAPHIS PHOTO 94

EINSENDESCHLUSS: 31. AUGUST 1993

WERBEPHOTOGRAPHIE: Anzeigen, Kataloge, Einladungen, Plattenhüllen, Kalender. **REDAKTIONELLE PHOTOGRAPHIE**: Pressephotos, Firmenpublikationen usw. **KÜNSTLERISCHE PHOTOGRAPHIE**: Persönliche Studien. **UNVERÖFFENTLICHTE PHOTOS**: Experimentelle Photographie und Arbeiten von Studenten. **IN FRAGE KOMMEN**: Arbeiten, die zwischen September 1992 und August 1993 entstanden sind.

GRAPHIS POSTER 94

EINSENDESCHLUSS: 30. APRIL 1993

KULTUR: Plakate für Ausstellungen, Film-, Theater-, Ballettaufführungen etc. **WERBUNG**: Plakate für Konsumgüter, Eigenwerbung **GESELLSCHAFT**: Ausbildung, Politik, Umwelt **IN FRAGE KOMMEN**: Arbeiten, die zwischen Mai 1992 und April 1993 entstanden sind.

GRAPHIS ANNUAL REPORTS 4

EINSENDESCHLUSS: 30. APRIL 1993

IN FRAGE KOMMEN: Jahresberichte einer Firma oder Organisation, die zwischen Mai 1991 und April 1993 publiziert wurden.

TEILNAHMEBEDINGUNGEN

Durch Ihre Einsendung erteilen Sie dem Graphis Verlag die Erlaubnis zur Veröffentlichung der Arbeiten in den Graphis-Büchern und in der Zeitschrift Graphis oder für die Wiedergabe im Zusammenhang mit Besprechungen und Werbematerial für Graphis-Publikationen.

■ **IN FRAGE KOMMEN**: Alle Arbeiten von Fachleuten und Studenten – auch nicht publizierte Arbeiten –, die in der angegebenen Periode vor Einsendeschluss entstanden sind.

■ **WAS EINSENDEN**: Senden Sie uns das gedruckte Beispiel oder Duplikatdias (bitte Dias mit Ihrem Namen versehen) zusammen mit dem ausgefüllten Etikett. KLEINBILDDIAS BITTE IM KARTONRAHMEN, KEIN GLAS! *Bitte beachten Sie, dass Einsendungen nicht zurückgeschickt werden können.*

■ **WIE SCHICKEN**: Befestigen Sie das ausgefüllte Etikett (oder eine Kopie) mit Klebstreifen (nicht mit Klebstoff) auf der Rückseite jeder Arbeit. Bitte per Luftpost oder auf normalem Postweg einsenden.

Keine Luftfrachtsendungen. Deklarieren Sie «ohne jeden Handelswert» und «Arbeitsproben». Die Anzahl der Dias und Photos sollte auf dem Paket angegeben werden. Bei Luftkurier-Sendungen vermerken Sie «Dokumente, ohne jeden Handelswert».

■ **GEBÜHREN**: SFr. 15.–/DM 15,– für einzelne Arbeiten; SFr. 40.–/DM 40,– pro Kampagne oder Serie von mehr als drei Stück.

■ **STUDENTEN**: Diese Gebühren gelten nicht für Studenten. Senden Sie uns bitte eine Kopie des Studentenausweises.

Bitte senden Sie uns einen Scheck (SFr.-Schecks bitte auf eine Schweizer Bank ziehen) oder überweisen Sie den Betrag auf PC Luzern 60-3520-6 oder PSchK Frankfurt 3000 57-602. Jeder Einsender erhält eine Empfangsbestätigung und wird über Erscheinen oder Nichterscheinen seiner Arbeit informiert. Durch Ihre Einsendung erhalten Sie 25% Rabatt auf das betreffende Buch. Bitte senden Sie Ihre Arbeit an folgende Adresse:

GRAPHIS VERLAG, DUFOURSTRASSE 107, CH-8008 ZURICH, SCHWEIZ

APPEL D'ENVOIS

GRAPHIS DESIGN 95

DATE LIMITE D'ENVOI: 30 NOVEMBRE 1993

PUBLICITÉ: journaux, magazines. DESIGN: brochures, catalogues, invitations, pochettes de disque, annonces, logos, campagnes d'identité visuelle, calendriers, livres, jaquettes, packaging (spécimen ou série, étiquettes ou emballages complets). DESIGN ÉDITORIAL: magazines de sociétés, journaux, revues, publications d'entreprise, rapports annuels. ILLUSTRATION: toutes catégories noir et blanc ou couleurs. ADMISSION: tous travaux réalisés entre le 1er décembre 1992 et le 30 novembre 1993, y compris les inédits de professionnels ou d'étudiants.

GRAPHIS PHOTO 94

DATE LIMITE D'ENVOI: 31 AOUT 1993

PHOTO PUBLICITAIRE: publicités, catalogues, invitations, annonces, pochettes de disque et calendriers sur tous sujets. PHOTO RÉDACTIONNELLE: reportages pour périodiques, livres et publications d'entreprise. PHOTO D'ART: études personnelles. PHOTOS INÉDITES: travaux expérimentaux ou projets d'étudiants. ADMISSION: tous travaux réalisés entre le 1er septembre 1992 et le 31 août 1993.

GRAPHIS POSTER 94

DATE LIMITE D'ENVOI: 30 AVRIL 1993

AFFICHES CULTURELLES: expositions, films, musique, théâtre etc. AFFICHES PUBLICITAIRES: produits de consommation, autopromotion. AFFICHES SOCIALES: formation, conférences, politique. ADMISSION: tous travaux réalisés entre le 1er mai 1992 et le 30 avril 1993.

GRAPHIS ANNUAL REPORTS 4

DATE LIMITE D'ENVOI: 30 AVRIL 1993

Rapports annuels, brochures et tout matériel d'identité corporate. ADMISSION: travaux publiés entre le 1er mai 1991 et le 30 avril 1993.

REGLEMENT

Par votre envoi, vous donnez aux Editions Graphis l'autorisation de publier les travaux reçus dans nos livres Graphis, dans tout article du magazine Graphis ou toute publicité, brochure ou autre matériel publicitaire destiné à promouvoir la vente de ces publications.

■ ADMISSION: sont acceptés tous les travaux de professionnels et d'étudiants – même inédits – réalisés pendant les douze mois précédant le délai limite d'envoi.

■ QUE NOUS ENVOYER: un exemplaire imprimé ou un duplicata de la diapositive (n'oubliez pas d'inscrire votre nom dessus) avec l'étiquette ci-jointe, dûment remplie. NE PAS ENVOYER DE DIAPOSITIVES SOUS VERRE! *Les travaux ne peuvent pas être retournés.*

■ COMMENT ET OÙ ENVOYER: veuillez scotcher (ne pas coller) au dos de chaque spécimen les étiquettes (ou photocopies) dûment remplies. Envoyez les travaux par avion ou par voie de surface. Ne nous envoyez rien en fret aérien. Indiquez «Sans aucune valeur commerciale» et «Echantillons pour concours». Inscrire le nombre de diapositives et photos sur le paquet. (Pour les envois par courrier, indiquer «Documents, sans aucune valeur commerciale»). Pour les envois en provenance de pays soumis au contrôle des changes, veuillez nous contacter.

■ ENVOI D'UN SEUL TRAVAIL: droits d'admission, SFr 15.–/US$ 15.00

■ ENVOI D'UNE SÉRIE DE TROIS TRAVAUX OU PLUS POUR UN SEUL CONCOURS: SFr 40.–/US 35.00

■ ÉTUDIANTS: les étudiants sont exemptés de la taxe d'admission. Prière de joindre une photocopie de la carte d'étudiant.

Veuillez joindre à votre envoi un chèque tiré sur une banque suisse ou verser ce montant au compte chèque postal Lucerne 60-3520-6. Nous vous ferons parvenir un accusé de réception. Tous les candidats seront informés de la parution ou non-parution de leurs travaux. Votre envoi vous vaudra une réduction de 25% sur l'annuel en question. Veuillez envoyer vos travaux à l'adresse suivante:

EDITIONS GRAPHIS, DUFOURSTRASSE 107, CH-8008 ZURICH, SUISSE

ENTRY LABEL

SENDER:

FIRM, ADDRESS, TELEPHONE/TELEFAX

ART DIRECTOR:

ADDRESS, TELEPHONE/TELEFAX

DESIGNER:

ADDRESS, TELEPHONE/TELEFAX

ILLUSTRATOR, PHOTOGRAPHER, STYLIST:

ADDRESS, TELEPHONE/TELEFAX

COPYWRITER:

ADDRESS, TELEPHONE/TELEFAX

AGENCY, STUDIO:

ADDRESS, TELEPHONE/TELEFAX

CLIENT, PUBLISHER:

ADDRESS, TELEPHONE/TELEFAX

DESCRIPTION OF ASSIGNMENT AND YOUR SOLUTION:

SIGNATURE:

I HEREBY GRANT **GRAPHIS PRESS** NON-EXCLUSIVE PERMISSION FOR USE OF THE SUBMITTED MATERIAL, FOR WHICH I HAVE FULL REPRO-DUCTION RIGHTS (COPY, PHOTOGRAPHY, ILLUSTRATION, AND DESIGN).

ETIKETT/FICHE

ABSENDER/ENVOYÉ PAR:

FIRMA(E), ADRESSE, TELEPHON(E), TELEFAX

ART DIRECTOR/DIRECTEUR ARTISTIQUE:

ADRESSE, TELEPHON(E), TELEFAX

GESTALTER/DESIGNER:

ADRESSE, TELEPHON(E), TELEFAX

KÜNSTLER/ARTISTE, PHOTOGRAPH(E), STYLIST(E):

ADRESSE, TELEPHON(E), TELEFAX

TEXTER/RÉDACTEUR:

ADRESSE, TELEPHON(E), TELEFAX

AGENTUR/AGENCE:

ADRESSE, TELEPHON(E), TELEFAX

KUNDE/CLIENT:

ADRESSE, TELEPHON(E), TELEFAX

BESCHREIBUNG DES AUFTRAGS UND DER AUSFÜHRUNG:
DESCRIPTION DE LA COMMANDE ET DE SA REALISATION:

UNTERSCHRIFT/SIGNATURE:

ICH ERTEILE HIERMIT DEM **GRAPHIS VERLAG** DIE NICHT-EXKLUSIVE ERLAUBNIS ZUR VERÖFFENTLICHUNG DER EINGEREICHTEN ARBEITEN, FÜR DIE ICH DIE REPRODUKTIONSRECHTE BESITZE (TEXT, PHOTOGRAPHIE, ILLUSTRATION UND DESIGN).

J'ACCORDE PAR LA PRÉSENTE AUX **EDITIONS GRAPHIS** L'AUTORISATION NON EXCLUSIVE D'UTILISER LE MATÉRIEL SOUMIS Á LEUR APPRÉCIA-TION, POUR LEQUEL JE DÉTIENS LES DROITS DE REPRODUCTION (TEXTE, PHOTOGRAPHIE, ILLUSTRATION ET DESIGN).

GRAPHIS PRESS CORP., 107 DUFOURSTRASSE CH-8008 ZÜRICH, SWITZERLAND

BOOK ORDER FORM: USA AND CANADA

BOOKS		USA	CANADA
☐ GRAPHIS POSTER 93		US $69.00	US $94.00
☐ GRAPHIS POSTER 92		US $69.00	US $94.00
☐ GRAPHIS DESIGN 93		US $69.00	US $94.00
☐ GRAPHIS DESIGN 92		US $69.00	US $94.00
☐ GRAPHIS PHOTO 92		US $69.00	US $94.00
☐ GRAPHIS ANNUAL REPORTS 3		US $75.00	US$100.00
☐ GRAPHIS LETTERHEAD 1		US $69.00	US $94.00
☐ GRAPHIS LOGO 1		US $50.00	US $70.00
☐ THE GRAPHIC DESIGNER'S GREENBOOK		US $25.00	US $41.00
☐ GRAPHIS PUBLICATION 1/MAGAZINDESIGN 1 ☐ ENGLISH ☐ GERMAN		US $75.00	US$100.00
☐ ART FOR SURVIVAL: THE ILLUSTRATOR AND THE ENVIRONMENT		US $40.00	US $60.00
☐ GRAPHIS NUDES		US $75.00	US$100.00
☐ GRAPHIS PACKAGING 5		US $75.00	US$100.00
☐ GRAPHIS DIAGRAM 1		US $69.00	US $94.00

☐ CHECK ENCLOSED (GRAPHIS AGREES TO PAY MAILING COSTS)

☐ PLEASE BILL ME (MAILING COSTS IN ADDITION TO ABOVE BOOK PRICES WILL BE CHARGED. BOOK(S) WILL BE SENT WHEN PAYMENT IS RECEIVED)

PLEASE PRINT

NAME _____ DATE _____

TITLE _____

COMPANY _____

ADDRESS _____

CITY _____ POSTAL CODE _____

COUNTRY _____

DATE _____ SIGNATURE _____

SEND ORDER FORM AND MAKE CHECK PAYABLE TO:
GRAPHIS US, INC.,
141 LEXINGTON AVENUE,
NEW YORK, NY 10016, USA

REQUEST FOR CALL FOR ENTRIES

PLEASE PUT ME ON YOUR "CALL FOR ENTRIES" LIST FOR THE FOLLOWING TITLES:

☐ GRAPHIS DESIGN   ☐ GRAPHIS ANNUAL REPORTS
☐ GRAPHIS DIAGRAM   ☐ GRAPHIS CORPORATE IDENTITY
☐ GRAPHIS POSTER   ☐ GRAPHIS PACKAGING
☐ GRAPHIS PHOTO   ☐ GRAPHIS LETTERHEAD
☐ GRAPHIS LOGO   ☐ GRAPHIS TYPOGRAPHY

SUBMITTING MATERIAL TO ANY OF THE ABOVE TITLES QUALIFIES SENDER FOR A 25% DISCOUNT TOWARD PURCHASE OF THAT TITLE.

BOOK ORDER FORM: EUROPE AND WORLD

BOOKS	GERMANY	U.K.	WORLD
☐ GRAPHIS POSTER 93	DM 149,–	£ 49.00	SFR. 123.–
☐ GRAPHIS POSTER 92	DM 149,–	£ 49.00	SFR. 123.–
☐ GRAPHIS DESIGN 93	DM 149,–	£ 49.00	SFR. 123.–
☐ GRAPHIS DESIGN 92	DM 149,–	£ 49.00	SFR. 123.–
☐ GRAPHIS PHOTO 92	DM 149,–	£ 49.00	SFR. 123.–
☐ GRAPHIS ANNUAL REPORTS 3	DM 162,–	£ 52.00	SFR. 137.–
☐ GRAPHIS LETTERHEAD 1	DM 149,–	£ 49.00	SFR. 123.–
☐ GRAPHIS LOGO 1	DM 108,–	£ 36.00	SFR. 92.–
☐ THE GRAPHIC DESIGNER'S GREENBOOK	DM 54,–	£ 18.00	SFR. 46.–
☐ GRAPHIS PUBLICATION 1/MAGAZINDESIGN 1 ☐ ENGLISH ☐ GERMAN	DM 162,–	£ 52.00	SFR. 137.–
☐ ART FOR SURVIVAL: THE ILLUSTRATOR AND THE ENVIRONMENT	DM 89,–	£ 33.00	SFR. 79.–
☐ GRAPHIS NUDES	DM 162,–	£ 48.00	SFR. 137.–
☐ GRAPHIS PACKAGING 5	DM 160,–	£ 48.00	SFR. 132.–
☐ GRAPHIS DIAGRAM 1	DM 138,–	£ 49.00	SFR. 112.–

☐ CHECK ENCLOSED (PLEASE MAKE CHECK PAYABLE TO EUROPEAN BOOK SERVICE, DE MEERN)

☐ PLEASE BILL ME (MAILING COSTS WILL BE CHARGED)

FOR CREDIT CARD PAYMENT (ALL CARDS DEBITED IN SWISS FRANCS):

☐ AMERICAN EXPRESS   ☐ DINER'S CLUB
☐ EURO/MASTERCARD   ☐ VISA/BARCLAY/CARTE BLEUE

ACCOUNT NO. _____ EXPIRATION DATE _____

SIGNATURE _____ DATE _____

PLEASE PRINT

NAME _____ DATE _____

TITLE _____

COMPANY _____

ADDRESS _____

CITY _____ POSTAL CODE _____

COUNTRY _____

DATE _____ SIGNATURE _____

PLEASE SEND ORDER FORM TO:
GRAPHIS PRESS CORP.,
DUFOURSTRASSE 107,
CH–8008 ZÜRICH, SWITZERLAND

REQUEST FOR CALL FOR ENTRIES

PLEASE PUT ME ON YOUR "CALL FOR ENTRIES" LIST FOR THE FOLLOWING TITLES:

☐ GRAPHIS DESIGN   ☐ GRAPHIS ANNUAL REPORTS
☐ GRAPHIS DIAGRAM   ☐ GRAPHIS CORPORATE IDENTITY
☐ GRAPHIS POSTER   ☐ GRAPHIS PACKAGING
☐ GRAPHIS PHOTO   ☐ GRAPHIS LETTERHEAD
☐ GRAPHIS LOGO   ☐ GRAPHIS TYPOGRAPHY

SUBMITTING MATERIAL TO ANY OF THE ABOVE TITLES QUALIFIES SENDER FOR A 25% DISCOUNT TOWARD PURCHASE OF THAT TITLE.

SUBSCRIBE TO GRAPHIS: USA AND CANADA

MAGAZINE	USA	CANADA
☐ NEW ☐ RENEW		
☐ GRAPHIS (TWO YEARS/12 ISSUES)	US $149.00	US $166.00
☐ GRAPHIS (ONE YEAR/6 ISSUES)	US $79.00	US $88.00

IMPORTANT! CHECK THE LANGUAGE DESIRED:

☐ ENGLISH   ☐ GERMAN   ☐ FRENCH

☐ CHECK ENCLOSED

☐ PLEASE BILL ME

☐ 25% DISCOUNT FOR STUDENTS WITH COPY OF VALID,
   DATED STUDENT ID AND PAYMENT WITH ORDER

FOR CREDIT CARD PAYMENT:

☐ VISA   ☐ MASTERCARD

ACCT. NO   EXP. DATE

SIGNATURE

PLEASE PRINT

NAME   DATE

TITLE

COMPANY

ADDRESS

CITY   POSTAL CODE

COUNTRY

SEND ORDER FORM AND MAKE CHECK PAYABLE TO:
GRAPHIS US, INC.,
141 LEXINGTON AVENUE
NEW YORK, NY 10016-8191
SERVICE WILL BEGIN WITH ISSUE THAT IS CURRENT
WHEN ORDER IS PROCESSED.   (POSTER 93)

REQUEST FOR CALL FOR ENTRIES
PLEASE PUT ME ON THE "CALL FOR ENTRIES" LIST FOR THE
FOLLOWING TITLES:

☐ GRAPHIS DESIGN	☐ GRAPHIS ANNUAL REPORTS
☐ GRAPHIS DIAGRAM	☐ GRAPHIS CORPORATE IDENTITY
☐ GRAPHIS POSTER	☐ GRAPHIS PACKAGING
☐ GRAPHIS PHOTO	☐ GRAPHIS LETTERHEAD
☐ GRAPHIS LOGO	☐ GRAPHIS TYPOGRAPHY

SUBMITTING MATERIAL TO ANY OF THE ABOVE TITLES QUALIFIES
SENDER FOR A 25% DISCOUNT TOWARD PURCHASE OF THAT TITLE.

SUBSCRIBE TO GRAPHIS: EUROPE AND WORLD

MAGAZINE	GERMANY	U.K.	WORLD
☐ NEW ☐ RENEW			
☐ GRAPHIS (TWO YEARS/12 ISSUES)	DM 326,–	£ 106.00	SFR 280.–
☐ GRAPHIS (ONE YEAR/6 ISSUES)	DM 181,–	£ 63.00	SFR 156.–

IMPORTANT! CHECK THE LANGUAGE DESIRED:

☐ ENGLISH   ☐ GERMAN   ☐ FRENCH

☐ SUBSCRIPTION FEES INCLUDE POSTAGE TO ANY
   PART OF THE WORLD

☐ AIRMAIL SURCHARGES (PER YEAR)	DM 75,–	£ 26.00	SFR 65.–
☐ REGISTERED MAIL (PER YEAR)	DM 20,–	£ 7.00	SFR 20.–

☐ CHECK ENCLOSED (PLEASE MAKE SFR.–CHECK PAYABLE
   TO A SWISS BANK.

☐ STUDENTS MAY REQUEST A 25% DISCOUNT BY SENDING STUDENT ID

FOR CREDIT CARD PAYMENT (ALL CARDS DEBITED IN SWISS FRANCS):

☐ AMERICAN EXPRESS   ☐ DINER'S CLUB

☐ EURO/MASTERCARD   ☐ VISA/BARCLAY/CARTE BLEUE

ACCT. NO   EXP. DATE

SIGNATURE

PLEASE PRINT

NAME   DATE

TITLE

COMPANY

ADDRESS

CITY   POSTAL CODE

COUNTRY

SEND ORDER FORM AND MAKE CHECK PAYABLE TO:
GRAPHIS PRESS CORP.,
DUFOURSTRASSE 107
CH-8008 ZÜRICH, SWITZERLAND
SERVICE WILL BEGIN WITH ISSUE THAT IS CURRENT
WHEN ORDER IS PROCESSED.   (POSTER 93)

REQUEST FOR CALL FOR ENTRIES
PLEASE PUT ME ON THE "CALL FOR ENTRIES" LIST FOR THE
FOLLOWING TITLES:

☐ GRAPHIS DESIGN	☐ GRAPHIS ANNUAL REPORTS
☐ GRAPHIS DIAGRAM	☐ GRAPHIS CORPORATE IDENTITY
☐ GRAPHIS POSTER	☐ GRAPHIS PACKAGING
☐ GRAPHIS PHOTO	☐ GRAPHIS LETTERHEAD
☐ GRAPHIS LOGO	☐ GRAPHIS TYPOGRAPHY

SUBMITTING MATERIAL TO ANY OF THE ABOVE TITLES QUALIFIES
SENDER FOR A 25% DISCOUNT TOWARD PURCHASE OF THAT TITLE.